THE GROCER
WHO SOLD
McCARTHYISM

THE GROCER WHO SOLD McCARTHYISM

THE RISE AND FALL OF ANTI-COMMUNIST CRUSADER LAURENCE A. JOHNSON

Fred M. Fiske

CHESTNUT HEIGHTS
PUBLISHING

Copyright © 2024, Fred M. Fiske

The moral right of the author has been asserted.

All rights reserved.
No part of this publication may be reproduced, stored in a retrieval system, or transmitted, in any form or by any means, without the prior permission in writing of the publisher, nor be otherwise circulated in any form of binding or cover other than that in which it is published and without a similar condition including this condition being imposed on the subsequent purchaser.

In quoting from published sources, the author has attempted to adhere to original spelling and grammar, making minor edits only for clarification when necessary.

Published by Chestnut Heights Publishing, Liverpool, New York

ISBN 978-1-7322416-8-8 (hard cover)
ISBN 978-1-7322416-6-4 (paperback)
ISBN 978-1-7322416-5-7 (ebook)

Library of Congress Control Number: 2024910389

First edition: July 2024

Cover photo: Laurence A. Johnson poses at a desk in 1943. (Syracuse *Post-Standard* photo)

Cover design and manuscript editing: William D. LaRue (williamlarue.com)

Author photo: Ron Trinca

Typesetting services by BOOKOW.COM

To Rosemary, who was there during the first phase, and to Chris, with me through the second.

Contents

Introduction	1
CHAPTER ONE: A Rooted American	9
CHAPTER TWO: The Innovator	27
CHAPTER THREE: The Activist	59
CHAPTER FOUR: The Threat Perceived	75
CHAPTER FIVE: Anti-communism Inc.	85
CHAPTER SIX: Johnson Joins the Anti-communists	109
CHAPTER SEVEN: Syracuse and the McCarthy Era	133
CHAPTER EIGHT: Harvey Matusow's Odyssey	147
CHAPTER NINE: Out-merchandising the Competition	161
CHAPTER TEN: McCarthyism Beyond McCarthy (1954-1955)	193
CHAPTER ELEVEN: The Crest of the Anti-communist Wave	215
CHAPTER TWELVE: Enter John Henry Faulk	225
CHAPTER THIRTEEN: The Cogley Report	241
CHAPTER FOURTEEN: The John Henry Faulk story	251
CHAPTER FIFTEEN: The Antiquarian	271
CHAPTER SIXTEEN: Pretrial Maneuvers	279
CHAPTER SEVENTEEN: Faulk Case Goes to Trial	287
CHAPTER EIGHTEEN: The Verdict	303
Epilogue	313

THE GROCER WHO SOLD McCARTHYISM

A Note on Sources   321
Index
About the Author

Introduction

By the spring of 1951, Laurence Ayres Johnson, a self-made supermarket mogul in Syracuse, New York, had joined the fight against communism. Fueled by patriotism, he leveraged his platform as a major merchandiser to put pressure on the nation's broadcasters, whom he believed employed too many "suspect" actors. He drew inspiration from his adult daughter, Eleanor Buchanan, an outspoken critic of any American who was aligned with the Communist Party—or who just opposed U.S. involvement in the Korean War. Her husband was then with the U.S. Marines fighting the communists in Korea. Grim radio reports and battlefield images on the new medium of television stoked her alarm.

Johnson quickly transcended the ranks of ordinary anti-communist citizens. He brought to the cause the skills he pioneered in the booming retail marketplace following World War II. His manipulation of the levers of merchandising soon had an outsized effect on the broadcasting industry and its major advertisers. Many complied with the demands of Johnson and his associates to "blacklist" hundreds of actors, writers, and others in show business. These lists, widely circulated among employers, contained the names of individuals deemed to be associated with or sympathetic to communism or leftist ideologies. It was a secret club no one wanted to join, as the listed individuals were effectively barred from obtaining work.

For a time, Johnson's efforts were met with widespread support amid a climate of fear. Newspapers in the early 1950s offered one sensational headline after another alleging communist spy rings, a "fifth column" of Americans working to undermine the capitalist way of life. FBI director J. Edgar Hoover claimed that for every U.S. communist, there were ten "fellow travelers."

However, while Soviet spy rings and espionage did exist, whatever influence communism ever had in America was on the wane by the 1950s. The party never came close to overthrowing capitalism; it never had the chance. A half-dozen federal laws between 1939 and 1954 set up American communists for harassment, investigation, and jail. It was officially illegal to be an active party member. In 1951, U.S. Supreme Court Justice William O. Douglas described American communists as the "best known, the most beset, and the least thriving of any fifth column in history."

Soviet dictator Joseph Stalin's show trials and other repressions had disillusioned many U.S. party members. Circulation of the *Sunday Worker*, the American communist newspaper, fell from 65,000 in the 1940s to less than 29,000 in 1953, the year of Stalin's death. By 1962, an estimated one of every six party members was a government agent assigned to secretly infiltrate the communist organizations.

Communism's prospects had been brightest in the grim 1930s when Depression-era throngs turned to the party for solidarity and hope. Most American communists were nonviolent idealists on the left fringes of politics and society, ideologically devoted to the working classes and civil rights for all, while also deferring to Moscow and the shifting party line. They were effective labor organizers, and they advocated for Black citizens long before Selma and Montgomery. However, the party never had much electoral clout. The Communist Party candidate in the 1932 presidential election earned 102,785 votes, trailing the Socialist Party's 884,000, both of whom finished far behind Democrat Franklin Roosevelt's winning total of 22 million.

During World War II, Americans warmed to Russia as their ally against Germany's Hitler, Italy's Mussolini, and Japan's Tojo. That support waned in the post-war years when the growing influence of communism abroad sparked renewed investigations on federal, state, and local levels. In 1947, the U.S. House Committee on Un-American Activities (HCUA) held hearings that exposed alleged communist writers and directors in Hollywood. New allegations of subversion seemed to surface daily, and loyalty boards emerged at all levels of government across the country. Thousands of Americans lost their jobs, including teachers, lawyers, social workers, longshoremen, electricians, mine workers, sailors, journalists, and factory workers.

In 1950, the outbreak of war in Korea became a litmus test for American patriotism. When the Communist Party called for resisting war production, it further dimmed its political prospects, particularly in labor unions.

Communists neither posed a significant threat to the American social order, nor were they ever perceived as such. In opinion polls listing the nation's No. 1 problem throughout the '40s and '50s, communism peaked at just 9 percent. Yet in mid-century America, there was no shortage of politicians, newspaper columnists, veterans, business leaders, and others eager to follow the lead of U.S. Senator Joseph McCarthy in targeting the inroads of communism, real or not.

This anti-communist fervor found an eager disciple in Laurence Johnson. Though family necessity limited his schooling, he possessed a keen mind, lively ambition, and a gift for innovative thinking. Known to his friends as Larry, he loved Americana, becoming an author of numerous articles on American folklore. His particular interest was the old country store, like the one in rural Wayne County in Upstate New York where he got his first job.

Never a churchgoing man, Johnson became an evangelist of Americanism. The Declaration of Independence was his Apostles' Creed, the Constitution his bible, Columbia the earthly manifestation of the divine. In these he took to heart the values that would sustain him through his anti-communist campaigns.

Never a military man either, Johnson made common cause with anti-communist veterans' groups in the same spirit that led his ancestors to fight first the Redcoats, then the Confederates. In 1954, the National Veterans of Foreign Wars awarded Johnson a citation and good citizenship medal for his anti-communist efforts.

His was a palpable patriotism, much like that captured in an American Legion flag salute from the 1940s:

> Our comrades saluted that flag…for its red stripes of sacrifice.
> The color made fast in the shed blood of thousands of our

THE GROCER WHO SOLD McCARTHYISM

U.S. Senator Joseph McCarthy, left, chats with Laurence Johnson in 1952 when Syracuse-area veterans invited the senator and the grocer to a clambake at Hinerwadel's Grove in North Syracuse. (Eleanor Buchanan photo)

strongest, best, virile manhood.... We salute the white stripe of purity, washed clean with the tears of the wives and mothers and daughters who stayed behind and mourned those who never came back. We salute it for the blue field of constancy that has never wavered in its idea of freedom, and we salute it for the twinkling star of hope that even in this dark hour shines out to all the world undimmed in its luster and in its glory.

Johnson and his allies took at face value the Marxist-inspired dictum: "There is not, nor can there be, a sphere or field of work that cannot be won by the communists." In Johnson's case, he was determined to silence the voices of American communism on radio and TV. No matter that those voices were weak and largely ignored. Johnson believed the language of subversion adopted subtle and seductive tones, influencing the American public through the dream factories of Broadway and Hollywood—and now also television studios. Johnson feared that communist performers, writers, producers, and directors could promote the party line, luring fellow-travelers to play supporting roles and to further the cause, their words reaching millions, their generous salaries fattening party coffers.

The few Communist Party true believers writing in Hollywood would have loved to tilt their scripts toward the party line. But overthrowing capitalism always came second to earning a living. More often, the frustrated writers worked on scripts for "Juke Box Jenny" and "Bachelor Daddy." For every socially conscious film like "What Price Glory" or "The Grapes of Wrath," there were a dozen escapist productions like "Earth vs. the Flying Saucers" and "Zombies of Mora Tau."

The 1950 publication of the anti-communist pamphlet *Red Channels* provided an easy-to-use guide for Johnson and others to identify actors and other show people with links to groups on the Attorney General's List of Subversive Organizations.

Despite this blacklist, many of these performers were still active in show business in 1951. To Johnson, this represented both a national security threat and a personal affront. Applying his business acumen to the situation, Johnson devised a counterattack. Since broadcasting was a commercial enterprise, he reasoned that the it would be vulnerable to commercial pressure. If he could persuade advertisers and manufacturers who sponsored the programming to pressure the radio and TV networks, the message might get through.

On this front, Johnson was in familiar territory. He had been one of the first to distinguish the outlines of the dawning consumer era in the 1920s. At that time, the retail industry prioritized the needs of food brokers, wholesalers, and producers. Grocers were beholden to their suppliers, and customers had limited options on the shelves. Assembly lines accelerated production, increased profits, and offered lower-cost goods. However, many shopkeepers were slow to modernize their approach to delivering products to customers.

Enter Laurence Johnson. He set about transforming the country store into the cash-and-carry supermarket. By reversing market priorities and relationships, he put the needs and desires of the customer first. Manufacturers and suppliers henceforth would ignore the point-of-purchase consumer at their peril.

THE GROCER WHO SOLD McCARTHYISM

The retail revolution that Johnson led meshed with the productivity boom in the 1940s and 1950s. As advertisers devised strategies to market competing brands, Johnson's supermarkets became a stage for their bright new packages, assembling an ever-wider array of merchandise and moving an ever-larger volume of goods to the consumer.

Initially met with skepticism, the supermarket model rapidly gained popularity. Soon, these new palaces of consumption, lauded for their efficiency, logic, and cost-effectiveness, became commonplace. By prioritizing the customer, Johnson helped move the American Dream several steps closer to reality. In his view, offering a selection of frozen fryers was a way to put a "chicken in every pot." This vision of democratic pluralism gave customers freedom of choice within their budget, granting them access to a widening selection of products and sales pitches fueled by American ingenuity, enterprise, and salesmanship.

Descended from the old country store, the modern supermarket remained a crossroads where manufacturer and consumer met, where a nation's productive energies were harnessed, its artifacts displayed, inspected, and acquired in glorious profusion.

By the 1950s, 60 percent of the products advertised on television were sold in supermarkets, which meant these store owners had major influence with manufacturers and broadcasters. Johnson owned a chain of six supermarkets in Central New York, and he was a national leader in the food service industry.

If he went to the networks as an ordinary private citizen and asked them to "fire the Reds," the executives would ignore him. But if he managed to interrupt the flow of sponsored products from the manufacturer to his customers and persuaded his fellow merchants to do likewise—or better yet, if he just mentioned it—well, the networks might take notice. He was right. They did.

Between 1951 and 1955, Johnson held something close to veto power over show-business casting in the studios, on Madison Avenue and in the network boardrooms. Key to his success was enlisting sponsors to pressure ad agencies and broadcasters. Everywhere he found eagerness to cooperate, to avoid controversy and forestall product boycotts.

Year after year, even those in advertising who deplored Johnson's anti-communist merchandising tactics were unable or unwilling to defy him. The corporate sponsors of television or radio shows would often panic whenever Johnson claimed their products promoted programming that featured what he called "Stalin's little creatures."

Ad agencies stopped buying time on programs employing blacklisted show people. The networks went along. Talent agencies navigated the currents, seeking safe passage for their clients. All played their parts in this shadowy dance, second-guessing a jittery nation whose people mostly wanted peace and quiet and a chance to get ahead—and who didn't care much for liberals, atheists, or nonconformists, much less communists and their sympathizers.

In yielding to Johnson and his commercial pressure, broadcasters sidestepped due process, freedom of speech and association, the presumption of innocence, and more. It was strictly about the bottom line, market share, or, as the studios often claimed when they sent out the termination slips, audience ratings.

Johnson's critics looked at him as a small-minded provincial tradesman out of his depth, obsessed with paranoid fantasies of communist subversion, cruelly assassinating reputations and careers.

To this day, many regard the anti-communism furor of the 1950s as the McCarthy Era, a dark period when the nation was held captive by an ugly combination of fear, intolerance, and indifference. According to these "anti-anti-communists," the blacklisters represented the real threat by exploiting the nation's insecurities, sweeping up innocent liberals in their nets, stifling free expression and creativity, and trampling on civil rights. To Johnson's critics, the anti-communists snatched opportunity from loyal Americans who dared to imagine a better, more equitable society. In their view, the targeted were the heroes; it took courage to defy congressional committees, proudly plead the Fifth Amendment against self-incrimination, refuse to name names, sacrifice their own careers, and sometimes go to jail.

On the other hand, decades later, many conservatives still see Johnson and his fellow anti-communists as justified in their dire warnings, if not always their methods. Plentiful evidence has emerged over the years to buoy their claims that, indeed, there was a communist influence in government, labor unions and various professions, including entertainment. The end of the Soviet Union in 1990 provided access to KGB archives. Along with the release of the code-breaking Venona papers starting in 1995, this new evidence documented Soviet-backed espionage and covert activity by hundreds of Americans, up to the highest levels of government. Even if they weren't hardline Communist Party members trying to establish a Stalinist regime in America, they were doing their best to promote Moscow's interests. Communists not only supported Henry Wallace's Progressive Party campaign for president in 1948, they helped to lead it.

Zealous anti-communists such as Johnson were, in many ways, unremarkable Americans, notable more for their representative traits than for any demonic attributes. Not a clubman by nature, Johnson joined organizations but shunned leadership roles outside his business interests. He had no congressional or executive mandate to pursue subversives. What was in it for him? Nothing financially. He never recouped the thousands he spent on his anti-communist work.

The flame of his influence flared for only half a decade. In 1956, he finally faced a challenge he could not overcome: a libel suit brought by blacklisted entertainer John Henry Faulk.

At the New York City show trial six years later, celebrated attorney Louis Nizer sued on behalf of Faulk. Johnson and his co-defendants were represented by attorney Thomas Bolan from the law firm of former McCarthy aide Roy Cohn.

Many in the entertainment business held out hope the trial would snuff out the final embers of anti-communist civic activism in America.

Even before the verdict, Laurence Johnson's reputation as a shrewd marketer and a supermarket patriot had been irrevocably tarnished, his legacy seen as something akin to damaged goods.

CHAPTER ONE:
A Rooted American

Laurence Johnson's family lore is entwined with American history, right back to the early years of Colonial settlement. A maternal ancestor, Walter Palmer, helped found Stonington, Connecticut, where he died in 1661. Another maternal forebear, Captain Roger Clap, sailed from England to the Massachusetts Bay Company around 1630, as John Winthrop was establishing the settlement of Boston. Clap was just 21 years old. He and his wife apparently thrived in the New World. The names of some of their 14 children bear witness to their sturdy Nonconformist faith—Preserved, Wait, Thanks, Desire, Unite, Supply, Experience, Hopestill, and Waitstill.

Many of Johnson's ancestors were farmers or commercial traders. Among the first merchants in Connecticut was Thomas Stanton, who had arrived in Virginia as a boy. His trading prowess with the Indians up and down the Eastern Seaboard earned him appointment as interpreter by the Massachusetts Bay Company; Johnson wrote later that it was to Stanton that Uncas, the "last of the Mohegans," went to have his will drawn up. In 1638, the Connecticut General Court granted Stanton exclusive trading rights with the Indians. He eventually built a trading establishment in Hartford. Family records note that Indians killed Roger Bartlett, another maternal forebear, in Northampton, Massachusetts, on March 4, 1684. Johnson's great-great-grandfather, Edmund Johnson, fought for Rhode Island in the Revolutionary War. Another ancestor, Nathaniel Ayres, was a private in New York's Sussex Regiment.

A thrilling tale is told about another maternal ancestor, Lucretia Miner. After fleeing from Indian attacks in Pennsylvania's Wyoming Valley, she and her family suffered through lean years, eventually finding themselves interned in Fort Oswego, New York, then in British hands. Evidently her trials had not dampened her spirit; in one confrontation, she was said to have pressed against the crossed swords of British bayonets until they drew blood. She and her family escaped when Fort Oswego fell to the Indians, or so the story goes.

Another ancestor, Amos York, also landed in British custody in Oswego during the Revolutionary War after he refused to swear allegiance to the Crown. Though the experience left him and his family penniless, they eventually managed to resettle and rebuild their lives in Connecticut.

By the mid-1800s, many of Laurence Johnson's forebearers were farmers whose homesteads dotted the Northeast—Stonington, Connecticut; Newbury, Massachusetts; Woodbridge, New Jersey; and Trumansburg, Stillwater and Savannah, New York. When the Civil War broke out, Johnson's great-grandfather, Morris Craw, looked after the farm while his twin sons went off to do battle for the Union. Johnson's Uncle Laurence became a Union officer.

A POLITICIZED FARMER

Laurence Johnson's paternal grandfather, Thomas Johnson, was born in 1812 in Stillwater, New York. Tall at 6-foot-2 and athletic as a young student, Thomas was known to walk forty miles in one day. Thomas moved to the Savannah, New York, area about 1835. There he met Anceanda Craw, perhaps on a visit to old Morris Craw's tavern on the Post Road between South Butler and Spring Lake, where Anceanda cooked for and served the traveling clientele. They married on March 5, 1840, and had two sons.

Thomas Johnson taught school in South Butler, and he took on the job of local justice of the peace. He served one term in the New York State Legislature. But Thomas didn't take to Albany; he had little patience for the florid rhetoric of 19th-century statesmanship. An intensely religious man, he shunned profanity. His favorite imprecations were "Gosh all hemlock!" and "Consarn it!" Family records tell that, upon hearing a speech by one spellbinder in Savannah, he remarked that he had "never heard such a diarrhea of words and such a constipation of thought."

Anceanda Craw Johnson made good use of the skills she had learned at her father's tavern. Her salt pork with milk gravy and mashed potatoes became family legends, as did her cakes, cookies, and pies. She also earned a reputation for maintaining order in the household and remaining calm in adversity.

According to family lore, Thomas returned to to the house one afternoon to read the paper. When he was ready to go out again, he couldn't find his straw hat. After working himself up into a lather, he confronted his wife, suggesting she had put it somewhere. She replied demurely that she hadn't even seen it on his head when he came in. He stormed out, only to return a moment later with a sheepish grin to confess: "It was up behind a beam in the hog pen."

In an 1875 letter to his sons, Thomas wrote an eloquent assessment of his life's work, concluding that "providence has led me to reflect on the past and as I do so I can't but exclaim O! how merciful and good God has been to unworthy me. Forty years ago I came into this country a poor boy and by the aid of your dear mother and a kind providence, I also may add my children, we have secured a good earthly home."

A BOLD VENTURE

Laurence Johnson's maternal grandfather, Stephen Beckwith Ayres, was born in Trumansburg, New York, in 1819. He showed his mercantile talents early, working in bustling country stores. He married Artemesia Dunlap of nearby Ovid, and the couple settled in Penn Yan. Stephen and Artemesia made a handsome couple and enjoyed the finer things in life. They accumulated an estimable library, a rarity in the farm country of Central New York.

After working for nearly two decades in other people's stores, Stephen Ayres was seized with the idea of moving west and becoming a frontier entrepreneur. In 1857, the family moved to Fort Dodge, Iowa, which had a population of less than 1,000. There, Stephen Ayres set up shop in a small two-story brick building with a wooden awning out front and a sign on the facade proclaiming "S.B. Ayres." The business prospered. A picture postcard of downtown Fort Dodge prominently featuring the Ayres emporium looks so perfect for the era it could be mistaken for a Hollywood backlot set.

By the time their daughter, Ida, was born April 11, 1858, her father had become a civic leader, with interests in real estate and banking. He became the local agent for the Aetna Fire Insurance Company of Hartford. Eager to attract immigrants, Stephen advertised passenger tickets from Liverpool, England, to New York "at current rates." As Fort Dodge grew, other merchants competed for customers. Stephen resisted his competitors' practice of carrying whiskey in a "customer's barrel" with a handy tin cup. With his sober business sense, he combined a keen understanding of the value of advertising and maintaining high visibility in newspapers. One indication of the healthy volume of his business was his advertisement that ran on January 17, 1865: "Wanted: $20,000 worth of prime furs for which the highest market price will be paid."

Two months after that notice appeared, Artemesia Ayres died. Her health had been declining, but her death nonetheless shocked the family.

Little Ida, not yet seven, was a bright girl whose mother had spent time reading to her from the family library—books on subjects ranging from botany to Latin. Artemesia had instilled in her daughter a love of learning that Ida would pass on to her own children.

Without his beloved Artemesia by his side, Stephen lost interest in the Fort Dodge adventure. He sold out and returned to Penn Yan as a wealthy man. He retreated to his library and cultivated other interests, among them ownership of the *Yates County Chronicle*. He died at sixty-eight on November 23, 1887, two years before Ida gave birth to Laurence Johnson.

A FARM COUPLE

Laurence's father, Francis Marion Johnson, was born May 17, 1852, in the family's log cabin home in Savannah, New York. Thomas and Anceanda Johnson named their son after General Francis Marion, the Swamp Fox of the Revolutionary War who had distinguished himself in battle

CHAPTER ONE: A Rooted American

at Savannah, Georgia. Francis Johnson attended the local public school, studied for a time at Cazenovia Seminary, then settled into farm life.

Like his father, Francis taught school during the long Central New York winters. However, he liked nothing better than to be out in the fields setting traps for woodchucks under the straw, or fishing for bullheads he had stocked in the farm's sheep-washing pond. Family records tell of Francis' encounter once with a skunk; his clothes had to be scorched before they were wearable again.

Francis and Ida Ayres married on November 21, 1878. Ida was twenty, Francis twenty-six. They settled in Savannah, New York, for by then Francis had just about taken over the farm from his father. A daughter, Margaret Louise, was born July 24, 1883. With Francis in charge, old Thomas Johnson could spend more time at the country stores in Savannah or South Butler, trading stories with the Civil War veterans; discussing the iniquities of Tammany Hall, the bewildering Tilden-Hayes presidential vote, the horrifying Garfield assassination, or marveling over the suspension bridge being built between Brooklyn and Manhattan.

Francis Johnson also found room for political discussions. A letter he wrote to his brother, Laurence, in 1878 displayed a keen interest in the standoff between President Hayes and New York State's uncrowned king of Republicanism, Senator Roscoe Conkling, over the issue of patronage and civil service reform.

Although Central New York was well-settled by the late 1800s, there was still plenty of wilderness and wildlife. On the farm, a shotgun was usually kept handy to ward off wildcats or the occasional bear lumbering out of the woods.

One day, Ida Johnson accompanied her nephew Edmund Roe Johnson on a mission to execute a woodchuck he had trapped. "While carrying the gun with the trigger cocked and down alongside of her she accidentally pulled the trigger and the bullet went into the ground through her flowing skirt," he recalled. "She showed no great concern, as if it were all in a day's work. However, I heard Uncle Marion give her a good dressing down when he noticed the powder-burn hole in the skirt as he returned."

Laurence Ayres Johnson was born on April 3, 1889. His parents named him after his Uncle Laurence, a doctor in Lyons, New York.

On a spring day while Laurence Johnson was still an infant, Francis caught a nasty cold while sitting too long on the ground topping onions. The family recorded that the cold "went to his hips" and became a nagging presence. There were complications, including a crippling abscess. Uncle Laurence, the doctor, did all he could, then took Francis to New York City to enlist the help of colleagues and specialists.

After much suffering, Francis Johnson died February 21, 1891, three months before his thirty-ninth birthday.

HEADED FOR DISASTER

Ida Johnson was then at age thirty-two a widow with two young children. After a decent interval, she married Michael Welch, also a farmer. Ida Ayres Johnson-Welch was ready for a new chapter in her life.

In 1894, the couple sold their interest in the Savannah farm and invested in a spread in Hyde County, South Carolina. Ida had as encouragement the example of her father, S.B Ayres, who prospered after his move to Fort Dodge a half-century earlier.

Under the terms of their contract, the Welches were supposed to end up with equity in the farming property. But there were loopholes. According to the Johnson family account, the seller's agent counted on the Yankees to fail. Then he would foreclose on them, ending up with both the land and the couple's life savings. But Michael and Ida surprised him. They were experienced farmers, hard-working and determined. Using the last of their resources, they bought modern farm machinery, hired skilled farm workers, and introduced efficient techniques. Their diligence was rewarded with a bountiful harvest and profitable crop sales.

By the time a son Donald, Laurence's half-brother, was born February 1, 1895, the young family seemed to be making a go of it. Michael and Ida could keep up with the mortgage payments, which meant no foreclosure. Their success was not part of the plan of the agent who had expected the property and the Welches' investment to fall into his lap.

Family records and recollections tell what happened next. The strange men came at night after little Laurence was in bed in the farmhouse. Suddenly, his stepfather was standing over the bed, shaking him awake, almost kicking him out from under the covers, onto the floor and under

CHAPTER ONE: A ROOTED AMERICAN

the bed. Somewhere in the house, a window shattered. The terrified boy heard the "pop! pop!" of shots fired somewhere in the dark.

Suddenly, it was no longer so dark. Through the window, the sky lit up. The barn was on fire. In the house with Margaret and Laurence, Ida Welch cradled baby Donald while her husband clutched his rifle, waiting.

The hoodlums never got into the house. It's unclear whether they planned to kill the Welches or merely to harass them. One theory is that the men had been hired to attack the farm, drive the family out of the house, and shoot them. But the clumsy ruffians initially mistook the barn for the house, spoiling the surprise and giving Michael Welch and his men the chance to defend themselves.

The Welches escaped with their lives. The case was investigated, there were arrests, and some men were jailed—though apparently the alleged mastermind was not among them.

The Welches were ruined. The barn and the equipment and crops stored there were a total loss. Michael Welch could no longer keep up payments on the mortgage, so he and his wife were forced to give up the farm.

With money running out, the family boarded a train heading back North. Accompanying them were two Black farmhands who had stayed loyal to their employer.

Starting over back in Wayne County, Michael was conscientious and experienced, so his farming prospects were good—if only he and his wife could put the Hyde County nightmare behind them. This was not to be. The man who owned the South Carolina property sued Michael Welch over the settlement. The case dragged on for years, draining the Welches' meager finances. Michael had to put off plans to build a house for his family. The lawsuit eventually petered out.

Many years later, during one of his frequent jaunts around the country, Laurence Johnson took his wife and children back to the site of the farm in South Carolina. "Dad wanted to show it to us," recalled daughter Eleanor. "He inquired at the local grocery store. Dad came out laughing. It seems they wondered if he had come back to reclaim any interest in it. There were sidelong glances.

"We went to the farm," she continued. "It seemed to be a commercial enterprise, with a beautiful plant. As we approached the farmyard, Dad was holding a movie camera. I wonder if they thought it might be a gun."

Having already endured the premature death of her first husband, Ida Welch endured more tragedy when her daughter fell seriously ill, probably from tuberculosis. Margaret Louise had graduated from high school and was studying to enter Wells College in nearby Aurora, New York. She died the day after her sixteenth birthday, July 25, 1899. Her brother Laurence was ten.

"They were wild with grief," Eleanor Buchanan said of the family. "It was a terrible blow to my father."

Then Ida Welch's own health failed. Laurence Johnson dropped out of high school to help care for his mother.

Ida died August 10, 1905, in Savannah. She was forty-seven.

FINDING HIS WAY

Uncle Laurence quickly took his nephew, then sixteen, under his wing, sending him to the Cazenovia Seminary. During the summer, young Laurence worked on farms around Savannah.

He also took odd jobs at the Wilson Brothers General Store. The shop had been in business since 1864 in South Butler, a tiny community near the Johnson family farm. The Johnsons shopped and traded in hamlets such as South Butler, Clyde, and Spring Lake. Writing years later, Laurence Johnson was still able to describe in minute detail the magical dexterity with which Judson Green, who kept store in Spring Lake, improvised paper "pokes" to wrap up his wares:

> After he had the desired amount of bulk commodity in the hopper of the scale—rolled oats, sugar, beans, maybe nails— he would reach under the counter and bring up a sheet of wrapping paper. With his right hand he'd toss it in the air, holding one corner in his hand. A quick flip and a twist of the wrist, and he held a cornucopia. Folding the small end upward, he'd pick the hopper off the scales and pour whatever was in it into

the cornucopia, jounce it once or twice to settle it, fold the top over, reach above him for the string dangling from the string-holder and tie up his package—all in the twinkling of an eye.

Johnson also recalled an early encounter with a master in the art of merchandising. The boy was scarcely ten years old when a traveling salesman arrived at the farm:

> Pete, the Johnson hired man, was called away from his work at cutting and stringing tobacco to talk with a "celluloid peddler," a Mr. Howe from Port Byron. The next Sunday afternoon when Pete started out to call on his girl, sitting stiff and straight in his buggy behind his little trotting mare...he was resplendent in celluloid collar, celluloid tie, celluloid shirt bosom, and celluloid cuffs, all in brilliant pink. His cuff links, also celluloid, had been "thrown in to boot" by the enterprising Mr. Howe.

After dropping out of Cazenovia Seminary following one term, Johnson found work as a clerk and delivery truck driver for the general store in Clyde, New York. His wage was six dollars per week, soon to rise to $7.50. Johnson never forgot the day he got the raise—he said he had never been happier.

However, farming drew him away from shopkeeping after just six months. Dressed in dusty overalls, he would bump along a rutted road to deliver milk to the creamery in South Butler every day at noon, do some trading, or pick up his mail. Farming may not have been his main interest in life, but he did well for himself. Before he was twenty, Johnson had saved enough to set up his own 67-acre farm, including eight acres of apple orchards on Taylor Road, two miles outside of South Butler.

Johnson shared his mother's love of books, music, and theater. Given the opportunity, particularly during the winter when farm chores were at a minimum, he would take in a performance of "Uncle Tom's Cabin" or similar fare at the Odd Fellows Hall in South Butler, put on by groups like the Syracuse Lyceum Bureau in circuit travels throughout Central New York.

Johnson himself was known to have performed onstage. Howard Williams, a contemporary from South Butler, recalled seeing him and a couple of his friends doing a clog dance to entertain the audience between the acts. The 200-seat auditorium would be packed, and the trio made quite a racket on the wooden slats of the stage floor while the pianist set the pace. "It took some dancing skill," Williams said. "As a kid I thought they were pretty skillful at it. The crowd liked it. They always got a big hand."

During his travels, Johnson encountered Hermione D. Cartner. The spirited and vivacious young woman was born in Victory, New York, of Dutch and English ancestry. One of her English ancestors, Edward Doty, was aboard the Mayflower as a bondsman, according to daughter Marilyn Giancola. Doty was said to be argumentative and hot-tempered. He was involved in shady deals but generally prospered in the new colony. "He was the first one convicted of a crime," daughter Eleanor Buchanan noted cryptically. "He worked off his passage."

Hermione grew up in Auburn, New York, where she graduated from high school and demonstrated early talent as a substitute teacher. "She taught kids sometimes as old as she was," said daughter Lois Wangerman, "and definitely bigger."

Laurence and Hermione were married on December 10, 1913. The young couple settled on Johnson's farm, and Hermione, for the moment, shelved yearnings for a cosmopolitan lifestyle and concentrated on helping to grow fruits and vegetables.

Hermione brought to the marriage a quiet, good humor and sparkling charm. "She looked and acted ten years younger than her age," daughter Marilyn recalled.

In 1914, for reasons the family was unable to fathom, Laurence Johnson's sandy hair suddenly turned snowy white. At age twenty-five, he stood 6 feet tall, with broad shoulders and barrel chest, his skin burnished by the elements, his hands toughened by farm labor.

With the birth of daughter Lois on June 30, 1915, the couple's lifestyle changed. Hermione now worked less on farm chores. This increased burden on her husband merely aggravated his restlessness.

CHAPTER ONE: A ROOTED AMERICAN

Laurence Johnson's wife, Hermione, stands next to a doll table with Staffordshire china in their Syracuse home as part of a "Victorian Shop" display that was open to the public for tours on May 23, 1953. (Syracuse *Post-Standard* photo)

Laurence's grandfather, Thomas Johnson, viewed the farm as his "earthly home." Not Laurence Johnson. He soon began hunting for a way out of farming.

As an agricultural worker with a wife and baby, Johnson was exempt from military service in World War I. Thus, Johnson remained in overalls until late in the war. When he decided to leave farming, the Germans were retreating at St.-Mihiel and Meuse-Argonne, the British were breaking through the Hindenburg line, and the Bolsheviks were plotting an end to the Romanovs. By 1919, Johnson and his family had settled in Syracuse, New York. Hermione was delighted. She had longed for the cultural milieu of an urban environment. It was with her blessing, if not prodding, that they made the move.

Laurence Johnson went to work for Edgar Jennings, who lived in Lyons but owned The Market Basket in Solvay on the western edge of Syracuse. Johnson now wore the starched white shirt and stiff collar of the up-and-coming shopkeeper.

After several months, Johnson took a better position managing a small store in Syracuse owned by William A. Genant. Hermione also began helping in the store—a chore she would never learn to love.

Laurence Johnson itched to have a store of his own. A year after moving to Syracuse, he took his accumulated savings, borrowed an additional $200, and opened his first store in a small building on Lemoyne Avenue. His business flourished.

Hermione also blossomed in Syracuse, where she became president of the Lemoyne Elementary School PTA, sat on the board of the Girl Scouts, and was a founder of the Corinthian Club, an enduring cultural bastion. Lois said both parents were fine bridge players, and Hermione won master's points in duplicate bridge. In 1934, they visited the New York World's Fair—indulging in the same curiosity and enthusiasm that inspired Johnson's mother, Ida, 40 years earlier to attend the Columbian Exposition in Chicago.

THE CHANGING MARKETPLACE

Syracuse was a dynamic commercial crossroads in the early 1900s. Up to the turn of the century, cargo barges plying the Erie Canal would unload at canal-side warehouses. Horse-drawn carts carried produce and wares to market, and the barges pulled up to the Weighlock Building on Clinton Street. But by 1920, the canal had been abandoned for commercial purposes, soon to be filled in throughout downtown Syracuse. However, the city remained commercially viable because of the railroad, whose tracks led past Hanover Square and City Hall. Syracuse was "the city where the train runs through town."

In Dearborn, Michigan, the Ford Model T began rolling off assembly lines. Before long, motorized vehicles were a competitive means of delivering products to markets in Syracuse and elsewhere.

The first mail-order catalog stores—Sears & Roebuck and Montgomery Ward—were sending out their "dream books" to urban and rural America. Their catalogs opened new vistas of consumption to customers who had been captives of the local market.

CHAPTER ONE: A Rooted American

A flood of products from new factories filled the shelves of F.W. Woolworth's 5&10s. By 1911, there were a thousand of these discount stores.

Goaded by the competition, large manufacturers introduced national advertising campaigns and colorful packaging to catch the shopper's eye. Many consumers stopped asking for soap, flour, corn flakes and coffee, and started demanding Ivory, Gold Medal, Kellogg's, and Maxwell House.

The 1920s were a decade of hard work for Laurence and Hermione Johnson. He opened a second store at 1701 Court Street, doing business six days a week.

The couple's second daughter, Marilyn, was born on January 2, 1924, and the young family moved to a spacious frame house at 165 Kuhl Avenue. The third daughter, Eleanor, arrived on June 29, 1925. On busy days, Lois would watch her two younger sisters while their parents worked.

Laurence Johnson decided the family could afford a car in addition to the delivery truck; he bought a new Buick. With the luxury of mobility, Johnson began to indulge a restless desire to see the country and experience history firsthand. On Sundays, holidays, and rare vacations, he packed up his young family for trips to the locks along the Erie Canal, to Ticonderoga or Gettysburg.

"He was marvelous to go places with," Lois remembered. "He'd know all about it, tell stories about the town or the fields."

By the mid-1920s, Laurence Johnson was making a decent living in the grocery business while the family settled into their lively residential neighborhood. One of the Johnsons' neighbors was Burnett Haylor, who co-founded an insurance business in 1928 that became one of the region's largest. The Haylors and the Johnsons both had children in Lemoyne Elementary School.

Haylor remembered how, in those days, he would pass the hard-working Johnson driving his car to the wholesale houses to pick up a 100-pound bag of sugar or another bulk commodity. Johnson was a canny buyer, and his thrifty habits and budding talents as a merchandiser served him well. When he purchased wholesale goods, he made a point of paying his debt within ten days, earning a two percent discount. What profit he made mostly went back into his stores.

Johnson and his wife continued to enjoy an active social life, particularly after they moved to 1202 Broad Street, where he built a country store replica in the basement. Haylor remembered house parties with a half-dozen couples—Dr. Warren Saile, advertising executive Jack Flack, and others. "We'd have cocktails and go to dinner," Haylor recalled. "During Prohibition, we'd drink bootleg alcohol."

Henry "Tink" Keller, who was advertising manager at the Syracuse *Post-Standard* newspaper, remembered the night Johnson produced a bottle of moonshine. "He brought out a jug of White Mule he had bought down in Kentucky," Keller said. "And he had a picture of the place where the stuff was made. We each took a couple of slugs."

Family friend Jasena Foley described house parties that turned into weekend slumber parties. "We'd all spend the night and through the weekend. In the morning he'd get up and get breakfast for everyone. Oh, boy, he loved that." One night, Johnson brought out trunks full of old clothes, and there was a costume party. "He said, 'Now Jasena, you pick a hat for every woman,'" she said. "So that was fun."

Like many others, Johnson invested in the overheated stock market. With the market crash in October 1929, he lost what little he had accumulated. When Johnson tried afterward to get bank financing to expand his business, the bankers asked for collateral—which had vanished in the crash. Later, they rejected him again when he sought bank financing for bulk purchases. On both occasions Johnson managed to raise the necessary capital through friends and from his own perseverance. The experience was enough to shake forever his confidence in the financial community. "He never really trusted banks or bankers afterward," daughter Lois said.

The banks came around eventually. Thomas Higgins, a banker who moved to Syracuse in 1937, became a friend. By 1939, he and Johnson were lunching regularly. "I knew him as a customer," Higgins said. "He was a good customer at the bank. He built up a great credit reputation."

Notwithstanding those generous words, Johnson made sure he never grew overly reliant on the fickle financial marketplace. At the time of his death decades later, Johnson's entire investment portfolio consisted of

CHAPTER ONE: A Rooted American

300 shares in the "Tweetsie Railroad" amusement park in Blowing Rock, North Carolina.

TAKING THE PLUNGE

By the end of the 1920s, Johnson was eager to move beyond the boundaries of conventional shopkeeping, which was largely unchanged from a half-century earlier. Markets were laid out in the same haphazard fashion, bursting with a profusion of pickle barrels, canisters of beans and other dry goods, and shelves stacked high behind the counter. The inventory might change from store to store, but within each one there was seldom any variety. Brand names were still something of a novelty. Name recognition was just dawning on the American shopper. Most of the time, the customer could either buy the pickle or not buy the pickle; there was no such thing as choosing one brand over another.

The customer would enter the store, approach the counter, catch the clerk's eye, and place an order. The clerk would assemble the items, measuring and wrapping as required. Most often, the clerk would add the cost of the order to the customer's credit bill; only occasionally would cash change hands then.

Johnson ran his markets along these lines, though he thought it a highly inefficient way to do business. Johnson was as generous with credit as any merchant during the Depression, in some cases allowing bills to reach $400 or even $500 with little hope of immediate repayment. Said his daughter Marilyn, "Ten years later, some began to pay it back. They were proud, honest people."

The problem, Johnson knew, wasn't the customer. It was the system. And the problem with the system could be divided into two parts: inefficient credit practices and inconvenient customer service. Johnson's solution was to turn the old country store into the self-service, cash-and-carry supermarket.

A few merchants—Johnson included—had been tinkering with self-service for years, but it had not caught on, as he explained in his 1961 book, "Over the Counter & On the Shelf: Country Storekeeping In America, 1620-1920":

Practically all foodstuffs once handled in bulk were packaged. Occasionally an independent storekeeper arranged packaged goods so that the customer could make his own selection, carry it to the counter for payment, and avoid a long wait for service. Though this practice worked well for the few who tried it, it was generally considered a pretty slipshod way of doing business.

Johnson was not the first to open a modern "supermarket" in the United States. That honor reportedly belongs to Michael J. Cullen, a former Kroger Co. manager who devised a scheme for a self-service market and asked his company to back him. But he got nowhere. So, he resigned and rented a huge garage in Jamaica, Queens, and converted it into the nation's first supermarket, King Kullen.

Customers flocked to his novel market, and word of the concept's success spread along the retail grapevine. Johnson finally saw his chance. He had been talking up the self-service store for some time. Now, with a supermarket operating, Johnson persuaded a couple of potential investors to make the trip with him to Queens, where he sold them on the concept.

In December 1931, Johnson and his two partners entered business as Associated Foods Incorporated. Johnson, at age forty-two, was president, part owner and manager of the group's store on the intersection of Burnet and Hawley avenues in Syracuse. Thus was born what Johnson would proudly call "the second self-service market in the East."

Johnson soon converted his credit store on Court Street into a cash-and-carry market as well. (He kept the old black cash box, complete with credit slips, as a souvenir. The family eventually donated the artifact to the Onondaga Historical Association.)

As is usual when someone comes up with a new idea, some say it won't succeed. After Johnson took the plunge and opened his first supermarket, his daughter Eleanor remembered, a food salesman walked up to him at a diner. "He warned Dad not to put all his eggs in one basket," she said. "He thought supermarkets were a flash in the pan."

As soon as he could afford it, Johnson departed Associated Foods and opened the first Johnson's Super Market in a roomy building at 1114 South

CHAPTER ONE: A ROOTED AMERICAN

Shoppers leave Johnson's supermarket, 1114 South Salina Street, Syracuse, in this undated photo. (Onondaga Historical Association photo)

Salina Street. Eventually, he would have six stores: four in Syracuse and two in neighboring Oswego County.

For Johnson, the South Salina Street store would become what Menlo Park was to Thomas Edison—the laboratory of a commercial pioneer.

CHAPTER TWO:
The Innovator

Times were tough for Laurence Johnson and his family in the 1930s. Not as bad as for those without jobs during the Great Depression, but it was bad enough to make it a constant struggle to get by. It would be years before Johnson could afford to tinker fully with his new supermarkets, and even more years after that before success allowed him to join the anti-communist movement.

Even in those challenging early days, Johnson was making discoveries that would profoundly affect not only his own markets but also the entire American retail trade. The novelty of the supermarket in 1931 is hard to imagine today. Said Johnson's business manager, Mary Coyne: "He probably brought the first self-service meat to Syracuse. Things you take for granted, he brought so many of those innovations himself."

Johnson quickly recognized a dehumanizing aspect of the supermarket. In the old country store, the merchant-shopkeeper was a living, breathing point of contact. Not only was he the agent who made the store work for his customers, he was a bulletin board, a community message service, a consultant, and an adviser. The self-service market moved the focus from the shopkeeper to the products—where it belonged, to be sure. But in the process, shopping lost a vital human dimension. Much later, Johnson noted wistfully: "Self-service presented its own problems. One, for which there seems no remedy, is the lack of contact between customer and those who work in stores."

However, Johnson never gave up trying to overcome shopper-shopkeeper alienation. He decorated his stores with artifacts of Americana he collected, and he set up special displays on holidays and patriotic occasions. His most ambitious strategy came in 1938 when he built a replica of an entire "old country store" within the walls of his flagship market on South Salina Street. Installing original hardwood shelves and a counter, he "stocked" his replica with dozens of items, some dating back to the early 1800s—an antique coffee grinder, bolts of fabric, tin kerosene cans, straw baskets of eggs, and an old-fashioned cracker barrel.

By blending his love of shopkeeping folklore with his knack for merchandising, Johnson found a combination that worked. Customers could shop at Johnson's market for the spectacle of the "country store" and for bargains on up-to-date brands. In juxtaposing the self-service market and the nostalgic set-piece, Johnson also underscored the appeal of modernity. The mom-and-pop store might still be doing business in the traditional way, but at Johnson's Super Market, the Old Country Store was already an antique. With this adaptation of a play-within-a-play, Johnson deftly consigned the old-style market to the past, even as he promoted its super successor.

Coyne, who signed on for a clerical job for Johnson in 1940 after working for several years at a wholesaler, remembered what a difference his store made to the shopping experience.

"Food was in the case. There was no fuss. Help yourself," she said. "Everything was self-service, and everything was displayed. You might have fifty cases of soups, fifty cases of soaps. He was a leader in starting much of this. He would build all kinds of pyramid displays. He invented them."

One other thing was different in this new supermarket.

"It was definitely cash. No credit," Coyne said. "You paid cash and you saved money."

Another early Johnson discovery was that many products on his shelves had not kept pace with his new means of delivery to the customer. Without the shopkeeper to pre-select products or fill orders, customers were on their own as they went along the aisles. In choosing between competing brands, all other factors being equal, Johnson noted, the customer seemed to prefer the product with the most familiar name. The key, Johnson recognized right away, was advertising. Self-service customers "selected advertised brands, ignoring nationally unknown merchandise of quality and value on which stores had formerly made a good profit," Johnson wrote later.

While Johnson may have lost the kind of contact his predecessors had with their customers, he was among the first to realize that the customer is king (or queen) in the self-service market. In the following decades, Johnson would ride this discovery into unexplored regions of retail merchandising and marketing, with implications that were practical and profound —and, ultimately, political.

FIGHTING BOTTLE THEFT

One problem the new self-service merchant encountered was not unique to the cash-and-carry market. It involved empty soda bottles, which had a value back then of two cents each. For reasons of space, Johnson stored his empties outside. The problem was that the bottles kept disappearing. The likely culprits: neighborhood boys. However, Johnson didn't want to have the youngsters arrested—after all, they could be the sons of his best customers.

At first, he tried to solve the problem by stacking his bottles on the roof, out of reach of young hands. This cumbersome practice went on until one lad approached Johnson, looked up at the imposing figure with the wire-rimmed spectacles and that shock of white hair, and made a bold suggestion: "Hi, Mr. Johnson! Can we sort bottles for you?" With a scowl, Johnson initially contemplated the question, but he eventually realized the enterprising boy had offered a solution to the bottle pilferage. From then on, Johnson shared his bottle profits with the boys, who in turn zealously guarded "their" inventory from theft.

Johnson went on to reap more dividends from the arrangement, as some of the boys grew up to be clerks and cashiers in his stores. One of them was Robert Giarrusso, who started sorting bottles when he was about ten. "We weren't on the payroll," he said of bottle duty. "I guess it was a violation of the labor laws."

Later, Giarrusso clerked for Johnson in the South Salina Street store, then worked weekends at the checkout counter. Giarrusso's older brother

THE GROCER WHO SOLD McCARTHYISM

Mario, who also had joined the bottle-sorters, used the knowledge and experience gained working for Johnson to build his own successful supermarket, Mario's Big M.

HIS INNOVATIVE WAYS

Competitors noticed this grocery idea man on South Salina Street. Some were nettled by Johnson's innovative ways—for example, his early discovery and use of "loss leaders" to lure customers.

"All the rest of the grocers used to get quite upset," Coyne recalled. "He would take four or five items and cut them right to the bone, merchandise them, and he would get quite a response. And of course, he made money on other things."

Johnson was among the first retailers to explore the intricacies of the checkout counter. What good is a self-service store, he reasoned, if the customer saved time in the shopping aisles only to waste it in a bottleneck at the cash register? Over the years, Johnson continually refined his checkout operation to improve flow and customer convenience. "His main thing was: Get the people the hell out fast!" Giarrusso said. "He did the biggest volume of any individual store on South Salina Street. And up at the counter—especially on weekends—he would have five employees at every register."

Years later, Giarrusso would remember every detail of the Johnson checkout routine operating at full tilt.

"He had an employee taking the items out of the shopping cart and putting them on the belt according to price to make it easier for the cashier, who would know how to put all the items together. Another employee would put a stick between one order and the next, so you've got them in line. The cashier would ring up the items.

"Next to the cashier was another cashier who used to have the money drawer. Off comes the bill to go to the next cashier. Now, in the interim, the second cashier didn't have to ring up, just handle the cash flow and send the packages to the two sorters assigned to each register."

The sorters bagged the groceries, putting in the items according to hardness and softness. Johnson then employed two "floaters" who would take the groceries out to the customer's vehicle.

CHAPTER TWO: THE INNOVATOR

"He cut down the time unbelievably. You can't believe how fast that line moved," Giarrusso said.

In the 1940s, Johnson would pioneer another innovation at the checkout counter—the express lane. He mounted a cardboard cutout of an old choo-choo train and tacked it to a table next to a box holding the cash register. He coined a succinct (although technically ungrammatical) phrase "Express Lane: Six Items or Less." The customer with only a few groceries could walk up to the cashier, who would ring up the items right out of the basket. "Then, pfuitt! On to the next six items," Giarrusso said.

Johnson's emerging brilliance as a supermarket and merchandising pioneer arose from native intelligence, intuition, and self-education. He was an avid, restless reader. Friends and family said they could usually find him with a newspaper in his hand.

Anti-communist crusader Vincent Hartnett, who came to know Johnson much later, was struck by the man's intellect. "He was a man not only of great abstract conceptual ability, but of course also great practical ability, as shown by his business success," Hartnett said in the 1980s. "He had a genius or near-genius IQ. He was a man with a great capacity to learn, too."

To every problem, Johnson typically applied what, to him, seemed common sense. Said Giarrusso: "He used to tell me, 'What do we want to appeal to? The low-income? The middle-income? Higher-income? Let's appeal to them all!' People would come from all over the city to Johnson's supermarkets. Wherever he could save time, he did. And a lot of competitors used to come to his store just to see what he did."

In his market on South Salina Street, Johnson built his own "bridge" —a rear office suspended over the aisles, with a clear view of the whole floor below. "He could watch you. He could see what was going on all the time," said Giarrusso, breaking into a wide grin, noting that the surveillance helped to keep employees from goofing off.

Coyne said errant stock clerks quickly mended their ways when she or Johnson assistant Joe Reschke took them aside, pointed to the suspended office of "the boss" and advised: "Hey, you should always keep that damp cloth with you."

31

In the summer, Giarrusso said, Johnson would come back from a trip to an out-of-town store with the germ of a new idea, march through his South Salina Street market to his office—surreptitiously palming a piece of fruit on the way—and retreat to his sanctum to make plans. Then, depositing the peach pit in the wastebasket for the fruit flies to feast on, he would descend to his domain and confront a hapless clerk with an outburst: "They had a big bin, built right up to the ceiling for a display. Now I want one built!" Or he would exclaim, "Everything on the shelf should be eye level!" The stock boys would scurry around, pulling products off the shelves and rearranging displays.

"He would experiment; he would change the store around," Giarrusso said. "If something wasn't moving, he'd say, 'Hey, let's give it another chance and move it to another part of the store.'"

HERALDING A NEW ORDER

As he turned his stores into an attractive arena of competing brands, Johnson put manufacturers on notice: Market your product or the customer will ignore you. He would make the shelf space available, but the manufacturer and its salesmen must do their part. "He'd tell them, 'Hey, you've got the stock, OK, you come in with a stand and display it,'" Giarrusso said. Johnson himself put it this way: "The...challenge was met successfully with new techniques—low-pressure selling, planned display, and 'talking' sales signs." Johnson played a major role in making this style of merchandising the standard in the industry.

For inspiration, Johnson wrote later, he reached back into his knowledge of the folklore of shopkeeping:

> The story is told that Sir Thomas Lipton, as a boy in his parent's little grocery in England, watching his father count out eggs and put them in the customer's basket, remarked sagely, "Let Mother serve the eggs. Her hands are smaller—the eggs will look larger." The same positive approach had been long a precept to country store clerks, weighing commodities in front of a customer: "Always put a short quantity in the hopper and

add to it to reach the required weight. If you pour in too much, then take some out, the customer is bound to feel cheated."

In self-service, the importance of the placard was learned early. Once in the Johnson market, a quantity of Old Trusty Dog Biscuits, shaped like a dog bone, were purchased in bulk, weighed out in two-pound cellophane bags, and placed for sale under a "2 lbs. for 25¢" sign. Next day a belligerent matron slapped a package of dog biscuits on the counter. "We can't eat these cookies. They're stale. They won't even dissolve in coffee." The identifying "Dog Biscuits" appeared immediately thereafter on the sign.

Johnson learned early the value of frankness and "undersell." After he began displaying a can of standard peas with a particularly attractive label, the complaints rapidly came in. Customers looking at the label expected fancy peas, and therefore believed they got shortchanged. After that, Johnson put a sign over the display: "These peas are NOT fancy, mostly standard grade. Some are overcooked, and some are hard." The reaction? "Curiosity sold the peas fast," Johnson wrote. "Nothing could be quite as bad as the sign indicated!"

Sometimes, Johnson showed his mastery of display merchandising through mischievous little experiments, according to business manager Coyne. "When there was something he wanted to sell, what we would term a 'dog,' something that doesn't move, he'd put it in a basket and say 'Only Two to a Customer'—and they went like hot cakes." She laughed. "He was very clever."

Coyne added that Johnson became an authority on labeling. "He felt it was very important, if you had a product, that you labeled it—good, attractive and simple—and tell the people what's what. He used to go to seminars throughout the country, as a representative of the food industry. His theory was that you had two packages on the shelf, and one was attractively packaged, properly worded, how much more sensible it is than if you're selling tomatoes and it's got a flowery, silly label."

Johnson's message was underscored, Coyne said, the time he sold a can of spinach with a label displaying the product topped with a poached egg:

"Some little old man came in the store and brought the can back because there was no egg in the can. That's the mind of the people.

"Mr. Johnson's idea was you sharpened up the product and sold a lot more. He was a salesman. If you're going to catch the customer, you've got to have a good product, colorfully, attractively packaged. He was very with-it."

BREAKING INTO PRINT

Word of Johnson's experiments reached the editors of *Printer's Ink*, a trade journal of the advertising industry. The result was an article in the April 4, 1941, edition titled "Super-Market Owner Tells Manufacturers How to Sell Him." The article carried Johnson's byline, along with a grabber: "Why Good Packaging Is Vital Factor in Supers and All Other Branches of Successful Retailing; Some Valuable Advice (Free but Worth Thousands) on How to Adapt Advertising to Dealers' Needs."

In the article, Johnson in plain language drew on his experiences in his Syracuse markets, making a case for the emerging revolution in merchandising. Johnson began his article modestly: "We do not pretend to appreciate all the difficulties which the manufacturer encounters." Then he passed along a bit of advice. "In my opinion, the first essential in selling super-markets is a good package." To test his thesis, he had conducted an experiment, placing two packages of the same popcorn side by side. One was in a plain package, the other in an attractive wrapper. "At equal prices, the good package outsold the poor one seven to one," Johnson said. Even when he reduced the price of the plain package, its sales still lagged.

Put descriptive labels on packages and cans, he recommended. Include suggested uses, such as at a party or as a snack; note the number of servings. ("Women, I am convinced, don't think in pounds, ounces, pints and quarts. Those are masculine measures," he wrote. "The average woman thinks in terms of how many people can be fed from the contents of the can.")

In marketing the product, Johnson wrote, the manufacturer should abandon the old-fashioned method of mass selling. The average supermarket shopper only buys small quantities of each item. Forget the glamorous national advertising campaigns. "I would rather see an advertisement which contained a couple of recipes instead of a half-dozen advertisements talking rosy cheeks, vitamins and 'Be the party queen of your neighborhood.'"

Johnson concluded, "It's my business to know my customers, and I know they want facts. And they aren't afraid of the truth....What pleases the customer, pleases the super-market operator. If the manufacturer, large or small, will gear his advertising and selling methods to this simple fact, he will find the super-market a consistently profitable outlet."

The impact of Johnson's article was immediate. An employee of J.P. McKinney & Sons, a national advertising representative, rushed to Syracuse. The employee arranged for Johnson to appear in a nationwide promotion of the new concept of "food day" newspaper advertisements. On April 12, 1941, Johnson's face appeared in an advertisement in *Editor and Publisher*, a weekly magazine of the newspaper industry, along with an excerpt from his article urging national manufacturers to run their ads in the Syracuse newspapers the same day Johnson's supermarket ads appeared.

With the article and the national promotion under his belt, Johnson was the acknowledged grocery czar of Syracuse. "Larry Johnson Fame Farflung," trumpeted the headline in *Grocers' Topics*, the monthly newsletter for Central New York grocers. Describing Johnson as "one of the best-known grocers in the country," the newsletter continued: "His eternal philosophy of selling what people want to buy, not what he thinks they should buy, has apparently reaped rewards."

THE ART OF SALESMANSHIP

The editors of *Printer's Ink* were "so well-impressed with the reception of the article that they have come back to Mr. Johnson for an additional piece of writing," according to *Grocers' Topics*. The lengthy article appeared in the May 23, 1941, issue of *Printer's Ink*. This time, Johnson's subject was how to bring the salesman into the supermarket age.

Conventional sales techniques are out of date, Johnson argued, such as the sales pitch geared simply toward making the sale ("The story ends when the boy and girl are married," he wrote. "But, in real life, isn't that just the beginning?")

Johnson also lamented the practice of "loading"—forcing large quantities of one item on a merchant—as a relic of the days when credit was the rule and there weren't many competing brands. "As I sit here writing this, I am looking down to the floor of the store," Johnson noted. "In the baskets of the shoppers, you will rarely see over two or three items of any one kind. We should very much like to buy replacements to the merchandise in somewhat the same proportions. But instead, in some instances we are forced to buy a year's supply of some foods, juices and vegetables."

Johnson shared a definition of the grocer from a message he had tacked to the wall in the salesmen's waiting room in his South Salina Street store, attributed to the legendary publisher Elbert Hubbard:

> The typical buyer is a man past middle life, spare, wrinkled, intelligent, cold, passive, noncommittal, with eyes like a codfish, polite in contact, but, at the same time, unresponsive, cool, calm, and damnably composed as a concrete post or a plaster-of-paris cat; a human petrification with a heart of feldspar and without charm, or friendly germ, minus bowels, passions or a sense of humor. Happily they never reproduce, and all of them finally go to hell.

"Well," Johnson quipped, "I am short and fat and have three daughters, but the last line—it bothers me!"

Johnson also quoted another folksy message borrowed from a display by Jason Bushnell of Brattleboro, Vermont, whom Johnson described as "that successful grocer and prince of good fellows." The message read:

> *Merchants should remember*
> *When dealing with a supersalesman*
> *That, as in shooting at a target,*
> *They must allow for the wind.*

CHAPTER TWO: THE INNOVATOR

Johnson continued by noting that salesmen did bring a lot of color into his business life, providing a measure of entertainment along with the headaches:

> They run the gamut from the starry-eyed young boy fresh out of a sales meeting to the good old high-pressure "kiss 'em where you find 'em and leave 'em where you kiss 'em" type. Then there's that rare fellow who makes a study of the situation—the buyer's stores, his methods of operation, his customers, his warehouse facilities....It is this last salesman that I would like to say more about....He sees that the displays are kept up over the week end, signs in their proper places, never whines, has no grievances. Maybe he gets a little dirt under his fingernails, but in my opinion, he's "aces."

Three months after this second article, Johnson was still making national headlines in the food industry. According to the August 1941 issue of *Progressive Grocer*, Johnson had just completed a record-breaking purchase of 300,000 pounds of frozen foods—an accomplishment at the time since many other stores didn't have equipment to handle even modest quantities of frozen produce.

Johnson had installed special subzero refrigeration equipment at his markets so he could offer customers vitamin-fresh fruits and vegetables even during the winter months.

"He was way ahead of his time," Coyne said of Johnson. "He spent a lot of his own money trying to refrigerate frozen products. I remember he had a fellow always working on equipment, because he [Johnson] knew that sale space was so valuable."

By this time, Johnson also had joined with other independent merchants in the region, such as Ben and Bernie Golub in Schenectady and Jack Wegman in Rochester, in buying merchandise by the carload and disposing of it quickly, passing along the savings to customers and giving chain-store competitor A&P a big headache.

In the early 1940s, Johnson and two friends, George and Ruth Eakins of Geneva, purchased a diner and set it up next to Johnson's store on

South Salina Street. Paradoxically, this side venture had to be shut down due to its own success. "They were there for four or five years," Coyne said. "But the two businesses couldn't prosper on the same lot because of parking. On Friday nights, there just wasn't room for them both."

Johnson drew more national publicity in September 1941, when *Modern Packaging* magazine published a story and photo layout showing his old-country-store-within-a-store setup, as well as a gleaming, spacious aisle with seven-foot-high pyramid displays on one side and bold signs on the other. "Today meets yesterday in a supermarket in Syracuse, N.Y. owned by dynamic merchandiser Laurence A. Johnson," read the blurb.

In January 1942, *Reader's Digest* featured Johnson in a paean to the bright new arena of American prosperity. It was titled, "Behold the Supermarket—It's Colossal." The article noted: "In three days Johnson in Syracuse, N.Y. can get rid of 1,800 pounds of scrod, 1,500 packages of Kellogg's corn flakes, 1,900 cans of Libby's tomatoes. Many small wholesalers would consider such quantities a tidy week's business...."

Who could blame Johnson for starting a scrapbook in 1942 to preserve the evidence of his growing fame? Spanning the next dozen years, the clippings would fill five 26-by-50-inch ledger books.

THE WARTIME MERCHANT

Two months after the Japanese attacked Pearl Harbor in December 1941, Johnson adopted imagery from the battlefield in an article for the *Bulletin of the Point of Purchase Advertising Institute*. The headline read: "Supermarket Man Sees Growing Peril for National Brands." An editorial note emphasized the need for manufacturers to concentrate on follow-up advertising at the retail level, and to pay particular attention to independent grocers as a better market for their brands than chain stores, which push their own house brands. "We wish you would read this article," the editors urged. "It comes directly from the retail sales firing line—from the point at which the final sales battle is fought."

Johnson noted that only seven operators of the thirty supermarkets in the Syracuse area were independents. The independents advertised heavily in the local papers, and were a natural outlet for national brands, he wrote:

CHAPTER TWO: The Innovator

> The simple fact is, that the manufacturer is spending millions of dollars in advertising his goods so as to create salability and consumer acceptance for them. But a large part of this effort is wasted for the reason that the manufacturers have not followed through to the point of sale....The problem is to keep the food field from being monopolized by the manufacturer-retailer. I believe the battle can be won if we apply ourselves more diligently and use our present assets more intelligently.

As a major and innovative grocery advertiser, Johnson gravitated to the Advertising Club of Syracuse, where he found a forum for his ideas and experiments. In April 1942, he was elected a club officer.

Later in the year, for the benefit of a reporter for the local paper, Johnson had some fun imagining "wonder foods" of the future. His ideas drew heavily on the innovative techniques used in soldiers' rations—processed ham and eggs; dehydrated beans baked in tomato sauce and packaged in paper containers; and coffee prepared with grain or chicory.

During World War II, grocers chafed under the increasing restrictions imposed by government labor, trade, and market regulations. Rationing, shortages, and substitutes were the daily bread between 1942 and 1945. Retailers had to use all their ingenuity to merchandise their restricted inventory to consumers spoiled by pre-war plenty.

For Johnson, these new exigencies just meant working smarter. "Don't look for miracles to help you in these war times," he counseled fellow shopkeepers in one trade journal. "Search your market for new ways of profit."

He re-told the inspirational tale that traces back to Booker T. Washington:

> When I was a little boy, my mother told me a story of people who were in distress and how they obtained aid. It was the story of the sailing ship becalmed at sea, off the coast of South America.
>
> Its sail hung lifeless. Those aboard had run out of water. Desperately they looked everywhere for aid. At last they saw a

> steamship coming over the horizon toward them, and when near enough, they signaled "Send us water. We are dying of thirst." Instantly a message was signaled back: "Drop your bucket where you are. You are off the mouth of the Amazon River, and the water underneath your ship is fresh."
>
> Hundreds of thousands of retailers throughout this land are faced with the problem of survival in business. Priorities, cessation of manufacturing in various lines, General Maximum Price Regulation, and other war situations which may prove deadly in effect, threaten their future...
>
> Why not be realistic? There is only one chap you can turn to in the solution to these vexing problems: this is the fellow who is wearing out the seat of your pants as he squirms in his chair ....We who operate self-service markets have numerous items not under price ceilings. Let's drop our bucket. Maybe we all have fresher water under our keels than we realize.

Shortly after this story appeared, Johnson received a large envelope in the mail from the J.J. McCarthy advertising agency in Los Angeles. Inside was a full-color advertisement featuring a painting of an old-fashioned galleon, its sails limp, its crew leaning over the side and dropping a bucket. Attached was a letter from J.J. McCarthy himself: "Dear Mr. Johnson: I was quite interested in your story, 'Drop Your Bucket Where You Are.' By a coincidence we developed the same title in an advertisement...."

During these challenging times, Johnson kept looking for effective ways to display his wares. One effort during the war years produced a bit of ration cheating, as Johnson described later:

> The Second World War rationing offered special temptations. In the Johnson store a display of "Seven Day" coffee in the bean was placed on a counter in the center of the store. An attendant stood near to assist in the grinding—and to pick up the ration stamp. Payment was made at the regular checkout counter. Rather than change the counter display each week, a dummy display of bags filled with sawdust and shavings was

CHAPTER TWO: The Innovator

made up. In the first week of coffee rationing, twenty-two dummy bags, dexterously removed from the display, were paid for at coffee prices. There were no complaints from the ration stamp cheaters, and the Red Cross received from the store a check for the full amount of 'sawdust' profits.

THE MENU PLANNER

The national accolades continued in March 1943 when *Better Homes and Gardens* named Johnson as "Grocer of the Month." Later in the year he expanded on the theme of good packaging in an article for *Supermarket Merchandising* magazine, which produced at least a dozen fan letters and laudatory notices from advertising agencies.

A feature article in *Woman's Home Companion* appeared in February 1944 under the title "We Asked Mr. Johnson." The magazine's food editor, Dorothy Kirk, visited Syracuse to consult Johnson on how the shopping public could enliven the bland wartime fare on the home front. Johnson took Kirk on a tour of his South Salina Street store, where she admired the wide, brightly lit aisles and the modern two-tiered shopping carts.

"I can't praise women enough for the way they've accepted a completely different set of marketing conditions," Johnson told Kirk. "They take the disappointments and delays like soldiers. Of course a few still blame the dealer. We had one only this morning. She came in expecting to buy two packages of her favorite dessert. Our allowance is sold out and we have no way of replenishing it until our next allotment falls due. When we explained our predicament to her, she felt better and willingly made another selection."

While visiting Johnson's office, Kirk pressed him for practical advice on stretching the family budget to produce appetizing meals. "Here was a neighborly service exactly to Mr. Johnson's liking," Kirk wrote of his ideas. "Seated at his desk, we made out the list which you will find on the following pages. From it our kitchen has developed one comforting cold-weather breakfast and four delightful dinners."

THE GROCER WHO SOLD McCARTHYISM

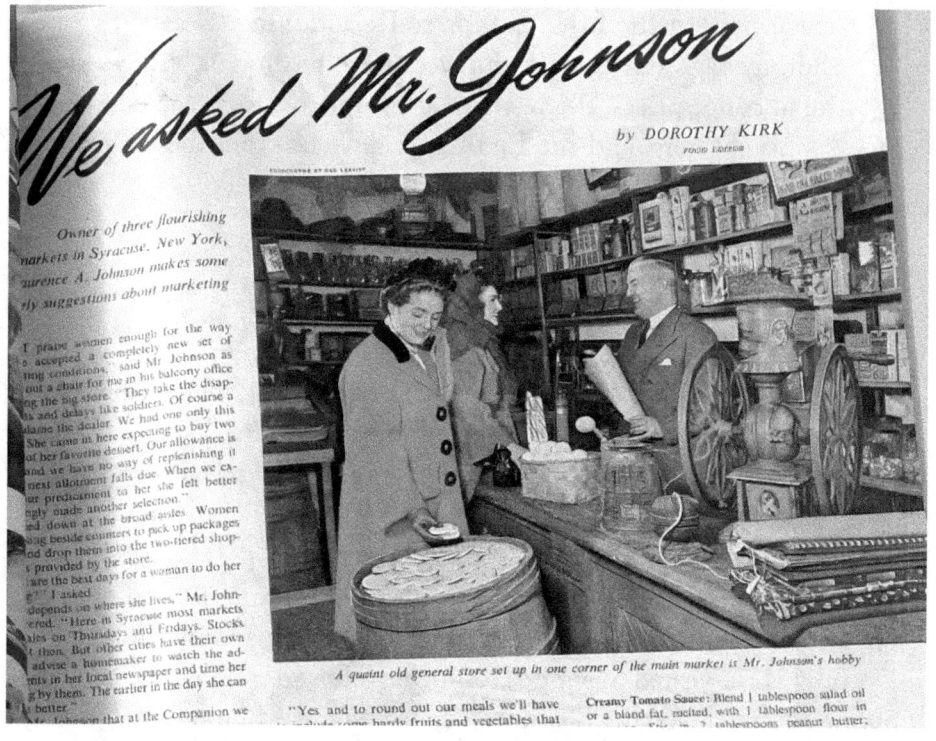

A feature story in the February 1944 issue of *Woman's Home Companion* shows Laurence Johnson behind the counter of his re-creation of the old country store.

Starting with soy grits, canned lunch meat, canned beets, raisins, tomato soup and fruit gelatin, Johnson concocted such culinary delicacies as "Ham Loaf Roll," "Soy Scallops and Browned Soy Slices," "Scotch Raisin Squares," "Macaroni and Cheese Timbales with Creamy Tomato Sauce" and "Twin Fruit Fluff." By today's standards, this is pretty humble fare. But in war-weary 1944, it was manna.

Kirk later sent Johnson a letter of appreciation: "I thought you might like to know that our February food article, 'We Asked Mr. Johnson,' got the highest readership of any article in the magazine that month."

Imagine, across America on dreary winter mornings, families were starting off their days with marmalade muffins and soy slices, and later sitting down to dinners of fish and potato puffs, stewed tomatoes, shredded carrot relish and Scotch raisin squares—all thanks to the ingenuity

CHAPTER TWO: The Innovator

of Mr. Johnson.

In July of that same year, Johnson was profiled as one of thirty-two outstanding business leaders in "The Technique of Building Personal Leadership," a book by Dr. Donald A. Laird. A business writer of the inspirational school and author of self-help guides, Laird included in this slim volume a formal photo of Johnson and a one-paragraph summary of his accomplishments to date:

> Laurence A. Johnson, founder and president of Johnson's Food, Inc., pioneered in developing supermarkets. He started as a grocery clerk, and, at the age of forty-two, used his initiative to build up his chain of supermarkets with a business of two and a half million dollars a year. From dusty attics and abandoned country stores he has gathered relics of bygone merchandising ages with which to outfit completely his Old Country Store; this unique antique store is attached to one of his supermarkets. His insatiable urge has been: "Know something about everything, know everything about something."

THE OLD COUNTRY STORE

In his business and sightseeing travels through Central New York in the 1940s, Johnson was ever on the lookout for examples of early shopkeeping—perhaps a sugarloaf, an ancient barrel or scale, or ledger books rich in the detail of long-ago mercantile exchanges. As his collection of shopkeeping memorabilia grew, the outlines of his replica country store project took shape, much as the accumulations of goods and wares combined to form the haphazard unity of the old country store itself.

Early in his collecting days, Johnson found a shop inventory dating to the 1840s on the premises of the Wilson Brothers store in South Butler. In a three-year period, Johnson wrote, the store carried 746 different items. "Whoever thinks the country store must have been a hodgepodge, thinks exactly right," Johnson observed, adding:

THE GROCER WHO SOLD McCARTHYISM

> From the earliest mud-chinked log cabin establishment to the late model brick emporium, "the store" was a housekeeper's horror.
>
> There were soaps and spices, salt and saleratus, dishes, books and dry goods on the shelves. Hardware and leather goods shared floor space with barrels of flour, sugar, and molasses. A cat in the cracker barrel was commonplace. Axes, log chains, kettles, pots, pans, kegs of nails were piled in corners or hung from the rafters on cords. Shoes were piled loose in a big "shoe box;" saddles and harnesses added to the variety.
>
> The drug corner lined up patent medicines, physics and sedatives....Coffee, cheese, and tobacco crowded the counter along with piles of Russian sheeting, shirting, bed ticking....
>
> Whiskey was usually out of sight, but not of smell, in the back room or basement. Pins, pens, paper, buttons and collars, black silk gloves and palm leaf fans were always "around somewhere."

In the roomier frame stores of the 19th century there also were hogsheads of molasses, casks of whale oil and camphene, Johnson noted, as well as cool storage space for cheeses, butter, and eggs. There were scales, coffee mills, an auger to loosen dried fruits, a sugar grinder, and, of course, the wood- or coal-burning stove.

AN INBORN TRAIT

Johnson's interest in the artifacts of American history began in his youth and never died. The patriot was a nativist, nostalgic for the values and common sense absorbed in his early life around the stove of the country store in South Butler. The insatiably curious and restless wanderer would travel to far corners of the nation—eventually overseas—where he would locate artifacts and implements like those of his forebears.

Johnson's collecting activities began in earnest in the 1930s when he started to assemble memorabilia of presidential election campaigns and other bits of Americana.

CHAPTER TWO: THE INNOVATOR

In May 1940, the Syracuse *Herald-Journal* featured a story about Johnson and his collection, which the newspaper noted included lyrics of "The Star-Spangled Banner," written in Francis Scott Key's hand.

That year, Johnson donated his collection of campaign memorabilia to the Onondaga County Public Library. A report in the *Herald-Journal* on September 12 noted the "gem" of the collection: a flag of the Wide Awakes, a marching club affiliated with Lincoln's 1860 campaign. The banner portrayed a clean-shaven Abe with running mate Hannibal Hamlin against a field of stars. *The Post-Standard* also covered the exhibit by publishing a photograph of Johnson's daughter Marilyn admiring another artifact from the Lincoln campaign: a large maul and wedge, reinforcing Lincoln's image as a "rail-splitter." Other choice items included a walking stick from a McKinley presidential campaign bearing a metal likeness of the candidate's head as a handle; and a flag carried through Manila to celebrate victory in the Spanish-American War.

The next month, part of Johnson's collection went on display at the First Trust & Deposit Company on Montgomery and East Washington streets in Syracuse.

As early as 1941, Laurence Johnson was at work on his project of re-creating a complete country store inside his supermarket on South Salina Street. He reported his progress to the trade journal *Salesgrams* for an article in its May 1941 edition headlined "From Bustles to Beeswax." The author wondered as an aside whether nostalgia buffs fifty years from then would long for the bygone days of the supermarket, "with its island displays, fluorescent lighting, air conditioning, related items and double-decked pushcarts. Then we'll pluck at our long white beards, and say 'That was back in the early '40s, by gum! Seems like it was only yesterday.'"

On August 18, 1946, the Sunday newspaper supplement *This Week* published Clementine Paddleford's interview and article, "Grandmother Shopped Here," with Johnson's Old Country Store in a photo spread. Paddleford wrote of how "grandmother" would have bought her food from similar bins and barrels while grandfather sat around the pot-bellied stove.

THE GROCER WHO SOLD McCARTHYISM

Laurence Johnson poses with some of his old country store antiques in his Syracuse home in 1957. (Syracuse *Post-Standard* photo)

Johnson received fan mail from the article, and several readers offered items. One writer from Middletown, Ohio, sent Johnson an old shop record book "that you might like to add to your collection." Vernon E. Baker of Elyria, Ohio, wrote: "I have an old grocery scale which has a scoop and is balanced by iron weights. If you can use it let me know what it's worth, and if the value is enough I can box it up and ship it."

Johnson's collecting efforts suffered a minor but exasperating setback on the night of Wednesday, September 25, 1947, when burglars broke into his South Salina Street store through second-story skylights. A report on the burglary noted that the intruders gobbled cookies and soda pop, then escaped through the log cabin of the Old Country Store installation, carrying with them fifteen dollars in pennies and two mementos of the 1940 Roosevelt-Willkie campaign: a silver bracelet bearing FDR's initials, and a jeweled Roosevelt pin.

By 1950, Johnson had assembled a traveling exhibit of his Old Country

CHAPTER TWO: THE INNOVATOR

Store. The replica was a popular attraction at the New York State Fair in Syracuse in September. In October, Johnson took his display titled "From Bustles to Beeswax" to the annual convention of the National Association of Food Chains at the Netherland Plaza Hotel in Cincinnati. Johnson himself provided a vivid precis of his project:

> Tucked away in the corner of our supermarket in Syracuse is an old country store. Here I have tried to recapture the atmosphere of the crossroads trading center where our forefathers loved to gather. The "heyday" of the old country stores was from 1840 to the turn of the century. To me, these old country stores symbolize American free enterprise. Here free men met—discussed their local and economic problems. President Lincoln and Cleveland worked in such stores. The items shown here are from old general stores in Central New York. Ninety-five percent of the items were found within 50 miles of Syracuse.

Even as Johnson devoted himself to building his collection of antiques and showcasing them in the 1940s, he maintained his momentum of innovation within the modern supermarket.

PROSPERITY AROUND THE CORNER

The end of World War II freed the vastly expanded industrial sector of the American economy to serve the domestic marketplace. Johnson was ready for the merchandising blitz that matched products with markets.

In August 1945, the weekly digest of the Super Market Institute reported on one of his marketing experiments: Johnson filled three 16-ounce packages with Mueller's macaroni; one package was made of cardboard, the second of plain cellophane, the third of cellophane with an attractive label. He gave each package a fair chance on his shelves in three tests. The resulting sales figures:

Cardboard: 176.
Cellophane: 211.

Cellophane plus label: 240.

Johnson's conclusion: "Visibility is important."

In November 1945, Johnson was invited to Syracuse University to talk about his innovations in retail merchandising. His presentation included advice on the still-novel idea of grouping related products in the supermarket, a concept others credited him with inventing.

"He was the one who taught the other guys to put things together that were related," former employee Robert Giarrusso said. "He might put the mustard by the hot dogs; he might have the buns nearby…or some relish or ketchup, anything that pertained or might have been innovative.

"So, you've got it all together and you're not saying 'Hey, over here is the mustard' and 'Over there are the rolls' and 'Over there's the hot dogs.' Then there's the power of suggestion: Chances are, if it's there and you buy hot dogs, you'll think, 'Hey, gotta get the mustard!' Or, 'Gee, I've gotta get the rolls!'"

Burnett Haylor, Johnson's neighbor and friend, said the resourceful merchant often came up with new things to share while hosting a party. "The first frozen waffle I ever had was up there one night. We might be eating, he'd toast up some waffles, pour on maple syrup. I'd never seen a frozen waffle before. Things like that he learned in the business. If they were new, he'd pull them out at home with friends."

In February 1946, Johnson served complete meals from frozen foods to members of the Syracuse Lions Club. A newspaper photo showed a genial Johnson poised above a quartet of community leaders at the table. William E. Pierce appeared to be digging in with gusto; Dr. Harold B. Sampson was eyeing his plate with some enthusiasm; Paul R. Browne politely examined a forkful; Edgar J. Doyle seemed to be sticking with coffee.

Johnson's preoccupation with frozen foods led to articles in trade journals like *Quick Frozen Foods* and *The Locker Plant* and numerous speaking appearances. At a luncheon forum of the Eastern Frosted Foods Association, he passed along this advice: "Throw out polar bears, skis, igloos and walruses that disgrace these fine foods. We're not selling Eskimos, we're selling food!"

CHAPTER TWO: THE INNOVATOR

Along the way, Johnson found time to poke a little fun at the customers who meant so much to him. He wrote up an idea for a cartoon and mailed it to Jimmy Hatlo, whose popular newspaper comic strip, "They'll Do It Every Time," harpooned human foibles. On March 22, 1947, Hatlo's strip featured Johnson's idea in a two-panel sequence. The scene: a supermarket checkout counter. In the first panel, a woman pushes her way to the front of the line, explaining haughtily to a surprised shopper: "Mind if I go ahead of you, dearie? I'm only buying a can of soup and I'm in such a terrible hurry. I have to catch a bus." In the second frame, the same woman is still in the supermarket, gossiping at length with an acquaintance. The caption reads: "Every cash-and-carry grocer knows the dame who muscles into the line thusly....And an hour later is still blocking traffic in the door with some gal friend she bumped into...."

During this period, Johnson was named co-secretary of the Super Market Institute, where he shared duties with a man he considered a kindred spirit, fellow supermarket entrepreneur William Henry Albers.

The New York Times referred to Johnson as an "industry leader" in its report of a panel discussion he participated in during the Super Market Institute's annual convention in Chicago in May 1949. At the time, many lamented how slowly the economy was growing following the war's end. In the inflationary years between 1945 and 1950, per capita income declined from $2,416 to $2,392 in constant dollars, while the gross national product shrank by more than 4 percent.

Johnson was remarkably on-target when he counseled other Americans in 1949 to persevere through what he predicted would be only temporary adversity.

"Prices are slipping. People are holding on to their money and looking for better values," Johnson said. "But progress will not be denied. The spirit of true progress now is to get costs down, give the people what they want, take full advantage of the possibilities that lie within the walls of our stores today, whether they be old or new.

"What has happened in the last ten years is no guide to what is going to happen tomorrow. Let's stop looking back at profitable times."

HOW CAN WE SERVE YOU BETTER?

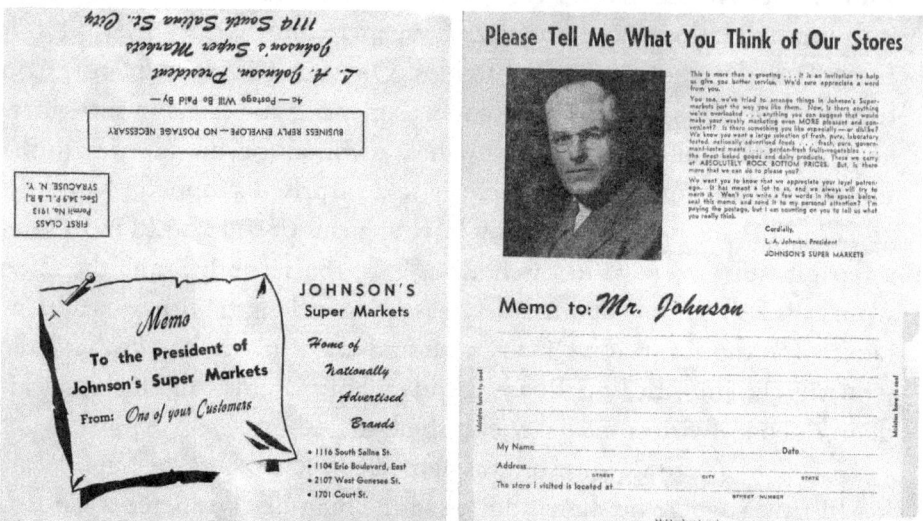

This postage-paid questionnaire was distributed at Johnson's supermarkets to shoppers in the early 1950s.

Shoppers at a Johnson market in 1950 discovered with their bagged groceries a sheet of paper with a photograph of the owner and the message: "Please Tell Me What You Think of Our Stores." Johnson had launched another innovation in the retail business: the postage-paid service questionnaire. It said:

> This is more than a greeting…It is an invitation to help us give you better service. We'd sure appreciate a word from you.
>
> You see, we've tried to arrange things in Johnson's Supermarkets just the way you like them. Now, is there anything we've overlooked?…Is there something you like especially—or dislike? We know you want a large selection of fresh, pure, laboratory tested, nationally advertised foods…fresh, pure, government-tested meats…garden-fresh fruit-vegetables…the finest baked goods and dairy products. These we carry at ABSOLUTELY ROCK BOTTOM PRICES. But, is there more that we can do to please you?

CHAPTER TWO: The Innovator

Johnson reported to *The Self-Service Grocer* that the questionnaire "turned out to be a powerful sounding board," improving customer relations. "We found out what our customers disliked about our stores, and we're doing something about it." Johnson elaborated in an article in the July 1950 issue of *Grocer's Digest* with the lead-in: "How to find out what your customers want....Do you know what people like and don't like about your stores?"

Johnson's restless energy also found an outlet in the movies. Along with business manager Coyne and his daughter Marilyn, Johnson appeared in a movie short by RKO Pathe for the National Association of Food Chains. The subject was the growth and history of the food industry. The production filmed Johnson and others in his old-country-store-within-a-store on South Salina Street. Shooting took place the week of May 11, 1950. "Shopkeeper" Laurence Johnson, resplendent in a high stiff collar, pearl-gray suit, and derby, attended to his vintage "customers," offering pickles from the barrel, slices from a huge cheese wheel, and choice items such as Dewey's plug tobacco and Nervine patent medicine.

DICK, JANE, SPOT AND PUFF

Having mastered the art of catering to the needs of the average adult shopper, Johnson turned to two other potentially lucrative markets: children and pets.

With a dash of whimsy and a sure grasp of human psychology, he arranged a candy display at the front of his store to catch the attention of the young, who presumably would be quick to alert their parents. A sign suspended over the display depicted a clown holding a hoop for a little dog to jump through, along with the message: "For the kids. Mom and Pop too!" As usual, the retail industry took note. *Packages and People*, a DuPont publication, printed an article headlined, "How Do Children Influence Food Purchases?"

With Dick and Jane eating out of his hand, Johnson went after Spot and Puff. Up to that point, pet food was not reliably available in grocery stores. As Johnson explained later at a meeting of Operation Inc., an idea came to him when he was remarking to an old friend about how many products were not even considered as inventory in the country store of old.

"I think the real reason behind the good demand for light bulbs, cigarettes, razor blades, drug items and many other non-grocery items...found in the stores today...is that our customers look to us to supply every household need," Johnson said. "We decided at Johnson's to set up a test of this idea of a complete pet supply department....We set up our department January 8, 1951."

Noteworthy features of Johnson's pet department included a singing canary, a tropical aquarium, and an electric buzzer to summon a clerk to carry large packaged items. In May 1951, Johnson wrote in *Food Field Reporter*: "I am sold on this pet supply department idea. As I write this, these pet supply items, not usually found in grocery stores, are continuing to sell well....My biggest surprise was my 61 percent increase in gross profit. Now when my dog barks, even in the middle of the night, it's music to my ears."

Many retailers were watching Johnson's various experiments, according to *Food Field Reporter*, and it expected many to follow Johnson's lead.

However, a decade after he gained national publicity in *Printer's Ink*, Johnson still felt that not enough manufacturers, advertisers and market owners were getting his message about how to merchandise their wares. At the Point of Purchase Advertising Institute's annual symposium on display advertising in April 1951, he lectured his colleagues on this.

An effective supermarket advertisement, he said, is like a road sign, brief and simple.

"If there is a danger point ahead on the road," Johnson said, "they do not put out a sign that reads: 'Put out by the New York State Highway Department under the supervision of So-and-So.' If they did, you'd be dead. They use simple words like Curve, Full Stop, Danger, Steep Hill."

Johnson continued: "This lady we are talking about—she is there to buy food for her family, and I don't care what you say, she has more money in her pocket now than ever before. I think the manufacturers and advertising people don't realize the attention they can get, the possibilities there are in self-service markets, if they would stop trying to be so cute and would be simple instead. This lady is not interested in working out puzzles on point-of-purchase material."

Johnson showed his audience at the Waldorf Astoria Hotel a coffee display poster he'd brought along. The message: "Buy instant coffee. Save time; save money: 53 cents." Johnson revealed that this simply written sign tripled sales within two weeks.

Anniversary sales? Forget them, Johnson said. "Shoppers don't care anything about anybody's anniversary except their own. But the lady doing her shopping does want good quality foods, and likes to save time and save money.

"I could go on all day on this subject because it's one of my pets. People are interested in simple things. I think they are interested in the displays that get the thought over to them quickly. If you write your copy and your sign so a child of twelve will understand it, then everybody will."

A GRAND EXPERIMENT

In 1951, Johnson had yet another merchandising experiment: a salesmen's display contest with money prizes. Originally, Johnson anticipated a dozen or so salesmen would sign up. When the competition began July 16, thirty displays competed for customer attention in three Johnson markets. His stores were a riot of cascading fruit stands, talking signs, pyramids, and floodlights. One enterprising salesman, Proctor & Gamble's Wayne Blessing, painted a set of footprints leading through the store to the Ivory Soap display.

Johnson's unique "merchandising clinic" was an industry attention-getter, featured in the August issue of *Food Field Reporter*. The story noted that some of the salesmen "are finding the sales firing line a surprise!" The five-week competition concluded in September. Syracuse Mayor Thomas J. Corcoran presented trophies and $200 checks to the winners of what the local paper termed "the first merchandising clinic of its kind."

Among the most popular displays was one by salesman Ralph Atwater for Hershey chocolate, featuring a large-scale model of a candy bar topped with baby pictures. The judges praised A. Ray Fairbanks' prize-winning cottage cheese entry as "unusual in that it stimulated new thinking in displays, emphasizing food value at a low price. However, there were no prices on display."

Johnson spent September 1951 toting up sales figures for the products featured in the clinic displays. His results, published in the October issue of *Progressive Grocer* magazine, were dramatic: Tuna fish sales up 277 percent; peanut butter up 253 percent; canned luncheon meat up 478 percent; popcorn up 873 percent; instant pudding up 654 percent; cake mixes up 514 percent; gelatin dessert up 968 percent; powdered milk up 405 percent; and pickles up 713 percent. Ralph Atwater's Hershey chocolate display upped sales by 700 percent, while Wayne Blessing's painted footprints helped sell 602 percent more Ivory Soap.

However, Johnson said the sales figures were of only secondary interest to him. "Making money from these displays is not the main point of the clinic," he noted in *Chain Store Age* magazine. "What we are really after are some good merchandising ideas....We are interested too in giving the manufacturers a chance to test their own ideas and material, and getting them to look at point-of-sale display from the retailer's angle."

The industry got the message. A representative of the giant New York ad agency Batten, Barton, Durstine & Osborn approached Johnson and proposed a special display for health and beauty aids. Johnson readily agreed and, in sixteen weeks, sales increased over 51 percent. Johnson and BBD&O released their results at the grocers' convention in 1952 in Miami, and the data appeared in the July issue of *Food Topics*. The editors noted that the grocers assembled in Miami "paid rapt attention to what has been happening...in one of Larry Johnson's supermarkets in Syracuse, N.Y."

LUCKY MONDAY

Years earlier, in the summer of 1939, Johnson reacted warily when S. I. Newhouse bought the two afternoon daily newspapers in Syracuse, the *Herald* and the *Journal*, and merged them into a single paper. By combining the two papers' circulations, editorial operations and production facilities, the new owner could offer local advertisers a bargain rate. This resulted in a flood of business to the new *Herald-Journal*, at the expense of the locally owned morning daily, *The Post-Standard*.

CHAPTER TWO: THE INNOVATOR

Johnson decided to get involved. He was wary of Newhouse because the newspaper owner was a "Downstater." Johnson preferred local ownership. Furthermore, he considered Newhouse's merger of the *Herald* and *Journal* as a blow to competition and the varied fare of two afternoon dailies. So, Johnson switched all his advertising to *The Post-Standard* when Newhouse took over the *Herald-Journal*. Johnson also resisted the *Herald-Journal* salesmen's pitch of lower rates and sliding scales.

Thus, when *Herald-Journal* salesmen knocked on his door and offered him a special promotion deal dubbed "Lucky Monday," Johnson grew suspicious.

According to former news executive Bill Dyer, here's how it worked: Every Monday, the *Herald-Journal* would print coupons for area advertisers—department stores like Flah's or Dey Brothers. The coupons would be distributed to stores and passed out for shoppers to fill out and hand in. On Thursday, coupons would be drawn at Loew's theater to determine the $500, $250 and $100 winners—courtesy of the *Herald-Journal*. To be part of the lucrative promotion, a company had to keep 75 percent of its advertising in the *Herald-Journal*.

"Lucky Monday" was an instant success. It helped spread business throughout the week by building up trade on Monday, which was normally a slow day.

Many advertisers began shifting their business from *The Post-Standard* to the *Herald-Journal*. A&P and American Stores kept their *Post-Standard* advertising but increased their *Herald-Journal* share to qualify for the coupons. The promotion was legally questionable as an unfair business practice and a restraint of trade. However, *The Post-Standard* was unable or unwilling to mount a legal challenge or to offer its own version of "Lucky Monday." Dyer recalled an A&P executive telling him: "We're not cutting down on *Post-Standard* advertising; we're increasing our *Herald-Journal* advertising, under protest, because we feel we have to get the coupons."

Johnson wasn't about to let Newhouse beat him at his own specialty—merchandising. Said Dyer: "He [Johnson] called me one day and said, 'Let's have lunch at the University Club. I want to fight them; I don't want to give in.'" Over lunch, they nibbled at ideas. Dyer suggested

Johnson record a phone conversation of a *Herald-Journal* salesman offering a coupon deal. With this recorded evidence, *The Post-Standard* could sue.

Johnson turned him down, Dyer said, explaining that win or lose, "I have to live with them afterward."

How about Johnson's markets offering a weekly prize, too? Johnson again told him no. "Too much money," he said.

"OK," Dyer said, "How about we take the national advertising away from the *Herald-Journal*?"

Johnson's eyes brightened behind his rimless spectacles.

"Fine," he replied.

Johnson promptly shared with salesmen for the major brands—Domino, Maxwell House, and others—an offer of his own: You want a display in the center of Johnson supermarkets? You want a mention in all of my advertising? Switch your advertising from the *Herald-Journal* to *The Post-Standard*, and I'll do it.

When the salesmen carried Johnson's pitch back to their bosses, the food executives were inclined to dismiss him as a provincial pleader.

Johnson increased the pressure.

"He could be pretty direct, pretty tough," *The Post-Standard*'s Tink Keller recalled. "He went to the national advertisers that put stuff on the shelves and said, 'I want you to take your advertising out of the Newhouse paper. I want it out. If you won't take it out, I won't ever buy a thing from you.'"

Twenty-two national accounts reportedly switched from the *Herald-Journal* to *The Post-Standard*. "Larry Johnson loved it," Dyer said. "I remember at one point I told him one account—Chef Boyardee—said, 'It's going to cause me great trouble.' Johnson said, and I'll never forget the saying: 'You can't detour around friends.'"

By and by, the Newhouse empire purchased *The Post-Standard*, and national advertising dollars trickled back to its new sister newspaper, the *Herald-Journal*.

By then, Johnson had mastered a potent way to use his merchandising talent and clout in the retail industry to accomplish a secondary objective.

CHAPTER TWO: THE INNOVATOR

He saw that advertisers were vulnerable to the unique influence he and other grocers could apply.

He eventually would aim this pressure tool to clean up a broadcast industry he was certain was awash in communists.

CHAPTER THREE:
The Activist

WITH assistants Mary Coyne and Joe Reschke minding the shop, Johnson turned his attention in the early 1950s beyond the supermarket shelves. He was satisfied with the size of his business and the profits it brought.

"As far as I could tell, he had no ambition to be a very wealthy man," anti-communist activist Vincent Hartnett recalled later. "Wealth as such I don't think attracted him. He was not an acquisitive man. The money just flowed naturally. His tastes were simple. His house was not palatial."

Johnson wasn't attracted to politics, but he read newspapers voraciously and began to respond in his own way to reports that the spread of communism threatened the American way of life.

"He wasn't flamboyant," Johnson's daughter Eleanor said. "He wasn't a zealot. But he would become angry from what he'd hear on the news. The injustice is what it was to him. A lot of injustices he'd notice, things we didn't take action on. For a peaceful man, it changed him. It enraged him."

The Post-Standard's Tink Keller said, "As far as I know he never wanted to be a public figure. He never wanted to run for any office or such. But he got mighty interested in good government and a good way of life."

Keller added, "The thing that stood out about Johnson was the intensity. The man got an idea, he was the damnedest pusher you ever saw."

THE RISE OF COMMUNISM

From the very start, Americans were eager to defend their invented democracy against subversion, real or imagined. The new republic was fertile ground for conspiracy theories, and patriots of the young land betrayed an insecurity that the nation has never managed to outgrow.

Less than a decade after George Washington took office in 1789 came the three Alien and Sedition Acts, theoretically intended to contain the subversive threat of French revolutionaries and others, but in practice stifling political dissent. When the Frenchman Alexis de Tocqueville crossed the Atlantic several decades later, he found a people both proud and apprehensive, bursting with enthusiasm for their government and daring anyone to challenge the new status quo. He wrote:

> It would seem as if, doubting their own merit, they wished to have it constantly exhibited before their eyes. Their vanity is not only greedy, but restless and jealous; it will grant nothing, whilst it demands everything, but is ready to beg and to quarrel at the same time....It is impossible to conceive a more troublesome or more garrulous patriotism; it wearies even those who are disposed to respect it."

Xenophobia has always dwelt on the edges of American nationalism. The 18th-century enemies of the Illuminati, the anti-Masons of the 1830s, the Know-Nothings of the midcentury years, the Populists of the 1890s, the anti-immigrants of the Wilsonian era—all were kindred precursors of Laurence Johnson and his fellow patriots. "McCarthyism," though named for and nurtured by Wisconsin Senator Joseph McCarthy, had roots in the virgin soil of the nation, with new branches sprouting even today.

In McCarthy's worldview, the "20 years of treason" that marked America's slide toward subversion began with President Roosevelt's New Deal. Along came FDR, this jaunty aristocrat with the Dutch surname, who, within 100 days after he took office, concocted a Rube Goldberg-type federal thingamajig that would have been laughable had it not relentlessly

CHAPTER THREE: The Activist

extended government influence into vast new areas of what had been private enterprise. As time went on, critics grudgingly conceded some of these new alphabet-soup federal programs seemed to work. But to the diehard capitalists, the New Deal still smelled of "pink socialism."

Politically, the 1930s were a free-for-all. The disastrous effects of the Depression—unprecedented joblessness, bankruptcies, foreclosures, bank closings, bread lines—were enough to shake the confidence of the most enthusiastic advocate of free-market capitalism. Thousands of men and women, disillusioned with a system that seemed to have brought itself to the brink of its own destruction, committed their energy and their idealism to the dogmas of Bolshevism, Trotskyism, Stalinism, Spanish Republicanism, or one of the socialist/communist hybrids.

Communism built a base in America in the 1930s largely within the labor movement where its trained organizers were in high demand. The list of union locals led by communists, or dominated by Communist Party members, is a long one, including the National Miners Union; the National Textile Workers Union; the United Auto Workers; the Fur Workers Industrial Union; the International Longshoremen and Warehouse Workers Union; the United Farm Equipment and Metal Workers Union; the National Union of Marine Cooks and Stewards; the International Fishermen and Allied Workers; the Food, Tobacco, Agricultural and Allied Workers; the United Office and Professional Workers; and the American Communications Association.

By 1934, communists claimed control of 134 locals within the American Federation of Labor (AFL), and exerted influence over 40 percent of unions affiliated with the Congress of Industrial Organizations (CIO). There were sixty communists on the New York Central Trades and Labor Council. Of the 9,000 members of the National Teachers Union in New York City in 1934, a thousand were communists.

Although communist union organizers tended to prioritize their unionism over their party, there was evidence to raise concerns about potential industrial espionage or sabotage. Communist influence was a particularly sensitive issue during strikes. After alarmed AFL leaders expelled communist-led unions, party members continued to prosper in the CIO. The CIO's political director and general counsel were both party members.

Within the labor movement, the communists promoted elements of the New Deal agenda that, when viewed today, seem anything but radical. They supported Social Security and unemployment insurance, sought civil rights for Black Americans, and called for an end to lynching. Communists also helped found the American Civil Liberties Union and the Consumers Union, publisher of *Consumer Reports* magazine.

Outside the labor movement, however, American communists never gained a solid footing. By the late 1930s, Stalin's show trials and executions in the Soviet Union had tarnished his image in the West. The frequent shifts in the party line also made for awkward moments in American communism. Early calls by Moscow for revolution in America gave way to orders simply to undermine American capitalism; absolute loyalty to Stalin and the USSR also was required. After that, many Americans who had flirted with communism left the party. Those who stayed or tried to hide past membership now lived with the fear of exposure.

EARLY ANTI-COMMUNISTS

Before Pearl Harbor, fear of communism sparked congressional hearings by Representative Martin Dies' new House Committee on Un-American Activities. In June 1940, Congress made headlines when it passed the Smith Act. It was now a crime to "teach and advocate the overthrow of the United States Government by force and violence." The pattern set by the Alien and Sedition Acts was reasserting itself in American history.

Other investigations focused on a few communist lawyers, government workers, and proteges of Henry Wallace, FDR's secretary of agriculture who was elected vice president in 1940.

Newspapers in 1940 played up an early inquiry into communism in academia, a probe that resulted in Bertrand Russell's blocked appointment as a philosophy professor at City College, the firing of more than thirty teachers, and Teachers Union leader Morris U. Schappes' perjury conviction and jailing. In California, state legislator Jack B. Tenney

CHAPTER THREE: THE ACTIVIST

launched what would become an eight-year career as chairman of the communist-hunting committee that would bear his name.

Early blueprints for the blacklists of the 1950s had appeared in the decade before World War II. In 1938, J.B. Matthews' "Odyssey of a Fellow Traveler" listed 563 political heretics. Among the first books listing names of alleged subversives in America was "The Red Network: A Who's Who and Handbook of Radicalism for Patriots," published in 1934 by Elizabeth Dilling, who later wrote "The Roosevelt Red Record and Its Background."

U.S. Representative J. Parnell Thomas loudly opposed government support for the Federal Theatre Project. He claimed in 1938 that "practically every play presented under the auspices of the Project...is sheer propaganda for Communism of the New Deal." In less than a year, the workshop was out of business, marking a significant early victory for the anti-communists.

But these early efforts were unable to muster widespread public support. Godfrey P. Schmidt, a prominent New York lawyer who later would help found the anti-communist group Aware Inc., met frustration in the 1940s in his first effort to mobilize the troops. Schmidt was serving as deputy industrial commissioner of New York City when he launched a loyalty probe of some 4,000 public employees. He was thwarted by political inertia and public apathy. Eventually, he was denied permission to continue because of the time and costs involved. Speaking to the Catholic Central Verein of America, Schmidt complained of the feckless bureaucracy: "The whims of convictions of 20 percent of the people" were "the guiding policy of government, bestriding and coercing the other eighty percent."

The first prosecutions under the Smith Act were confusing affairs, marked by infighting among the communists themselves. One party faction applauded the conviction and imprisonment of 18 fellow socialists in Minneapolis—because they were renegade Trotskyites. The cases went to trial in June 1941, just as Nazi Panzers invaded the USSR. The invasion outraged American communists, and the party line changed abruptly in favor of U.S. intervention into World War II.

Once the war began, public opposition to the Soviets generally softened among Americans, who welcomed Russian help in defeating the Nazis.

Following FDR's stirring war declaration and the general mobilization, Dies suspended HCUA hearings. The war years would produce patriotic film tributes to America's Soviet allies from Warner Bros. and MGM—films like "Mission to Moscow" (1943), "Song of Russia (1943) and "Days of Glory" (1944).

The U.S. State Department did diplomatic gymnastics to rationalize the alliance with the Soviets. The Nazi rulers, according to the official line, were "not interested in improving the lot of ordinary people, only in war, plunder and world power....The Soviet idea is that the dictatorship must serve the people; no 'master race' idea, all people considered equal."

MERCHANDISING THE WAR EFFORT

Home-front patriots like Laurence Johnson threw themselves into the war effort. When Johnson's clerks, stock boys and cashiers took off their aprons and donned military uniforms, their boss told them their jobs would await them when they returned. In 1940, Mary Coyne was the only woman on Johnson's staff. "Then the war came, and the men had to go," she said, resulting in the need for replacement workers. "It turned out to be all girls and Mr. Reschke and Mr. Johnson. I loved the business. There was lots to do during the war. It was very interesting."

Johnson signed up as deputy Civil Defense warden of Section 15, and he posed in a group portrait for *The Post-Standard*. In those frightening early days of the war, Johnson and like-minded citizens emphasized readiness. Who could rule out a Japanese air strike sweeping out of the plains of Canada? Or a stray Nazi U-boat slipping down the St. Lawrence River to Lake Ontario? U.S. territory had been attacked at Pearl Harbor, and public indignation mingled with fear and determination.

Johnson also responded by applying his remarkable talent for merchandising to the war effort. Thus was born the campaign he invented in which the public would tip using U.S. Savings Bond stamps.

"Stop and Think!" Johnson exhorted in one promotional pitch. "Countless thousands of us lay down countless thousands of dimes and quarters daily for tips. It staggers the imagination to think what would

CHAPTER THREE: THE ACTIVIST

happen if we lay down defense saving stamps. Furthermore, many people have told me that my stamps gave them their start in buying and saving defense stamps and bonds." Johnson delivered his message in an open letter, which he circulated among professional men and others with whom he frequently dined out.

He took out a half-page ad in the local papers with a drawing on top of two men sitting at a restaurant. One of the men looks up at an attentive waitress. He says: "I want to slap a Jap," using the wartime slur common in the United States at the time. "I'll give you a defense stamp for my tip."

The advertisement, delivered as an "open letter," went on to explain how the tipping program worked. "I think we here in Syracuse can start something which will sweep the nation like wildfire, and rock the foundations of Tokio and Berlin." It was signed "Sincerely, L.A. Johnson."

The campaign was an instant success. Five weeks after Pearl Harbor, *Herald-Journal* editors noted that the tipping practice was already well-established in Syracuse and had served to educate the public on the defense stamps.

On a snowy Thursday morning in March 1942, *Post-Standard* columnist Joseph H. Adams dropped by the Onondaga Hotel at the corner of Jefferson and Warren streets and caught Johnson in action. In his column the next day, Adams wrote, "L.A. Johnson, the food king, busied himself around the Onondaga, inside and outside, yesterday morning, and among his many activities was the passing out of the defense stamps as tips, and the little envelopes for the use of those who want to pass them out."

How was the campaign going? Adams asked Johnson.

"Well," Johnson said, making a snowball from the slush on the rear of his car, "it's going swell. I've started a good many cards personally and others have, too. Even the doorman here—I call him Nervous Nellie—said he preferred a stamp to a quarter tip. Provided of course it was a two-bit stamp. Guess we're doing all right."

Meanwhile, *The Post-Standard* warmly endorsed the stamps-for-tips campaign. "We think you've got something there, Mr. Johnson, any way you look at it," the editorial read. "We all know the inclination to purchase more is much greater after the first purchase." The United States won't start winning, they warned, "until we all look at this war as an opportunity to give, not as a chance to get more for ourselves."

More accolades for the Syracuse grocer came in letters to the editor. Gushed Mrs. J.A. DeWitt: "In these war days a man like Mr. Johnson must be busy, but he took time to think up this idea....He is a 100 percent American, striving to do his bit here on the home front."

Johnson had missed military service in World War I because he was a farmer. In 1941, he was fifty-two, too old to enlist in World War II. But if he was disappointed in twice missing out, he kept it to himself.

"His feelings about his own private life were his own business—he played his cards very close to his vest," Hartnett said. "I don't know whether Larry Johnson was sensitive because he hadn't been in the armed services or not. But he just casually mentioned to me one time that he had not been inducted into the military in World War I because he was an agricultural worker. They were all given deferments. He was a farmer—an essential occupation."

THE MERCHANT LOBBYIST

Although Johnson was passionate about the war effort, he also kept a critical eye on market patterns, both to give himself a business edge and to provide his customers with an adequate supply of goods. He grew increasingly frustrated as the wartime bureaucracy and mandatory rationing closed in. He became a kind of consumer advocate, and his wartime patriotism did not translate into automatic support of the Office of Price Administration (OPA) and General Maximum Price Regulation (GMPR). This set him at odds with some professors at the Maxwell School of Citizenship and Public Affairs at Syracuse University who were helping to make policy in Washington.

Johnson's daughter Lois claimed the wartime red tape literally made her father sick. "World War II was a very tough time with the OPA restrictions on business and rationing," she said. "Professors from the

CHAPTER THREE: The Activist

university were coming down to tell him how to run his business. By the end of the war, it had affected his health."

In April 1942, Laurence Johnson sounded a high-minded note in an interview for *Topic*, the retail merchandising magazine. His subject: how to manage the supply of rubber and other products in high demand. "The Super Market is now a fundamental part of our American way of life," he said, "and I believe the answer to these questions lies within ourselves —how well we do our jobs, how gracefully we accept changes, and how quickly we adapt these changes to our merchandising methods will answer for themselves."

In October, Johnson was tinkering with consumer substitutes for scarce commodities such as coffee and tea. He test-marketed "Gaucho Yerba Mate," a hot-beverage substitute, at his South Salina Street store, claiming with a salesman's flourish that customers preferred it over coffee and tea in Argentina, Paraguay, and elsewhere in South America.

Johnson also found a way to combine his love of Americana with a bit of adaptive consumerism. When the OPA banned commercial bread-slicing in 1943 as a wartime conservation measure, Johnson promoted a 100-year-old Vermont wooden bread-slicer he had acquired on one of his antique-gathering and sightseeing trips. He started a campaign to "Bring Back the Bread Slicer." He took his idea and the antique device to Jean Joyce at the Home Institute, a consumer service of the *New York Herald-Tribune*. They prepared design drawings for an easy-to-assemble modern version of the ingenious contraption. On March 7, 1943, Johnson and his bread-slicer were featured in the *Herald-Tribune*'s Sunday magazine. "We advise 20th century readers to make one like it, and slice bread for themselves ever after," Joyce wrote. The day after the article appeared, the government ended its ban on commercial bread-slicing.

While stressing the need for initiative and self-reliance to cope with the war effort, Johnson had little patience with the federal bureaucracy. Speaking to members of the Super Market Institute in St. Louis in September 1942, Johnson aired his grievances.

"Our immediate problem," he said, "is how to continue in business under these national alphabetical agencies— under GMPR and price ceilings. To continue in business with what labor is available, we cannot bid

67

for efficient labor because our ceiling prices do not permit us sufficient margin of profit for this labor.

"We have assets, too. The first asset is that we are in the retail food business itself. People have to have food. Food will be grown and processed and will be distributed by someone to the people of the United States. This can and should be our job. But make no mistake about this: If we who are gathered here today do not do it, someone else will."

Then Johnson turned patriotic, even visionary.

"We know our troops must be fed and clothed before the civilians," he said. "Our country will be shipping more and more food to our Allies. With all this our government is honestly endeavoring to halt inflation. The sacrifices that we are making and will have to make look pretty small when you measure them with the ones our boys are making who are fighting and dying to make this a better world to live in. Some of the things that look impossible have got to be done."

Those watching and waiting on the home front tolerated the petty irritations of wartime shortages as part of the daily grind. However, Johnson still complained that the system was inefficient and unfair—particularly in the distribution of food and other commodities to urban dwellers.

"This is the kind of thing he would stick his neck out for," said daughter Eleanor. "He was not a crusader, but this was just common sense. This was something he knew about. He was always a merchandiser, a store owner. His was a little business compared to others, but he was a crackerjack merchandiser, ready to take them on."

Johnson particularly objected to the distribution methods of the New Deal managers. He claimed the clumsy national plan ignored regional market characteristics. A shortage of canned goods in Syracuse meant real sacrifice for city families that depended on processed foods during Central New York winters. But in the Sunbelt, where fresh produce was plentiful, these shortages were considerably less of a burden.

Johnson spoke with local OPA officials, but he decided he wasn't making any headway, so he resorted to his characteristic device: a merchandising campaign. He set up a display in the front of his South Salina Street store, explaining the issue in vivid, down-to-earth language.

CHAPTER THREE: The Activist

The national media picked up Johnson's message, and it earned him a mention in *Reader's Digest*. After the government announced a per-capita point rationing system, Johnson carried his campaign to New York City, where he held forth at the Barbizon Plaza. He made headlines in the *New York Sun* when he predicted a "disaster to civilian morale."

Johnson's increasingly vocal protests caught the attention of Katherine Fisher of the Good Housekeeping Institute. She was struck by his combination of patriotism and hard-nosed business sense. She urged him to contact Dr. Russell M. Wilder, who headed the civilian foods requirements branch of the U.S. Department of Agriculture. Johnson wrote:

> The requirements of our Army and our allies in the matter of these foods do and should come first. Now, whatever amount is left, should that not be distributed as evenly as possible in the proportion that it has always been consumed?...The maintenance of civilian morale is an important part of the war effort. Just as an Army travels on its stomach, so do these war workers in the war industries of Detroit, Cleveland, Buffalo, Pittsburgh, Syracuse and other centers require adequate and substantial food.

OPA administrators subsequently modified their regulations. While it's unclear whether Johnson influenced their decision, some of the more burdensome wrinkles in distribution eventually were ironed out. However, the OPA retained rationing and price ceilings for the duration of the war in some form.

Meanwhile, Johnson expanded his wartime efforts. In Syracuse, he joined the Foods Division of the United War Fund Campaign. On August 23, 1943, *The Post-Standard* printed his letter to the editor dutifully explaining the reasons for a butter shortage. In April 1944, Johnson was named vice chairman of the Civilian Records Project for Onondaga County. Johnson's mission was to compile a civilian archive of World War II, drawing on the resources of nearly a hundred civic and patriotic organizations in the county. The records would be stored in the county courthouse until after the war, to become the basis of an official history.

Two weeks before the Allied invasion of Normandy on June 6, 1944, Johnson joined fellow Kiwanians in placing the names of 235 Onondaga County men killed in the war on a memorial at South Salina Street and Onondaga Avenue.

By early 1945, city officials had begun talking about building a War Memorial—a community center and auditorium. Johnson supported the idea wholeheartedly. On May 20, a few days after the German surrender, the *Herald-Journal* printed Johnson's pitch. His letter captures the pragmatic side of Johnson's patriotic zeal:

> This memorial to the thousands of men and women who are in the service will be a living contribution to our country in the form of a sorely-needed auditorium. What a fine opportunity this presents to save war records....Unlike some monuments erected by grateful communities after past wars, this will not have the sad experience of becoming stained and corroded by the weather. This war memorial will be used, and being used, it will have to be kept up. What better place could there be for the meetings of service clubs and associations that have the interests of the community at heart? This can be accomplished if we get behind this war memorial effort to build a community center. Let's not wait too long. Let's start now.

The War Memorial was built with the names of battlefields carved into its art deco facade: Bataan, Corregidor, Normandy, and others. During and after Johnson's lifetime, the building would see continuous and productive use.

"Larry wasn't a veteran, but he was active with the veterans because he was so patriotic," Johnson's friend Burnett Haylor said. "These guys at the Legion were tickled to death to have a fellow like Larry, with force and prestige, pushing for the same things they were pushing for."

Former Legion leader Jim McHale said Johnson's reputation, contacts and financial support boosted the group's mission. "Larry helped us in our Americanism activities," he said. "He helped bring in big-timers to speak at luncheons or over dinner—Victor Lasky, Roy Cohn, George

CHAPTER THREE: The Activist

Schuyler, Ronald Reagan. Larry made it possible through fundraising, buying tickets. Johnson's donation would help with the expenses."

POLITICS IN SYRACUSE

In the first half of the 20th century, Central New York was a bastion of conservative Republicanism. It's been said that in the 1936 presidential election, Alf Landon carried only Maine, Vermont, and Onondaga County. (Actually, most of Upstate New York, including Onondaga County, went for Landon.) Democrats occasionally won elections, but only with the acquiescence of the heavyweights from the Century Club and the rest of the GOP establishment.

"Syracuse was one of the most conservative…areas in the whole eastern part of the United States," said Marguerite Fisher, who in the 1940s was a young professor at Syracuse University's Maxwell School. "Just being a Democrat was enough to label you a radical.

"A friend of mine, a Democrat, once made some statements criticizing the Republican Party—nepotism and bribery and so on. Then things started happening to this man afterward. He had his car parked at the curb near his home, and they gave him a summons for blocking the streets or something like that. He had a business downtown, and all of a sudden, they ordered him to install a new fire sprinkler—and so on. Really, they intimidated anyone in the city who dared to register as a Democrat. And if you were in business, it was dangerous."

Syracuse University trustees numbered among the pillars of the Republican establishment, but the Maxwell School was a lightning rod for criticism. The university founded it in 1924 as a laboratory for progressive theory in policy-making and public administration. Maxwell's detractors later insinuated it had communist leanings by nicknaming it "The Little Red Schoolhouse on the Hill."

A number of professors were Democrats who took leaves to work in Washington during the New Deal years of the 1930s and 1940s. "This alone was enough to convince the local natives here that it was a hotbed of communists," Fisher said. Conservatives at the time considered President

Roosevelt "one of the most radical and dangerous men ever to be in the White House," she said.

WAVING THE RED FLAG

Fisher's academic work added fuel to the fire in December 1952 when the university's press published her book "Communist Doctrine and the Free World." Its nearly 300 pages explored the framework of communism by highlighting the words of its prophets, including Karl Marx, Vladimir Lenin, and Joseph Stalin. Fisher did provide some commentary, including a challenge to some communist precepts in the final chapter.

"It was neither pro-communist nor anti-communist," she asserted later.

Interestingly, some Syracusans most wary of the book were on the Maxwell faculty, fearing it would draw negative attention to the school.

Fisher said later that "quite a few colleagues came to me and said, 'Can't you recall publication of this thing? You shouldn't publish a book like that at this time' At least a dozen of my colleagues came up to me and whispered, 'Why don't you wait and publish this a few years from now?' They didn't want a shadow cast over their names. That amazed me, and indicated, I think, the general feeling that the faculty, not only at Syracuse but elsewhere, they were intimidated by all this, frightened."

Fisher had a sense of humor about this. When she attended a reception for the book at the Maxwell School, she wore a bright red dress that drew gasps from those assembled.

A woman then approached Fisher.

"Dear, do you think you should be wearing that color dress, with all that's going on?"

After that, Fisher said, she made it a point to wear that dress as often as possible.

Professor Fisher soon used her book in an evening course on modern European political theory. One of her students in 1953 was Martin Levine, a young electrical engineer who commuted from nearby Rome, New York, where he worked at Griffiss Air Force Base. Someone saw Levine reading "Communist Doctrine and the Free World," told someone else, and the word eventually reached Air Force security. Two men

CHAPTER THREE: THE ACTIVIST

visited the base and talked to him, asking about the book and whether it advocated communism. When Levine told her about this, Fisher suggested that the men buy a copy of the book if they wanted to know what was in it. At least she could make some money from it.

The Air Force suspended Levine after filing charges citing him for reading to others from Fisher's book. Later, he appeared before a congressional panel in New York City, where Levine testified that he was not a communist, had never been a communist, and, in fact, was a loyal American. The subcommittee accepted his story—a year later.

Griffiss reinstated him, but Levine resigned, upset that he wouldn't get back pay or the promotion he deserved.

Outside the Maxwell School, Syracuse had small pockets of leftist activists in organizations like the Syracuse Peace Council, founded in 1936, and Syracuse Women for Peace, as well as church leaders like Episcopal Bishop Malcolm Peabody and his wife, Mary. Other outspoken liberal leaders included Paul Shipman Andrews, dean of the Syracuse University College of Law, and Dean Charles Noble of SU's Hendricks Chapel.

"There were a lot of liberal organizations here," Legionnaire Carl Tarver recalled during an interview in the 1980s. "They were small, but they were prominent in that they were in the higher echelons of the community. They had a lot of influence toward liberal views. A lot of wonderful people belonged to these organizations.

"They were idealists. They didn't know what they were doing. They thought they were going to do great things. They were against our getting into the war—until Germany attacked Russia and then, all of a sudden, they wanted us to get involved. 'Second front!' they were hollering."

While iconoclasts like Professor Fisher may have felt out of place in Syracuse, those who played by the rules enjoyed the benefits of an informal network of business, political, and civic leaders.

Around 1942, a coterie of Kiwanis Club and Rotary Club members began dining together at Schrafft's luncheonette, conveniently located on South Warren Street near Jefferson Street in the heart of the business district. Johnson made the short trip from his store on South Salina Street for the club's Tuesday luncheons; Burnett Haylor walked over from his insurance office in the old Herald Building on Warren Street; *Post-Standard* business manager Tink Keller and city editor Leonard Gorman arrived from the newspaper offices on Montgomery and Fayette, joined by Thomas Higgins from Merchants National Bank, physician Dr. Warren Saile, jeweler Henry Wilson ("Wilson's Leading Jewelers"), and advertising executive Jack Flack (credited as inventor of the "Keepsake Diamond" slogan).

Soon, Schrafft's held tables for the regulars, and the luncheon gathering was dubbed the "roundtable."

"There were sixteen to eighteen in the group," Haylor said. "We'd average six to eight every day. The conversation was general. There was a lot of horseplay."

CHAPTER FOUR:
The Threat Perceived

NEAR the end of World War II, summit meetings among the Allied leaders added to skeptics' mistrust of the Soviet Union. The Tehran Conference in December 1943 had hinted at Russia's territorial ambitions. By the time Stalin, Roosevelt, and England's Winston Churchill met at the Yalta Conference in February 1945, Soviet troops were pushing across Eastern Europe as Western advances chipped away at the German border. In Asia, Moscow recaptured territory lost in the Russo-Japanese War of 1904-05, and it worked to undermine the struggling non-communist regime of Chiang Kai-shek in China. So, when President Harry Truman met Churchill and Stalin in Potsdam in July 1945, the boundaries of the Cold War were all but determined.

In the United States, the anti-communists could argue persuasively that their country had fumbled these conferences—that wishful thinking misled the ailing FDR and the inexperienced Truman about their Soviet ally; that the united fight against the Nazis and the jovial grin of stalwart "Uncle Joe" Stalin obscured the menace of communism; that U.S. interests were betrayed by the State Department of the Stettinius-Byrnes-Marshall era; after all, wasn't accused spy Alger Hiss among the ardent young players at frail old FDR's elbow in Yalta?

Four days after the Potsdam Conference concluded on August 2, 1945, the United States unleashed the horrors of the atomic age at Hiroshima. The Soviets, forewarned at Potsdam, hastened to join the final assault on Japan.

When the war finally ended, the majority of the U.S. public at first resisted turning against its Soviet ally. Not even after Churchill's 1946 speech in Fulton, Missouri, where he warned of a descending "Iron Curtain" between democracies and the Soviet-dominated countries in Europe. Americans were just as inclined to mistrust British imperial designs as Soviet hegemony. Late into the 1940s, Russophiles in the Progressive Party and in and out of government still exerted considerable influence over American public opinion—and public policy.

THE THREAT FROM ABROAD

It wasn't until 1948 that the term Cold War came into common currency, notably from the typewriter of Walter Lippmann (whose own secretary, Mary Price, turned out to be a secret communist).

U.S. anti-communists were vindicated as Stalin committed three strategic blunders—at least as far as American public opinion was concerned.

First, in February 1948, the Soviets moved into Czechoslovakia. The arrogance of the communist invaders, who cut off all Czech contacts with the West, combined with the "suicide" of the popular Czech foreign minister, Jan Masaryk, disabused many Americans of the notion the Soviets were still friends.

Second, Stalin's break with the fiercely independent communist state of Yugoslavia set up a David-Goliath model that did nothing to soften the image of Stalin's brutal regime in the eyes of the West.

Finally, the Berlin Blockade, which began in the spring and lasted for a full year, captured the American imagination. As the American-led airlift brought relief to the German city besieged by Stalin's jackbooted troops, Berlin clarified the nature of the East-West struggle. Just about the final bit of U.S. goodwill toward the USSR evaporated in September 1949 when the Soviets exploded their first atomic bomb.

Also that year, communists gained another foothold when Mao Zedong proclaimed the establishment of the People's Republic of China.

A few months after that, on June 25, 1950, North Korean communists streamed across the 38th Parallel into South Korea, where they soon were killing American servicemen who had come to the defense of a democratic ally.

CHAPTER FOUR: The Threat Perceived

THE THREAT AT HOME

As if all this from abroad wasn't bad enough, patriotic U.S citizens like Laurence Johnson were stunned at post-war revelations of Soviet spies working right in America.

The most celebrated case involved Alger Hiss in 1948 when former Soviet spies Whittaker Chambers and Elizabeth Bentley accused the haughty young New Dealer of being a communist who had fed sensitive microfilm and documents to the Soviets. For denying the accusations, Hiss was convicted of perjury in 1950. (Evidence that emerged in the 1990s from decrypted Soviet messages shows that Hiss had been passing information to Moscow since 1935.)

By the middle of 1950, the Federal Bureau of Investigation had arrested several U.S. citizens involved in an espionage network that provided the Soviets with technical details on how to make the atomic bomb. Klaus Fuchs, a British nuclear physicist working on the bomb at Los Alamos, New Mexico, admitted he passed secret information to a Soviet courier. Others arrested in the theft of atomic secrets included New York City couple Julius and Ethel Rosenberg.

FBI agents in June 1950 swooped into a Syracuse parking lot and arrested chemist Alfred Dean Slack on espionage charges. He quickly confessed to providing the Soviets during World War II with the secret formula for RDX, a powerful explosive he helped to make at a plant in Tennessee. A federal judge would sentence Slack to fifteen years in prison for that.

Although the arrests were relatively few, they stirred a perception in America of a widespread communist conspiracy in its midst, the result of its basic goodness making it vulnerable to subversion. Matthew Cvetic, whose life inspired the 1951 film "I Was a Communist for the FBI," put it this way: "The really frightening cleverness of the Communists is how they understand appealing to people's best emotions—their tolerance, their broadmindedness—and then use those good emotions for their own end."

The U.S. government launched investigations of suspected communists in federal departments, the civil service, and the armed services.

The probes soon widened to include state and local employees, labor unions, colleges and universities, elementary and secondary schools, libraries, Hollywood, Broadway, radio, and television.

Proceedings produced tons of "evidence" sufficient to call into question the loyalty of some Americans, raise doubts about the silence of recalcitrant witnesses, and imply guilt by association. These probes not only targeted Communist Party cells but also the "fellow traveler" and the "stooge" who may have stumbled with the best of intentions into an association with communism. Suddenly, anyone who had been a party member was obliged to recant or to suffer the consequences. Anyone who spoke up in defense of an individual under suspicion, or who criticized the anti-communist movement, became suspects themselves.

If specific documentation was lacking, an informer often emerged to supply compensating testimony. If informers could not be found, professional witnesses and "security experts" filled in.

According to recent estimates, as many as 12,000 public employees nationwide endured suspensions due to loyalty-security proceedings. Most resigned rather than seeking reinstatement. Between 1947 and 1956, 2,700 federal employees were dismissed on loyalty-security grounds.

SHOW BUSINESS AND MASS MEDIA THREAT

Those employed by the entertainment and media industries became a prime target for the anti-communists. Early on, the communist-supported Conference of Studio Unions made inroads into nine film industry unions with more than 9,000 members. Party members were an active faction in the Directors Guild, and they helped found the Screen Writers Guild. The American Writers Congress adopted a Stalinist line. The Communist Party also was instrumental in the creation of AFRA, the union of radio workers.

In a 1938 speech, American communist leader V.J. Jerome addressed the duties of party members in the media: "You have also a different contribution to make, whether you are a writer, a film artist, a radio performer....Let us not abandon a single cultural field to reaction....Let our party demonstrate its role of vanguard in modern culture."

CHAPTER FOUR: THE THREAT PERCEIVED

"We need *party* artists," proclaimed the soon-to-be blacklisted screenwriter Alvah Bessie, writing in the Marxist magazine *New Masses* in 1946. "We need artists deeply...rooted in the working class who realize the truth of Lenin's assertion that the absolute freedom they seek 'is nothing but a bourgeois or anarchist phrase'...."

Elsewhere, Bessie was quoted as saying: "We need writers who will joyfully impose upon themselves the discipline of understanding and acting upon working-class theory."

Writer and director John Howard Lawson, co-founder of the Screen Writers Guild, would join Bessie as a member of the Hollywood Ten, a group of writers and directors who were voted in contempt of Congress in 1947 for refusing to testify about their alleged communist connections. In the 1930s, Lawson had assumed the role of mentor to Hollywood communists at a time when many still considered party membership to be chic. A prolific playwright and screenwriter, he directed Humphrey Bogart in the wartime films "Sahara" and "Action in the North Pacific." He once offered this advice to young screenwriters and performers in the party:

> As a writer try to get five minutes of the Communist doctrine ...in every script that you write. If you can, make the message come from the mouth of Gary Cooper or some other important star who is unaware of what he is saying; by the time it is discovered he is in New York and a great deal of expense will be involved to bring him back and reshoot the scene....If you (actors) are nothing more than an extra wearing white flannels on a country club veranda, do your best to appear decadent, do your best to appear a snob; do your best to create class antagonism....If you are an extra on a tenement street do your best to look downtrodden, do your best to look a victim of existing society.

Lawson might as well have offered himself as a human sacrifice to the anti-communists with another statement he made in 1937: "As for myself, I do not hesitate to say that it is my aim to present the communist position and to do so in the most specific manner."

The way anti-communists saw it, movie after movie was steeped in Soviet-style propaganda, often portraying the U.S. banker as a greedy, grasping, unsavory capitalist. (Think Frank Capra's "It's a Wonderful Life.") Similarly, in screenwriter Robert E. Sherwood's "The Best Years of Our Lives," a bank officer got a bawling out from his relentless boss for approving a loan to a GI back from World War II because the employee didn't demand collateral. Arthur Miller's play "You're Next" was seen as a thinly disguised attack on the House Committee on Un-American Activities, and his play "The Crucible" helped return the term "witch hunt" to contemporary American life.

It didn't take long for the studios to adopt their own anti-communist agenda. Director John Huston, who managed to avoid the blacklist despite a penchant for mischief, told how Warner Bros. objected to a scripted line in 1948's "The Treasure of the Sierra Madre" in which an old prospector says, "An ounce of gold, mister, is worth what it is because of the human labor that goes into the finding and getting of it."

Said Huston: "It was all on account of the word 'labor.' That word looks dangerous in print, I guess."

By the 1950s, the communists were largely out of union leadership, and by one estimate, no more than 300 working in show business had gravitated to communism.

Yet many anti-communists were convinced even a tiny number of committed communists in show business could undermine the entire nation. As the anti-communist newsletter *Counterattack* warned in June 1950: "In an emergency (at any given time) it would require only three persons (subversives)—one engineer in master control at a radio network, one director at a radio station, one voice before a microphone—to reach 90 million people with a message."

And what would that message be? According to Vincent Hartnett and his anti-communist allies, all suspect writers, producers, and performers could be expected to promote the aims of the Communist Party in their work.

"Communist literature is replete with descriptions of Communist efforts to penetrate the theatre (in its broadest sense) and use art as a weapon in the class struggle," Hartnett wrote.

CHAPTER FOUR: THE THREAT PERCEIVED

Hearst columnist J.B. Matthews summarized the anti-communist view of the show-business threat in an article for *American Legion Magazine*. "It is silly to suppose that guys like Albert Maltz or dolls like Anne Revere were ever meant to do the dirty manual work of throwing up barricades in the streets," Matthews wrote. The communists' goal, he said, was to win the support of "fellow travelers"—the well-meaning, idealistic folks who would contribute part of their paychecks, back up the party line in union meetings, alter scripts, sign petitions, attend meetings of front organizations, and in general lend their name and prestige to the cause.

Eventually, television would find itself the center stage of this play for ideological cleansing. But not yet in 1949, when TV had penetrated just 6 percent of the nation. It gained its first foothold in major cities: Between 1948 and 1952, seven television stations opened in Los Angeles, and the same number in New York City. Austin, Little Rock and Portland, Maine went without. Among the first smaller "TV cities" was Syracuse, Johnson's hometown. By December 1951, Syracuse could boast two TV stations, WHEN and WSYR. Two-thirds of Syracuse households had TVs by mid-1951—a feat matched in only eight other cities at the time.

The Federal Communications Commission froze licensing of new stations in 1950 due to the outbreak of the Korean War, which required the diversion of engineering and manufacturing resources. The number of television receivers and radios manufactured in 1951 dropped by two million. After the fighting ended in 1953, the FCC lifted its restrictions, and by 1957 there were 500 stations broadcasting to 40 million TV sets sitting in 85 percent of American homes.

Meanwhile, the film industry had undergone a painful contraction. In the early 1950s, movie theaters attendance dropped due to people staying home to watch TV. As early as 1951, theaters in TV towns began to close in droves—70 in eastern Pennsylvania, 143 in Southern California, 61 in Massachusetts, 64 in the Chicago area, and 55 in metropolitan New York City.

From the start, TV merchandising was a potent and profitable enterprise. Radio drew the bulk of broadcast advertising revenue in 1950—$415 million. But the wondrous results of video commercials soon put television in front to stay. For example, the makers of Hazel Bishop lipstick reported that, by advertising exclusively on TV, their sales grew from $50,000 in 1950 to $4.5 million in 1952.

Quality programming was of secondary value in this new medium. Television's fortunes relied on having the right ratings, demographics, and market appeal. Motivational speaker and author Les Brown described the essence of the industry: "In day-to-day commerce, television is not so much interested in the business of communications as in the business of delivering people to advertisers. People are the merchandise, not the shows. The shows are merely the bait."

Setting the tone in program-pandering, a network sales barker once notified potential advertisers: "Audience of 12 Returning NBC Shows Reveal High Usage of Dry Dog Food."

Most of the show people snared by the Hollywood HCUA hearings in 1947 ended up shut out of television. With the stakes so high, neither the sponsors who paid the bills nor the networks airing the commercials could afford a false move. Negative publicity was anathema.

When Laurence Johnson started accusing the networks of employing communist propagandists to pitch toothpaste and frozen peas, the broadcasting industry wasn't interested in whether it was true. It acted in whatever way it could to avoid the unprofitable effects of controversy.

REACTING TO THE THREAT

As Johnson and his allies launched their campaign to save American broadcasting from what they considered an insidious plague, the targets of the accusations initially tended to dismiss their accusers as malcontents or zanies. In their dismissals, the critics of anti-communism underestimated the cultural, political, and economic sources from which it drew its strength.

In the late 1930s and 1940s, liberals linked anti-communism with conservatism, union-busting, racism, fascism, and Nazism. Liberal cartoonists drew HCUA investigators as bats in belfries, witches riding broomsticks, medieval torturers and goons smearing Congress with black ink.

CHAPTER FOUR: The Threat Perceived

Arthur Miller called the HCUA panel that descended on Hollywood in 1947 "cheap publicity hounds." But the hounds drew blood. One of the victims-to-be, writer John Howard Lawson, told HCUA on the witness stand: "I am not on trial here, Mr. Chairman. This committee is on trial here before the American people. Let us get that straight." Events quickly dispelled Lawson's naive notion. He ended up serving a year in prison for contempt of Congress.

When sportswriter Ring Lardner Jr.'s turn came to testify, he composed a memorable line in reply to the standard question, "Are you now or have you ever been a member of the Communist Party?"

"I could answer it, but if I did, I would hate myself in the morning," he said.

His bravado turned out to be gallows humor; he also was sentenced to twelve months behind bars, and both he and Lawson would subsequently find themselves serving hard time on blacklists.

CHAPTER FIVE:
Anti-communism Inc.

IN 1945, Alfred Kohlberg, a millionaire entrepreneur and supporter of Chiang Kai-shek, launched the anti-communist periodical *Plain Talk*. As researchers, he picked three ex-FBI agents: Kenneth M. Bierly, John G. Keenan, and Theodore C. Kirkpatrick. Kohlberg set them up in an office in Washington, D.C. The title on the door was John Quincy Adams Associates. JQAA acted as an anti-communist lobby and information clearinghouse, serving those who, in Kohlberg's words, "are anxious not to support a hidden Communist cause."

JQAA got off to a slow start. Its request for nonprofit status was shot down, and the business was dissolved. A year later, Bierly, Keenan, and Kirkpatrick moved to New York City and set up American Business Consultants Inc., which began the profitable practice of "clearance" in American show business and beyond.

For about five dollars a head, a corporation could have its employees checked by ABC Inc. to confirm their anti-communist reliability. This new agency also launched the bulletin *Counterattack*, naming names and citing alleged communist-front records.

In the early going, ABC Inc. criticized radio personality Mary Margaret McBride for advertising Polish hams, which were imported from behind the Iron Curtain. The company also lashed out at Frederic March and his actress wife, Florence Eldridge, for their memberships in organizations on the Attorney General's List of Subversive Organizations.

The Attorney General's List grew to seventy-eight organizations by March 1947, but that was not fast enough for anti-communists like the men at ABC Inc. By the end of the year, *Counterattack* listed 114 more organizations they considered to be communist fronts. *Counterattack* also expanded its list of undesirables in a veritable lexicon of suspect categories: "quislings...appeasers...pinks...fifth columnists...subversives... commies...stooges...fronters...dupes." The anti-communists would soon add yet another category: the "anti-anti-communist," which covered everyone who criticized their work.

Such public scorning seemed to have its desired effect. When the House Committee on Un-American Activities began the Hollywood Ten hearings in October 1947, many show business celebrities and others signed petitions and added their names to newspaper advertisements in support of the accused. More than twenty-one of the signatories to one such ad in *Variety* later had trouble finding work. Of 204 who signed a friend-of-the-court brief to the Supreme Court, eighty-four ended up blacklisted.

Business leaders in New York and elsewhere began receiving *Counterattack* in the mail with a recommendation that they take steps to check employees cited in the publication.

Many of the bulletins went to people in broadcasting. In *Counterattack*, the editors would identify Actor A as receiving a newspaper notice in a communist paper like the *Daily Worker* or *New Masses*, or appearing at a function with known communists B and C, with backing from communist front D. To ABC Inc., all this made Actor A suspect.

In those days, anti-communist researchers like those at ABC Inc. didn't bother to confirm the details with Actor A. Nor did they routinely check whether Actor A had indeed appeared at D's function or had anything to do with communists B or C. For ABC Inc., a printed program or advance notice was good enough. It also was good enough for other anti-communists such as Vincent Hartnett, J.B. Matthews, Godfrey Schmidt, Westbrook Pegler, and George Sokolsky. Later, Laurence Johnson would rely upon this same slipshod methodology.

Launched on a shoestring, ABC Inc. found an especially receptive ear in the half-billion-dollar broadcasting industry, which was eager to avoid employing anyone controversial. "We're a business that has to please the customers," one show business executive said. "That's the main thing we

CHAPTER FIVE: ANTI-COMMUNISM INC.

have to do—keep people happy and, to do that, we have to stay out of trouble."

Movie executives were similarly nervous. On November 24, 1947, the same day Dalton Trumbo, John Howard Lawson, Ring Lardner Jr. and the rest of the Hollywood Ten were cited for contempt in Washington, D.C., top movie executives huddled at the Waldorf Hotel in Manhattan. They decided to suspend without pay the "unfriendly" writers. The studio heads agreed that their employees would have to declare their non-communism. The film industry's loyalty oath would be a fixture of the Cold War for more than a decade.

COLD WAR CHILL

On Monday, February 3, 1948, the temperature in Syracuse was a relatively balmy 35 degrees Fahrenheit following a three-week deep freeze. At the Onondaga Hotel, James O'Neil, the visiting national commander of the American Legion, spoke about a different kind of chill—the Cold War. "The problem confronting us now is not how to get along with Russia, but how to get along in spite of Russia," he said.

An opposing viewpoint was on display on Saturday, March 6, when twelve members of the Progressive Citizens of America (PCA) and the American Labor Party (ALP) gathered in Syracuse on informational picket lines outside the old federal building on Clinton Square, carrying placards that read "Save American Democracy!" and "Stop Truman's Police State Methods!" The PCA was composed of liberals who welcomed communist allies; the ALP had members who were hard-core Communist Party members. They were protesting the detention without bail on Ellis Island of left-wing leaders Gerhart Eisler, John Williamson, Charles A. Doyle, and Ferdinand Smith. (Eisler had been identified as a Soviet agent.)

Among the protesters was Syracuse liberal activist Lillian Reiner, who remembered it as an exciting day. "It was my first picket line," she said. "A friend of mine had made me a cloth helmet."

Before long, the protesters were confronted by thirty or forty counter-demonstrators, including members of veterans and civic groups. They, too, carried placards, including one that read: "Russia Can Have PCA and ALP Pickets, They're Too Red for Us!" The crowd grew, heckling turned to jostling, and police gamely tried to keep both sides moving. Within a half hour, the protesters were outnumbered ten to one. As several hundred onlookers watched, the counter-protesters grabbed the other side's placards and destroyed them. The rally broke up soon afterward.

The protesters vowed to be back on the following Monday. The counter-demonstrators called for a corresponding "Rally of Americans."

Emotions on both sides simmered over the weekend. Reiner recalled that a local radio personality broadcast an appeal the night before the second picket. "He kept urging all evening, urging the American Legion to counter-demonstrate. And they did. They came in full uniform. And they wrestled our signs away."

Reiner did have at least one nice thing to say about the counter-picketers, who included Spanish-American War veterans and members of the anti-communist Citizens Foundation. "When they tripped us, they helped us up," she said.

The counter-demonstrators made no secret of their advance work. H. R. Ekins, executive secretary of the Citizens Foundation, said on the radio the following Tuesday that the tipoff had been a call for demonstrations on behalf of Eisler and the others, "published in last Tuesday's editions of the *Daily Worker* in New York—the official publication of the Communist Party of America."

Tensions continued to flare in Syracuse in the spring of 1948 as Washington pressed for a big noncommunist turnout in the Italian elections. In support of the noncommunists, local Italian-American civic leaders Joseph Sposato, Anthony J. Valentine and Matteo Milazzo made a recording for the Voice of America at Syracuse radio station WSYR. The Republican county chairman, Charles McNett, also called on Italian-Americans to write to friends and relatives in the old country, alerting them to the Red Menace.

Then a handbill appeared on the streets of Syracuse, warning of a plot to turn Italy into America's "colony." The handbill, signed by the Sacco-Vanzetti Club of the Syracuse Communist Party, urged Syracusans of Italian descent to ignore the GOP chairman's appeal. It also condemned the radio campaign.

McNett subsequently told *The Post-Standard* he was outraged that his critics "chose the eve of Good Friday to distribute handbills filled with familiar Communist trick phrases and appeals to support the phony 'People's Liberation Front.'"

THE WALLACE CAMPAIGN

In 1948, eighteen stations along the East Coast carried major network telecasts of the Republican convention in Philadelphia, where the GOP nominated Thomas E. Dewey and Earl Warren. Later in Philadelphia, television was present when the Democrats renominated Harry Truman and Alben Barkley.

Television also covered the Philadelphia convention of the Progressive Party, which nominated Henry Wallace for president and Idaho Senator Glen Taylor for vice president. By then, Wallace was a dirty word to the GOP establishment and many others in America.

Negative public and press reaction to the Progressive campaign demonstrated the risks of running a nonconformist race in an era when Americans seemed to prize political and social conformity, and eccentricity was considered one step from subversion. Syracuse declared itself off-limits to the Progressives, denying permission for a party speaker to visit a local school.

Progressives also weren't welcomed in many other areas of the country. A Wallace organizer was stabbed to death in Charleston, South Carolina. Gunfire broke out at a Wallace petition drive in West Virginia, where there were also threats to organizers. Evansville College in Indiana fired an outspoken Wallace supporter, Professor George Parker. The university offered this rationale for its action: "The college fully subscribes to the principle of academic freedom but believes that the individual who exercises the privilege must assume the responsibility for his utterances and actions when they destroy confidence and faith in the institution of which he is a member."

In Upstate New York, artist Rockwell Kent, an ardent Wallace supporter, ran a dairy farm in Ausable Forks, and anti-Wallace customers began boycotting his business. Kent turned over his dairy to a couple of his employees, and business returned to normal. In Binghamton, New York, a judge reportedly offered to hold custody hearings for children whose parents supported Wallace.

Truman eagerly pursued the claim that subversives ran Wallace's campaign. The president accused the Progressives of being a "communist front," and referred to Wallace supporters as communists.

The civic anti-communists were also in hot pursuit. ABC Inc.'s *Counterattack* put out a special report on the "commugressive" Wallace campaign. The anti-communists had an easy target; the Communist Party had given its full support to Wallace, whose campaign also had communists in key positions. In California alone, an estimated 3,000 party members worked on the campaign. One stated goal of the communists was to weaken Truman to make room for a more leftist candidate in 1952.

The New York Herald-Tribune and *The New York Times* generally ignored the Wallace campaign, a trend followed by the *New York Post*, the *Baltimore Sun*, the *St. Louis Post-Dispatch,* and the Syracuse press. A few newspapers were outwardly hostile. *The Pittsburgh Press* published on its front page the names of those who signed nominating petitions for Wallace. The editors announced that anyone "claiming they signed under misapprehension or through misunderstanding will have their statements printed the same day their names are used." When it printed the first 1,000 names, ten retractions accompanied them. A score of others who signed supposedly were hauled before their bosses and told: Repudiate or else! Other newspapers employing similar techniques were the *Milwaukee Journal*, some Scripps-Howard dailies, and papers in Boston and Cleveland.

Polls suggested 51 percent of the American people agreed that communists dominated Wallace's party. When Election Day came, just 2.4 percent of the popular vote went to Wallace. It was a pathetic showing, considering that third-party efforts in 1912 and 1924 yielded 27 percent and 16 percent of the vote, respectively. (Despite predictions otherwise, Truman upset Dewey to win re-election.)

Some said the dismal showing of the Wallace campaign broke the back of the Communist Party USA.

CHAPTER FIVE: Anti-communism Inc.

VINCENT HARTNETT, ANTI-COMMUNIST

By the time of the 1948 election, the anti-communists were alarmed that writers and actors they considered unreliable were appearing on this new medium of television. One of the first to sound the alarm was Vincent Hartnett.

In 1948, Hartnett was a young radio scriptwriter for the Phillips H. Lord Agency, an independent production house in Manhattan. An ex-Navy man, Hartnett worked on the "Gang Busters" radio series, and he worked in television writing for "The Black Robe," an early Perry Mason-type drama series set in New York night court. Hartnett recalled that the company would hire extras off the street at five or ten dollars a shot to appear in "court" live for the Dumont network. Said Hartnett: "I think we had the glorious number of three stations—New York, Philadelphia and Baltimore."

Hartnett had a slender build, with a crewcut and piercing eyes. His critics would later offer more ruthless descriptions. Journalist and author Stefan Kanfer called Hartnett "small, thin-lipped, resolutely drab." Socialist author Michael Harrington, who wrote about anti-communists in the 1950s, described Hartnett as "a prototype of the spoiled priest." Louis Nizer, the New York City attorney who would one day represent John Henry Faulk, wrote about seeing Hartnett for the first time in the early 1960s: "He was a frail, timid little man of about forty years of age, no more than 130 pounds in weight and less than average height. His dark eyes looked almost frightened, and his voice was thin and hesitant. He had an almost lipless mouth, which gave an outward curve to his cheeks."

Hartnett started college at Fordham University and transferred to the University of Notre Dame, where he received a bachelor's degree in 1937 and a master's in English in 1939, both with honors. During the war, he served three years in the Pacific, then worked in Washington for Naval Intelligence. He returned to New York after the war to become a freelance writer. He studied writing for radio for a year at Columbia University, then went to work for Lord.

Soon, Hartnett won a promotion to script supervisor for "Gang Busters," a position providing connections and information that would prove invaluable later for his anti-communist work. "Gang Busters" was radio *verite*: Each episode dramatized an actual police case. To produce scripts, Hartnett and his co-workers gathered material from reporters, highway patrol officers, and FBI agents, as well as a former New York City chief of detectives and an assistant U.S. attorney.

Hartnett said he joined the ranks of the anti-communists after an incident involving William Sweets, a director of "Gang Busters." In 1949, letters began arriving at the studio questioning Sweets' loyalty and protesting his continued employment. They cited his support for organizations linked to communists and his refusal to sign an anti-communist affidavit.

Agency management dismissed the protests as crank letters. However, sponsors and ad agencies were skittish. Some put up a fuss, including General Foods President Clarence Francis, Pepsi-Cola's Walter Mack, and ad executives from Young & Rubicam. With the backing of *Counterattack*, Hartnett alleged that Sweets had declined to employ those affiliated with the American Federation of Radio Artists who were opposed to communism. Not long afterward, Sweets was forced to resign.

Sweets' professional eclipse cast a shadow over the New York broadcasting community and beyond. A story in *Variety* was headlined "Red Scare Numbing Video." A TV network casting director said, "Now we spend our time trying to satisfy our top brass that the actors have never been on the left side of the fence."

The Lord Agency wasn't the only show business shop that faced off against the anti-communists in 1949. Fred Friendly, then the producer of the CBS quiz show "Who Said That?", said he was under strict orders from an oil company sponsor and his network bosses to avoid using controversial guests such as Norman Thomas, Al Capp, Oscar Levant, and Henry Morgan, as well as some senators and congressmen. The sponsor reportedly kept its own blacklist, which the network accepted as gospel. No one claimed the "listees" were part of a communist conspiracy, Friendly recalled. Instead, in the euphemistic phrasing of the times, the network said it worried the guests on a live show "just might say something."

Emboldened by the success of the Sweets protest, Hartnett went to his executive producer and complained about the agency's continued employment of actors with communist front records. Hartnett claimed 25 percent of the cast lists were suspect.

CHAPTER FIVE: Anti-communism Inc.

He recalled telling his boss: "I'm not going to put in the cast calls for these people."

The executive producer countered with a directive from the front office: Don't make waves.

"I protested it," Hartnett recalled. "They didn't want the boat rocked, so they said just go along with it or else get out."

Hartnett said he had no alternative but to leave the Lord Agency. "As a result of my protesting against our continued employment of communist-fronters on 'Gang Busters,' I was forced to resign. I hated to do it because it was a very lovely job; I enjoyed it very much."

Hartnett and fellow scriptwriter Paul Milton had been developing a TV show of their own. After he left Lord, Hartnett tried to sell the idea: a half-hour grand opera performance of the classics translated to TV format. Hartnett said he lined up as a sponsor the chemical tycoon Henry Reichhold. The American Broadcasting Company sounded interested. "We had an audition program, but the deal fell through," Hartnett said.

THE IRVING FEINER CASE

On a chilly March 8, 1949, a stocky, curly-haired young Syracuse University student named Irving Feiner took a loudspeaker to a busy downtown corner along Harrison Street and began making a public pitch for an upcoming visit and talk by O. John Rogge, the outspoken civil rights lawyer. The local paper reported how Feiner also allegedly "called various public officials insulting names."

Feiner was a member of the local chapter of Young Progressives of America, which the anti-communists considered a party front. The YPA and another communist-linked organization, the American Labor Party, had invited Rogge to speak at a local school.

With his loudspeaker and provocative remarks, Feiner soon drew a couple of dozen listeners, which swelled to seventy-five or more, many furious at his remarks.

When the police arrived, some in the crowd demanded that officers silence Feiner, with at least one person threatening violence against the student. Rather than take steps to control the crowd and to allow Feiner to speak, police took him into custody and booked him for disorderly conduct.

Feiner was a student in Maxwell School Professor Marguerite Fisher's political science course, and she immediately took an interest in the case. While she sympathized with Feiner, whom she called "very well-behaved, a good student," she thought he was asking for trouble delivering his political remarks in a manner that could be viewed as blocking traffic. "He should have started his speech in the park nearby, rather than in the middle of the street," she said.

Feiner's arrest quickly became a national cause of sorts. On March 18, 1949, Pete Seeger, then a member of The Weavers singing group, performed at a rally for the embattled student.

On April 4, Feiner went on trial in police court. Fisher testified as a character witness, the only faculty member from the Maxwell School to do so. Feiner was convicted and sentenced to thirty days in jail but released on $1,000 bail pending an appeal. The next day, Syracuse University expelled him.

Feiner's case eventually arrived at the U.S. Supreme Court, which affirmed his conviction and sentence. Three judges—William O. Douglas, Sherman Minton, and Hugo Black—issued strong dissents. Black called it "a dark day for civil liberties in our nation." He wrote that "this conviction makes a mockery of the free speech guarantees of the First and Fourteenth Amendments" in that it means "cities and states can with impunity subject all speeches, political or otherwise, to the supervision and censorship of the local police....Criticism of public officials will be too dangerous for all but the most courageous."

Feiner served his time at the Jamesville Penitentiary near Syracuse. Lillian Reiner, who joined supporters in visiting Feiner in jail, considered the conviction a tragedy.

"I felt so sad that this brilliant young man who wanted to be a lawyer had lost his chance to be a lawyer because of what happened at the hands of the stupid police in Syracuse," she said.

CHAPTER FIVE: Anti-communism Inc.

CLOSING IN ON THE REDS

In the spring of 1949, Syracuse moviegoers got to see "Lost Boundaries," a drama playing at the Paramount theater. One of the movie's stars was Canada Lee, a popular Black actor. Soon, anti-communists would pillory Lee for his associations with civil-rights organizations on the Attorney General's List. Lee suddenly found himself barred from movie and television work after his sponsor, the American Tobacco Company, withdrew its support. He died of a heart attack in 1952 at age forty-five.

In the summer of 1949, an appearance by singer and actor Paul Robeson, another Black American active in civil rights organizations, sparked an explosive confrontation in Peekskill, New York, at an open-air concert. At the time, Robeson had gained a reputation as one of America's more outspoken communists. After he was booked to sing for the Civil Rights Congress at the Westchester County event, the anti-communists turned out in force. Veterans patrolled in formation outside the entrance to the park, keeping out would-be concertgoers.

A riot broke out, cars were overturned, and there were some minor injuries. Robeson did not sing in Peekskill that day. Afterward, an elated Milton Flynt, commander of the American Legion's Peekskill Post No. 274, said: "Our objective was to prevent the Paul Robeson concert, and I think our objective was reached. Anything that happened after the organized demonstration was dispersed was entirely up to the individual citizens and should not be blamed on the patriotic organizations."

Robeson vowed that he and supporters from the American Labor Party in New York City would be back the following Sunday. The veterans promised a counter-demonstration, and as the date approached, New York Governor Thomas Dewey mobilized a small army of state police.

On Sunday, a group of 15,000 liberals, radicals, communists, and hangers-on showed up at Peekskill, and Robeson performed for them on schedule. Afterward, counter-demonstrators threw stones as the audience left the park. Nearly 150 people were injured. Governor Dewey took heat from all sides for his handling of the Peekskill affair. (Anti-communists were already angry at Dewey for vetoing as unconstitutional a bill that would have banned political parties advocating violent overthrow of the government.)

THE GROCER WHO SOLD McCARTHYISM

In Syracuse, many in the press and the public were eager to do more to keep a lid on communism. This impatience showed in *The Post-Standard*'s editorial cartoon of Thursday, December 1, 1949. It pictured a fellow with a flowing white beard enjoying his sunset years on a beach. The caption: "Twenty Years later—1969 social note: Convicted Communist enjoys luxuries of capitalism while waiting for Supreme Court to pass on constitutionality of law under which he was convicted in 1949."

In a letter to the newspaper, F.A. Brewer of Syracuse passed along this note of community interest:

> I feel inclined to relate a few features of Communism, as I heard read from a Communist book, describing the doctrine of this terrible class of people, by a lecturer in our local church.
>
> Communism is set to destroy every religious sect existing, wherever it is found, specially where it gains a foothold.
>
> It is opposed and a bitter enemy to morals, and decency, their purpose is to degrade marriage...
>
> Another thing, the Communists are a deceitful, lying bunch of criminals, and without exception.

By the middle of 1949, universities in twenty-two states had adopted loyalty oaths, many modeled on that of the National Education Association. Syracuse school officials also did their part to maintain the anti-communist vigil. Superintendent David H. Patton ordered school libraries to stop circulating "slick publications" such as *USSR Information*, published by the Soviet Embassy and routinely mailed to schools. It was the job of Harold J. Coon, assistant superintendent, to confiscate communist propaganda bulletins. Patton said, to his knowledge, school principals had destroyed all copies of the spurious Soviet publication—except for those "kept as evidence."

THE BIRTH OF McCARTHYISM

One person late to the anti-communism movement was a certain junior U.S. senator from Wisconsin. He would make up for it after January

CHAPTER FIVE: ANTI-COMMUNISM INC.

7, 1950, when Joseph McCarthy sat down to lunch at the Colony Restaurant in Washington, flanked by three friends, to plot a re-election strategy for 1952.

He needed an issue to improve his political image. During his freshman term, McCarthy had not distinguished himself in the Senate. McCarthy and his dining companions considered and rejected a few ideas. Push for a new St. Lawrence Seaway? Not exciting enough. A national pension plan? Too expensive.

When someone suggested that McCarthy should get tough on communism, the senator leaped at the idea. "The government is full of communists," he told his friends. "The thing to do is to hammer at them."

It did not take long for McCarthy to put the strategy to work. On the evening of February 9, 1950, McCarthy mounted the platform in the Colonnade room of the McLure Hotel in Wheeling, West Virginia, where he was a guest of the Ohio County Women's Republican Club. In his speech, he warmed to his theme of the worldwide clash between the forces of atheistic communism and Christian democracy. He questioned why Congress hadn't done something about the treasonous activity exposed in the Alger Hiss case. He blamed public apathy growing out of the postwar letdown of U.S. defenses.

Pulling out a sheet of paper and holding it aloft, he said in a drone of suppressed urgency: "While I cannot take the time to name all the men in the State Department who have been named as members of the Communist Party and members of a spy ring, I have here in my hand a list of 205...names that were made known to the Secretary of State as being members of the Communist Party and who, nevertheless, are still working and shaping policy in the State Department."

In his later speeches, the number of State Department communists he cited dropped to eighty-one, then as low as fifty-seven. At no time, however, did McCarthy produce the name of a single "card-carrying communist" employed by the State Department.

The Truman administration asked the Senate to investigate McCarthy's charges. The task was assigned to Millard Tydings, a Democratic senator from Maryland. His findings, released five months later, concluded that McCarthy's charges were "a hoax and a fraud." However, Republican senators refused to endorse the findings. (In November 1952, McCarthy won re-election while Tydings went down to defeat.)

One story has it that a friend later asked McCarthy what he had been holding in his hand that evening in West Virginia; he grinned and replied: "An old laundry list." In the end, it didn't really matter what McCarthy was holding. The fact a U.S. senator made the allegations was enough to give him the page-one headlines he so coveted. By the time people figured out he had no evidence, McCarthy had moved on to other targets, carrying media attention with him.

By mid-1950, the anti-communists had new legislative tools. One was the Subversive Activities Control Board (SACB), whose five presidentially appointed members were to supervise the registration of all suspect organizations. Another was the new Senate Internal Security Subcommittee (SISS) of the U.S. Senate Judiciary Committee.

This latter one would become McCarthy's chief anti-communist platform.

THE HOT WAR

The threat of communism became deeply personal for many Americans, including Laurence Johnson, after June 25, 1950, when North Korean troops invaded South Korea. Johnson's son-in-law, Jack Buchanan, was soon called to duty out of the Marine Reserves. The 26-year-old lieutenant was assigned to a mortar company, and he left for Korea early in 1951. During the next few months, Jack Buchanan would see some of the bitterest fighting of the war, as UN troops battled up to half-a-million Chinese who eventually joined the fighting on the side of communist North Korea.

Suddenly, millions of newly alarmed Americans hopped aboard the anti-communist train, sometimes in very personal ways. Maria Careccia of Utica reportedly persuaded the court to have her marriage annulled on the grounds that her husband was a communist.

In show business, Monogram Studio decided to shelve plans for a movie on the life of Hiawatha, deeming it too controversial. *The New York Times* explained why: "It was Hiawatha's efforts as a peacemaker among the warring Indian tribes of his day, which brought about the federation of five nations, that gave Monogram particular concern, according to a studio spokesman. These, it was decided, might cause the picture to be regarded as a message for peace and therefore helpful to present Communist designs."

On November 7, 1950, the new national commander of the American Legion, 29-year-old Eric Cocke Jr. of Dawson, Georgia, came to lunch in Syracuse, where Legion Post 41 was 2,000 members strong. To an overflow crowd of 300 in the post's clubrooms, Cocke warned that America was facing its hour of challenge and peril. "We must give a spartan touch to our cherished way of life," he said, "to save what we can of it in the showdown clash between democracy and communism."

THE ORIGIN OF *RED CHANNELS*

After his plans for a mini-opera entertainment series faded in the late 1940s, Vincent Hartnett visited the New York Public Library so often that its twin lions flanking the front steps began to feel like old friends. The library's high-ceilinged mustiness and echoing hallways added comforting authority and solidity to his newest project.

Hartnett began sifting through the back issues of the *Daily Worker*, *New Masses*, and various other left-wing publications. "In 1949, I had just started to do magazine work," Hartnett said in an interview in the 1980s. "Then I got the idea for writing the book *Red Channels*."

A radio actor friend introduced him to Ted Kirkpatrick of ABC Inc.'s *Counterattack*, and Hartnett pitched his idea of a reference guide listing broadcast journalists and people in entertainment suspected of having communist ties. "They said, well, they'd been thinking about it, too. So, we'd have a joint venture," Hartnett said.

Before long, Hartnett was working with ABC Inc. to write the pamphlet-style *Red Channels: The Report of Communist Influence in Radio and Television*, which could act as a convenient blacklist for employers looking to hire actors, writers, broadcast journalists, and others.

Ken Bierly, Kirkpatrick's colleague at ABC Inc., described the project this way: "We felt it might be good to come out with something documented and do it publicly. Lay it on the line and sell it over the counter to try to clear the air."

Although not technically an employee of ABC Inc., Hartnett's fingerprints were all over this new publication. "All I did was to help get together the names, because they didn't actually have any," he said later. "They (at ABC Inc.) weren't radio or TV people, and I knew people in radio and TV." Hartnett noted that he also wrote the introduction to *Red Channels*, although his name was not on it.

By the time *Red Channels* was developed, Hartnett had ample reason to expect the broadcast industry to pay close attention to its contents. The trailblazer in this field of naming names was Greenwich, Connecticut, homemaker Hester McCullough. Upon learning that the harmonica virtuoso Larry Adler and dancer Paul Draper—both "suspects" to the anti-communist faithful—had been booked for entertainment writer Ed Sullivan's CBS variety show, "Toast of the Town," in 1950, she launched a protest campaign. Her cause was joined by anti-communist columnists Westbrook Pegler, Walter Winchell, and others. Even so, Sullivan allowed Draper and Adler on the Sunday night broadcast, resulting in 350 telephone complaints and sixty telegram protests to CBS. The program's sponsor, the Ford Motor Company, received 1,294 irate letters and telegrams.

Within a week, Sullivan had dispatched a remarkable letter to William B. Lewis at the Kenyon & Eckhardt ad agency, which handled the Ford account for CBS. The letter, dated January 25, 1950, was noteworthy in baldly stating Sullivan's clear desire to avoid controversy at all costs, a stance that others in show business would adopt with far less candor. Sullivan wrote:

> Dear Bill:
>
> I am deeply distressed to find out that some people were offended by the appearance, on Sunday's *Toast of the Town* television show of a performer whose political beliefs are a matter

CHAPTER FIVE: Anti-communism Inc.

of controversy. That is most unfortunate. You know how bitterly opposed I am to communism and all it stands for. You also know how strongly I would oppose having the program used as a political forum, directly or indirectly.

After all, the whole point of the *Toast of the Town* is to entertain people, not offend them....If anybody has taken offense, it is the last thing I wanted or anticipated, and I am sorry.

I just want *Toast of the Town* to be the best show on television. I know that's what you and the sponsor want, too. Tell everybody to tune in again next Sunday night, and if I can get in a plug, it will be a great show—better than ever.

Sincerely, Ed Sullivan.

Adler and Draper filed a $200,000 libel suit against Hester McCullough for calling them "pro-communist." The case ended with a hung jury in May 1950. By then, Draper and Adler had become virtually unemployable in the United States and they went abroad to find work.

Although McCullough would not be a major figure in the remainder of the anti-communist movement, she had successfully entered the lion's den of broadcasting. She had shown to Hartnett and others that, with a threatening message, the lions became kittens.

RED CHANNELS ARRIVES

By mid-1950, ABC Inc. was ready for *Red Channels* to hit the streets. Hartnett and his colleagues leaked an exclusive to Ed Sullivan. In his June 21 column in the New York *Daily News*, Sullivan wrote: "A bombshell will be dropped into the offices of radio-TV networks, advertising agencies and sponsors this week with the publication of 'Red Channels'."

The journalist Stefan Kanfer, in his 1973 book "A Journal of the Plague Years," would describe this bombshell as "the most effective blacklist in the history of show business."

By October, ABC Inc.'s Kirkpatrick was equating *Red Channels* to a litmus test for loyalty. "I don't say you shouldn't hire the performers listed in *Red Channels*," he told the Radio Executives' Club. "I do say that those who continue to support Communist Party causes since June 23, 1950, must take the consequences. Anyone who has continued to support a communist cause since June 23 is just as much...an enemy of our country as if he were in Korea passing ammunition to the communists."

About 15,000 copies of *Red Channels* were initially published. Hartnett said everyone on the *Counterattack* mailing list got a copy. Freebies went to influential executives in advertising and show business. Hartnett said he distributed 1,000 copies during a lecture tour later in the year.

Red Channels sold for one dollar, so no one got rich off sales. After it became clear that *Red Channels* had an extraordinary impact on the broadcasting industry, ABC Inc.'s John Keenan would grouse: "We made a mistake in charging only a dollar....We didn't think there'd be such a hefty demand for it. We should have charged two bucks a copy. Now we're smarter than we were then."

At first glance, the paperback booklet, just over 200 pages long, looked like just another anti-Red tract in the tradition of Myron C. Fagan and Elizabeth Dilling. The cover showed a giant red hand poised over a microphone.

Hartnett's seven-page introduction added to the impact. In concise, unemotional terms, he articulated the views of anti-communist activists toward broadcasting. Quoting from Communist Party sources, and attributing verbatim quotations to Lenin and Stalin, Hartnett made the case that communism aimed to use the mass media in general—radio and television in particular—to indoctrinate the masses. Hartnett claimed that for every card-carrying communist in broadcasting there were ten "'reliables,' dupes or innocents who, for one reason or another will support its fronts." Thus, the networks, stations, ad agencies, production companies, unions and the trade press have been "colonized," in Hartnett's phrase. "The 'colonists' need not be party members or even deliberate cooperators," Hartnett wrote. "It is sufficient if they advance Communist objectives with complete unconsciousness."

Hartnett set forth four methods by which the USSR's new Cominform sought to undermine U.S. policies and support the Soviet Union:

CHAPTER FIVE: ANTI-COMMUNISM INC.

First, through cleverly disguised alliances with causes and issues such as "academic freedom," "civil rights," "peace," "the fight against anti-Semitism and Jimcrow," and "the outlawing of the H-Bomb."

Second, through financial support from the well-heeled show business community. Wrote Hartnett: "At one Communist-front meeting, a leading producer-director-announcer-actor pledged $500. A noted playwright contributed $1,000. Many $100 contributions were noted...."

Third, by open recruitment of major stars. Hartnett noted that the Communist Party had been soft-pedaling this direct approach since the Hollywood Ten troubles in 1947.

The fourth was through sheer domination of broadcast programming. "A few documentary programs produced by one network in particular have faithfully followed the Party line," Hartnett wrote. "Several commercially sponsored dramatic series are used as sounding boards, particularly with reference to current issues in which the Party is critically interested ....(One) program, sponsored by the advertising industry and American business and supposedly portraying the benefits of our economic system, turned out to be—in the words of one reviewer in the trade press—'more nearly a plea for collectivism'!"

Hartnett's critique meshed with a personal grudge dating to his troubled last days at the Lord Agency. He claimed that the Communist Party had ways to boost the careers of its favorites, that "articulate anti-communists are blacklisted and smeared with that venomous intensity which is characteristic of Red Fascists alone." The time had come, Hartnett declared, to turn things around. "The hour is not too late for those of the patriotic and intelligent majority to immediately undertake a suitable counter-attack," he wrote. "No time is to be lost."

Network executives and advertising vice presidents may not have committed Hartnett's words to memory. But they did pore over *Red Channels*' listing of names, page after page, together with a cross-indexed record of associations and other damning references, the result of Hartnett's hours at the New York Public Library and his conversations with former colleagues.

Among 151 people listed in *Red Channels* were many stars such as Larry Adler, Leonard Bernstein, Oscar Brand, Abe Burrows, Lee J. Cobb, Aaron

Copland, Jose Ferrer, John Garfield, Jack Gilford, Dashiell Hammett, Lillian Hellman, Judy Holliday, Burl Ives, Gypsy Rose Lee, Arthur Miller, Zero Mostel, Pete Seeger, Artie Shaw, and Orson Welles—and also the not-so-famous, such as Vera Caspary, Nat Hiken, Alexander Kendrick, Minerva Pious and Fredi Washington.

For many of the blacklisted, the most recent alleged link to communism dated back more than a decade. Many suspect organizations had long since disbanded, some before World War II. No matter. Unless the suspected person had come forward voluntarily to declare his or her loyalty in the prescribed manner, their past activities and associations remained grounds for current censure.

The entry for popular comic actor Jack Gilford provides a representative sample, with its frequent citing of findings by the House Un-American Activities Committee:

Jack Gilford (Guilford)

Actor-Comedian—Stage and Nightclub

- Scientific and Cultural Conference for World Peace. Reported as: Sponsor. Official program, 3/49.

- National Council of American-Soviet Friendship. Reported as: Participant: signer of statements, speaker, etc. Un-Am. Act. Com. *Review of Scientific and Cultural Conference for World Peace*, p. 51

- Celebration for William Gropper, *Daily Worker* cartoonist. Reported as: Supporter, 1939. Un-Am. Com. *Review of Scientific and Cultural Conference for World Peace*, p. 43.

- Stage for Action. Reported as: Affiliated. Un-Am. Act. Com. *Review of Scientific and Cultural Conference for World Peace*, p. 34

- People's Songs. Reported as: Affiliated. Un-Am. Act. Com. *Review of Scientific and Cultural Conference for World Peace*, p. 33.

CHAPTER FIVE: Anti-communism Inc.

- Progressive Citizens of America. Reported as: Affiliated. Un-Am. Act. Com. *Review of Scientific and Cultural Conference for World Peace*, p. 33.

- Artists' Front to Win the War. Reported as: Affiliated. Un-Am. Act. Com. *Review of Scientific and Cultural Conference for World Peace*, p. 23.

- Voice of Freedom Committee. Reported as: Performer, "The Case of the Loaded Mike," Town Hall, NYC, 10/22/49. *Daily Worker*, 10/12/49.

- American Peace Mobilization. Reported as: Member and sponsor. "American People's Meeting," NYC, 4/5/41. *House Un-Am. Act. Com., Appendix 9*, p. 433.

- Spanish Refugee Committee. Reported as: Entertainer, "Freedom Show," 2/16/49. *Daily Worker*, 2/13/49.

- Civil Rights Congress. Reported as: Entertainer, Lincoln's Birthday Party of Radio Industry Committee, 1949. Invitation.

In the entries for Gilford and others, *Red Channels* displayed a pithy patina of scholarship and authority, thanks to its orderly listings, references to official sources, citations, and a multi-page glossary detailing the nature of the offending organizations.

However, a close study reveals deep flaws in documentation. For instance, two citations in Gilford's entry list him as performing at events based solely on advance notices in newspapers. A third citation relied on an invitation to an event. In none of these three cases did *Red Channels* establish that Gilford, in fact, appeared at the functions.

In 1950, however, *Red Channels* went virtually unchallenged. Although many of those listed would claim they were being persecuted, few of them took more than token legal action, and the authors emerged unscathed.

In some cases, the listed persons feared a prolonged legal fight might further damage their careers. In others, the "listees" knew their entry in *Red Channels*, although often misleading, was essentially factual.

RESPONSE TO *RED CHANNELS*

Red Channels soon began making its mark on hiring. CBS producer Fred Friendly saw it firsthand in 1951 when planning a "See It Now" broadcast with newscaster Edward R. Murrow. The two men discussed hiring a composer for the opening and closing score. They took a list of three names to the programming vice president. In his 1967 book "Due to Circumstances Beyond Our Control…," Friendly recalled what happened next: The executive "glanced at the top name and asked, 'Is he in the book?' I started to ask a secretary for a telephone directory when the vice-president pulled open a drawer of his desk and said, 'This is the book we live by.' The book, of course, was 'Red Channels'."

Friendly's first choice for the composing job wasn't in *Red Channels*, though the two runners-up were. Friendly later said that *Red Channels* supplemented *Counterattack* as the "bible for broadcast companies, sponsors, advertising agencies and motion picture studios, among others." He added that, in the 1950s, being listed in *Red Channels* "was the death warrant for the careers of hundreds of talented actors, playwrights, directors, composers, authors and editors. Some of the most valued and loyal news broadcasters were rendered unemployable by 'Red Channels'."

Cedric Belfrage, the British film critic and a one-time communist, wrote that "tremors ran through media and show people" as *Red Channels* circulated. The impact spread beyond Broadway and Madison Avenue. In Newark, New Jersey, the superintendent of schools bought sixty copies of *Red Channels* to hand out as a reference book for teachers.

One of those tainted by *Red Channels*, the blacklisted writer Millard Lampell, wrote: "By 1951, standard equipment for every Madison Avenue and Hollywood producer's desk included, along with the onyx ash tray and penholder and the gold cigarette lighter, a copy of Red Channels in the bottom drawer."

CHAPTER FIVE: ANTI-COMMUNISM INC.

One of the first victims was actress Jean Muir, who helped found the Screen Actors Guild. Muir was poised to star in a TV version of the long-running radio show "The Aldrich Family" when *Red Channels* appeared, with her prominently listed inside. The sponsor, General Foods, claiming it was swamped with telephone calls protesting her employment, spoke of a pressing need to keep "controversial" individuals away from its programming. Despite Muir's claims of loyalty and innocence, her contract was canceled, and she received a cash settlement. Her "rehabilitation" would not come until 1953, when she testified before HCUA and praised her critics for their "fine and educational work."

Also among the early targets of *Red Channels* was the celebrated stripper Gypsy Rose Lee. She was scheduled to host ABC radio's "What Makes You Tick?" in 1950 when Edwin Clamage, chairman of the Illinois American Legion's Anti-Subversive Commission, pointed out she had a controversial background and citations as a fellow traveler.

When ABC radio asked Clamage for details, the veteran Red hunter deferred to the men from the other ABC—American Business Consultants Inc. "The entire matter could be easily clarified and the answer should not come from me," he replied, "but from the publishers of *Red Channels*." When the matter was put to ABC Inc.'s Ted Kirkpatrick, he said: "We are not adding any further documentation to the information already published."

Suddenly, whatever *Red Channels* contained became a de facto arbiter of guilt.

Although the show with Lee went on as scheduled, the network soon canceled the program. After that, she had few broadcasting opportunities. The *Red Channels* listing scared off potential employers.

Meanwhile, the Attorney General's List kept growing. By mid-November 1950, 197 organizations had this mark of official opprobrium. The attorney general was still far behind the House Committee on Un-American Activities, which had declared 624 organizations anathema.

Amid this furor, WPIX-TV in New York City canceled a weekly series featuring early Charlie Chaplin films after the Catholic War Veterans in Hudson County, New Jersey, protested showcasing the leftist actor.

THE GROCER WHO SOLD McCARTHYISM

Around that time, Joseph H. Ream became CBS's loyalty czar. The executive vice president asked the company's 2,500 employees to sign a statement clearing themselves of association with organizations on the Attorney General's List. Ream said later he considered the loyalty oath to be fairly innocuous. But he added: "*Red Channels* people thought it wonderful." Few dismissals and resignations were attributed to the CBS loyalty policy. One exception was CBS producer Tony Kraber, an alleged former communist listed in *Red Channels*. Although Kraber signed the loyalty oath, Ream asked him to resign, reportedly telling him, "The network is bigger than any of us." When Kraber pointed out he had signed the required documents, Ream quickly put things in perspective, saying, "Oh, that. That doesn't mean a thing."

In October 1950, Hartnett took *Red Channels* on the road, joining Clamage and the Illinois American Legion at the All-Peoria Conference to Combat Communism. Hartnett announced to his audience that *Red Channels* listees were being featured in their hometown even as he spoke: A road company was putting on "Death of a Salesman" by Arthur Miller at the Publix-Great States Theater in downtown Peoria. Not only was the playwright prominently featured in *Red Channels*, but so was one of the road company's actors, Albert Dekker. While producer Kermit Bloomgarden was not a "listee," nevertheless he was a veteran party-fronter, Hartnett assured his audience. The show's profits, he claimed, would benefit the Communist Party or its fronts.

"You have your choice of supporting or denying support to any entertainer, playwright or artist," Hartnett said. "Why should you support such a performance?"

Peoria Veterans Post No. 2 and the Junior Chamber of Commerce took the cue and demanded that "Death of a Salesman" be shut down. When the manager of the theater refused to comply, the protesters vowed to boycott the next performance. The anticipated confrontation never materialized, and the play completed its scheduled run. But attendance was reportedly sparse, to the satisfaction of Hartnett and his fellow anticommunist activists.

Similar scenarios would play out elsewhere, including Syracuse.

CHAPTER SIX:
Johnson Joins the Anti-communists

ONE evening in 1951, as the story goes, Laurence Johnson relaxed at home, his newly purchased television set flickering with a light-hearted variety show. His daughter Eleanor watched with him. She had moved back with her parents after her husband left to fight in Korea.

Eleanor, now an ardent young anti-communist, recognized on the TV show a performer who had been listed in *Red Channels*. Turning to her father, she reportedly declared, "You've got a communist-fronter right in your living room."

Others would later describe this conversation as a bolt of lightning that ignited Johnson's decision to join the crusade against communism.

However, Eleanor would deny her father underwent any such dramatic conversion. "It was not like someone being struck over the head on the road to Damascus," she said. "No, it didn't happen that way." She said she didn't even recall whether the living-room exchange ever took place. Her comment to her father might have been less dramatic, maybe just part of a gradual series of events that ultimately pushed Johnson into action.

One of his first steps as an anti-communist activist followed actor Jack Gilford's appearance on "Arthur Godfrey and His Friends" on August 29, 1951. Johnson sent a telegram to the show's sponsor, Liggett & Myers, criticizing the choice to hire an actor prominently listed in *Red Channels*. The letter reached CBS Television President J.L. Van Volkenburg, who responded promptly:

Dear Mr. Johnson,

Liggett & Myers Tobacco Company has written to us and sent a copy of your telegram regarding the appearance of Jack Gilford on ARTHUR GODFREY AND HIS FRIENDS on August 29. As you know, the makers of Chesterfields have no responsibility for the selection of the guests who appear on this show, inasmuch as they purchase it as a complete package from CBS.

We want to thank you for being instrumental in having this matter brought to our attention and fully understand the reasons for your deep feeling about it. Mr. Gilford's appearance on the show took place during the absence on vacation of the regular director-producer. He was engaged through a reputable talent agency for a one-time appearance on the basis of his previous performances on television with such stars as Milton Berle, Ed Wynn and Jack Carson, as well as for his performances in the comic role in "Die Fledermaus" for the Metropolitan. He was on tour with this opera company throughout the nation from April through July of this year.

With best wishes. Sincerely yours, J.L Van Volkenburg.

The letter made it clear just how seriously CBS took Johnson's communication. His innovative and outspoken ways as a grocer had long drawn the respect of manufacturers and advertising agencies. Being a founding member of the Super Market Institute, Johnson additionally was positioned to command a favorable audience in the broadcasting industry when he shifted his focus toward anti-communist activism.

Still, he might never have done so without the influence of his daughter Eleanor, whom Stefan Kanfer would later nickname "the Molly Pitcher of the blacklist."

THE DAUGHTER ALSO RISES

Eleanor Buchanan would one day look back at 1950 and recall with amazement how many Americans refused to act like the country was again at war. In World War II, when Eleanor was still a schoolgirl, it seemed

CHAPTER SIX: Johnson Joins the Anti-communists

like a glorious cause—one that united the American people and their allies, including the Soviet Union. "Everything was directed toward the war," she said. "People didn't mind because it was a more united effort... (and) people kept hoping during the war it was a mutual effort with the Russians. But after the war, of course, it fell apart."

After her husband, Lieutenant Jack Buchanan, began fighting in Korea, Eleanor got a letter in the mail from a group she believed to be a communist front in the United States. "It claimed our troops were using (poisonous) gas and other atrocities and so forth," she said. "I suppose it was an effort to partly demoralize."

Her husband and other servicemen received similar letters. "His men got mail from communist-front groups that didn't espouse communism, but didn't support the U.S. in Korea, either," she said. In those letters, Eleanor said, the United States was "always wrong."

The Korean War, as she saw it, exposed how communists and their supporters did not have America's best interests at heart.

"Organizations were making statements, communist-front organizations would raise money at functions, they would bring in people whose names were from the entertainment world. Artists, writers would give credence to the organization," Eleanor said. "They would raise money. Oftentimes they would shade the truth, that it would be a benefit for somebody, and the money would go for the organization's propaganda."

Jack Buchanan's perilous situation, combined with criticism from the home front, transformed Eleanor into an anti-communist activist. She studied *Red Channels* and issues of *Counterattack*, and before long she decided to focus on helping to clean up the entertainment industry.

With her father's introduction, she met on Friday, June 8, 1951, with members of American Legion Post No. 41 in Syracuse. The group mapped out plans for a mailing campaign to radio and television sponsors to protest their use of entertainers linked to communist-front organizations. Eleanor would do research and compile the mailings. The Legionnaires agreed to help with contacts and documentation. Laurence Johnson would bankroll the project.

Several days later, Eleanor sent a letter to officers at the Legion post. "Dad and I were pleased that you agree manufacturers can be persuaded to remove Communist sympathizers from their advertising programs on radio and television," she wrote. "As you gentlemen pointed out in our meeting last Friday, the task is too great for me alone. I am grateful for your aid."

Eleanor Buchanan decided to draw support from a broader section of the Syracuse community. Her first target: homemakers like herself—including shoppers at Johnson's supermarkets. She pulled together material from *Red Channels* and *Counterattack*, and she addressed the envelopes in her mass mailing to "The Lady of the House." To show what the anti-communists were up against, she included a story from the *Daily Worker* reporting on a rally in Madison Square Garden called to protest U.S. Representative J. Parnell Thomas' efforts in the HCUA.

She sent protest letters to sponsors such as Philco, Kraft Foods, Borden and Stopette, as well as to NBC and CBS. She compiled a "whitelist" of actors she considered above reproach and who deserved special consideration in hiring. (Critics later wryly noted that the list included ventriloquist Edgar Bergen's dummy, Charlie McCarthy.)

Eleanor began talking to civic groups, including the Syracuse Rotary Club and the Advertising Club of Syracuse, where her fear for her husband's safety helped to overcome her nervousness. "Public speaking is very difficult to me," she said later. "I was terribly worried about Jack."

On July 23, 1951, her audience was her father's Syracuse Kiwanis Club.

"My husband, a veteran of World War II, never received a penny for being a member of the inactive reserves," she told the group. "When he was recalled to service last October, it meant leaving the small town on the Hudson where we'd been so happy." There, Buchanan said, he was a businessman while she held a small teaching position at Vassar College in Poughkeepsie.

"And I know that Jack detested military life," she continued. "He's very un-military about hanging up his clothes....Only now, faced with the prospect of being apart from one another, I asked him one day why he'd ever signed up in the reserves. He answered quietly and simply in one word: patriotism."

Buchanan read from a letter she received from her husband: "I have not been sick, which is a blessing in this land of loose bowels and bodies.

CHAPTER SIX: Johnson Joins the Anti-communists

The flies go from the dead...(enemy soldier) 20 feet away, to the fish heads he left behind, to my C-rations, so I'm glad my stomach is strong."

Buchanan told the Kiwanians, "Well, my stomach isn't that strong. It sickens me to know of those banquets engineered by Red sympathizers on radio and television to raise funds for their henchmen, and those do-nothing patriotic citizens who discuss the wrongs of the world over a dinner table while my quiet, unassuming Jack ate his lunch, surrounded by dead Chinese."

The next day, *The Post-Standard* printed a supportive account of her talk under the headline, "She Battles Reds at Home as Hubby Fights in Korea." In her speech, the newspaper said, she singled out the well-known performer Jose Ferrer—linked in *Red Channels* to twelve organizations considered subversive or suspect—and noted he recently appeared on the silver screen in Syracuse in "Cyrano de Bergerac." Ferrer had testified before the HCUA and affirmed his loyalty, the story added, but had not cleared himself.

Buchanan expressed her disdain for suspected communists who made a living on TV and radio shows funded by advertising. "Her method of attack is to give their record to their sponsors. She has found advertisers quite ready to listen and act," the newspaper reported.

Her ideological fervor and dedicated efforts also energized the veterans of Onondaga County, particularly Legion Post No. 41. In September 1951, member John Dungey organized the post's Un-American Activities Committee, and launched a newsletter, *Spotlight*, modeled on *Counterattack*.

Legionnaire Carl Tarver remembered Dungey as a dedicated anti-communist as early as 1947. "I just don't believe there was anyone...that did as much as John Dungey did in this particular field of spotlighting the communist menace within the motion picture industry, the news media, the television-radio area," Tarver said, adding that he thought Dungey aimed for *Spotlight* to be as accurate as possible. "He wouldn't say anything about any one of these people other than give their record and say, 'Here it is. Take it for what it's worth.' He was a very fair person. He was not vindictive in any way—although he was totally, in my opinion, the most anti-communist, in the layman's term, that I've ever known."

John K. Dungey, left, editor of Syracuse American Legion Post No. 41 newsletter *Spotlight*, reviews a copy with Charles Ballard, right, Broome County Legion commander, and Laurence Jukoski, chairman of the Broome County Americanism Committee, in Binghamton, New York, in November 1960. (*Binghamton Evening Press* photo)

Even as Eleanor Buchanan was reading her husband's letter from Korea to the Kiwanians in Syracuse, negotiations had begun for a cease-fire in the war. However, talks were to drag on for two more blood-drenched years.

Meanwhile, Eleanor, her father and American Legion Post 41 were beginning to coordinate their efforts to rid the airwaves of suspected subversives, the American Legion's national organization took up the issue in fall 1951. The Legionnaires resolved to start a public information program to spread the word about entertainers with communist associations.

In November, the Legion's Hollywood post called for nationwide member picketing of theaters showing movies featuring actors on the HCUA's list. The post urged its counterparts to organize protest campaigns, including letter-writing, phone calls, and telegrams to networks and sponsors employing actors with communist-front records.

Not long afterward, however, Eleanor ended her direct involvement in anti-communist activism. In January 1952, when her husband returned from Korea, she would go back to her life with him as her father rode full tilt into the fray.

THE JOHNSON-HARTNETT CONNECTION

By 1951, whenever Laurence Johnson traveled to New York City to meet with food industry and advertising executives, he made no secret of his increasingly ardent anti-communism, and word got around. New York radio writer Paul Milton introduced him to Vincent Hartnett on one such trip.

"I was immediately impressed by Larry," Hartnett said. "First of all, that leonine head of his—a very large head, snowy white hair, sparkling eyes, a very genial personality. Slow to speak, he'd always think clearly first what he was going to say, and he impressed me right away as someone that observed Benjamin Franklin's admonition never to directly contradict anybody. He'd put a question or two, for example, if he had another opinion. He was very tactful."

Hartnett also found Johnson's earthy patriotism refreshing. "He had a different outlook than people around New York (City) would have," he said. "He was an unsophisticated man. He never could understand why Americans could possibly, knowingly be involved in any communist cause. It just was beyond his comprehension. I say 'unsophisticated'— I don't mean he was a naive man. He wasn't naive, but he didn't have that callous attitude toward political affairs people might have in a large metropolitan area."

The two men quickly developed mutual admiration, calling each other Larry and Vince, with anti-communism as a common bond. Their powerful collaboration was characterized later by John Henry Faulk as based on a "close, harmonious, congenial relationship." And although Johnson was decidedly an outsider in the show business world compared with Hartnett, the younger man quickly recognized that the merchant had influence far exceeding his own.

Early in their friendship, when Johnson was in Manhattan for a convention of grocery executives, he invited Hartnett to lunch. "He introduced me to some very important people in the food industry," Hartnett said. "And you could tell from their attitude that he was highly respected. Even though he was a relatively minor retailer, they profoundly respected him."

Johnson, Hartnett, Milton, and attorney Godfrey Schmidt soon formed the nucleus of what would become Aware Inc., a self-styled citizens group dedicated to rooting out alleged communists in the broadcasting industry. Johnson's more cosmopolitan colleagues had recognized in him a potent new agent to extend their influence.

A few years later, a community leader in Syracuse, speaking anonymously, would sum up his assessment of Johnson's role in Aware: "He is a perfect front man for the sharpies in New York."

However, Johnson was much more than a front man. He held significant power on his own, and he was more than happy to use his status and his skills at merchandising to achieve his ends.

Johnson's anti-communist strategy was still an improvised affair in 1951. Author and editor John Cogley, in a report on blacklisting published in 1956, said one of Johnson's early efforts focused on an actress whom Cogley described only as "Miss H."—later identified as actress Uta Hagen—who had been listed in *Red Channels*. When Johnson and his colleagues learned that the actress was to appear in a television program sponsored by General Mills, they complained to the network and the sponsor. The cast spoke up on behalf of the actress, the producers and sponsor stayed in the background, and the show went on as scheduled. However, Cogley noted Miss H. did little television work after that.

CHAPTER SIX: Johnson Joins the Anti-communists

On Tuesday, October 23, 1951, handbills appeared at several factories in the Syracuse area announcing that I.F. Stone was coming to town the following Saturday. The HCUA had cited the irascible columnist for leftist newspaper *The Daily Compass* for a score of ties to communist-front organizations. Stone's announced topics—peace and civil rights—were hot-button issues for Johnson and his colleagues, who considered them code words for pro-communist troublemaking. The local chapter of the Red-tinged American Labor Party was sponsoring the lecture. Worse, the way anti-communist veterans saw it, the talk was to be in their beloved Onondaga County War Memorial.

By Thursday, the American Legion went on the offensive. Post No. 41 issued a statement "violently protesting" Stone's appearance, *The Post-Standard* reported. In a statement by member John Dungey, the Legion said it "does not believe that the War Memorial was built or intended for the use of or in defense of such people." When a reporter asked a War Memorial official for comment, he said that the staff had rented out the hall before learning who was to speak there, and that the contract must be honored.

Stone's visit to Syracuse came off as scheduled. The audience sang "The Star-Spangled Banner" and listened to Paul Robeson records. Among the guests on the program was Syracuse resident Lillian Reiner, then running one of her many quixotic political campaigns, this one for education commissioner on the American Labor Party line.

To the apparent delight of his audience, Stone lit into the Truman administration for prosecuting communists under the Smith Act. He also took on his local critics, thanking *The Post-Standard* for the "free advertising" its coverage had provided. In an apparent reference to a recent series on communism in Syracuse by one of the newspaper's reporters, Luther "Gus" Bliven, Stone said: "I wondered where we'd seat all the Reds. *The Post-Standard* expose must have scared them, or else they are hiding in the Republican Party." Stone added, apparently tongue in cheek, that he was terrified of speaking in Syracuse again.

His witticisms did not amuse the Legionnaires. In the inaugural issue of *Spotlight*, the newsletter of Post No. 41's Un-American Activities Committee, Dungey provided this account of the talk:

> We were so effective, that Stone's audience was about 155, most of whom appeared to be college students. We had two friends there. Stone in his speech…(attacked) the American Legion and this Committee. Perhaps some of you will take this as a defeat by us, however, keep in mind that due to a contract with the War Memorial it was impossible to have Stone canceled. We did however force him to change his speech entirely. I don't believe Stone will be over anxious to return to Syracuse.

In *Spotlight*, Dungey explained that his committee had been formed several weeks before after he heard a record of Weavers singer Pete Seeger, a former member of People's Songs Inc. whose record producer was People's Artists Inc. "Both organizations have been cited as subversive by the U.S. government," Dungey wrote, adding:

> I quote from a Government publication: "All of the productions of People's Songs, Inc. follow the Communist Party line as assiduously as do the people behind the organization." Post 41, after hearing the record, at a regular meeting, passed a resolution, which in substance asked that all Radio, Television stations, Music stores, and "Juke" box distributors withdraw all Weaver records from their libraries. These people were then contacted and we wish to congratulate them, for without exception all the local radio and television stations, as well as the coin machine operators cooperated. This my friends is the kind of cooperation that is most heartening and this is how we can fight Communist fronts.

Not long afterward, the editors of *Spotlight* launched a campaign to get Syracuse broadcasters to stop playing jazz musician Artie Shaw. A couple of months later, in January 1952, they asked: "Why do the local radio stations still continue to play and promote recordings of Artie Shaw? All local radio and television stations were informed of Artie Shaw's front record in our November 1951 newsletter."

This time, *Spotlight* didn't get its way. In his study of blacklisting, Cogley noted that representatives of six local radio and TV stations, along with a delegation of Syracuse University student broadcasters, had met to discuss the call to ban Shaw. "They unanimously decided not to give in to the growing pressure," Cogley wrote. "In the future, they agreed, they would not listen to protests from Johnson which were not 'adequately documented'....After this decision was announced, local protests about records played on the air came to an end."

Speaking from the safety of anonymity, one Syracuse station executive scoffed at how Downstate broadcast executives had so often capitulated to the Central New York anti-communists.

"I don't know what's the matter with those people in New York," he told Cogley. "Maybe they're so big they have to be stupid."

Although broadcasters in Syracuse quashed future anti-communist protests over specific musicians, the radio and TV people still took care not to alienate the civic activists intentionally. One local media man stressed that his company was not challenging the legitimacy of *Counterattack* and similar publications.

'DIE FLEDERMAUS'

The stage was set for drama both outside and inside Loew's State Theatre on South Salina Street in fall 1951 when Syracuse was added to a tour of the German operetta "Die Fledermaus" ("The Bat") co-starring Jack Gilford, the actor whose appearance on Arthur Godfrey's TV show had stirred Johnson's protest a few weeks earlier.

Upon learning of the Syracuse booking, the American Legion's Dungey wrote to New York's Metropolitan Opera House, which was underwriting the tour. He sent it documentation of Gilford's alleged sympathies using the same sources Hartnett used for *Red Channels*. Dungey urged the Met to see that Gilford was removed from the cast.

The Met's business manager, Reginald Allen, politely declined. He proceeded to give Dungey and the Syracuse veterans post a little lecture on due process:

> We can, of course, assure you that the Metropolitan would not knowingly employ one, who, after a fair hearing in the manner

THE GROCER WHO SOLD McCARTHYISM

Jack Gilford performs as Frosch, and Patrice Munsel is Adele, in Strauss' operetta "Die Fledermaus" in the 1950s. (Metropolitan Opera Archives/Sedge LeBlang photo)

of American justice before an impartial tribunal, was found to be engaged in activities hostile to our country....But the Metropolitan cannot sit as such a tribunal nor could it make such a decision on the basis of publications which are mere compilations from frequently dubious sources, compilations which in no wise represent the judgment of such a tribunal as we have mentioned, made under the conditions required by American justice.

Allen stressed that Gilford's record showed "nothing illegal and...you do not claim he is a Communist." He continued:

You are proposing that Gilford's loyalty to the United States and his right to hold a job anywhere be tried and determined by the Syracuse Post # 41 of the American Legion. That, of course, is a matter of indirect concern to the Metropolitan which believes as strongly as you do in American concepts and a free trial.

Allen's lengthy and thoughtful response was evidence of how seriously the Met considered the Syracuse Legion's challenge—from a public relations standpoint if nothing else.

Gilford wrote to the Met's Rudolf Bing on October 30, alerting him that a sworn statement avowing his patriotism had been filed with the American Guild of Variety Artists. News of Gilford's statement reached Dungey and his colleagues in Syracuse. They were unmoved.

At their regular meeting on November 13, the Legionnaires adopted the following resolution: "Post 41 resolves to protest the appearance Nov. 30 and Dec. 1st of Jack Gilford, in the opera 'Die Fledermaus,' at Loew's State Theatre because of his activities with Communist front organizations. We further resolve and pledge not to support said opera unless Jack Gilford is withdrawn from the cast or makes an honest effort to clear himself to the satisfaction of the post."

Six days later, Dungey received a copy of Gilford's statement, which the post printed in *Spotlight*.

"To Whom It May Concern," Gilford wrote. "This is to certify that I am not a member of the Communist Party or of any subversive or Communist organizations....I have always tried to base my actions both as an artist and as a citizen on those fundamental principles upon which our nation is founded. It will always be my effort, both as a performer and in my personal conduct, to maintain my standing as a hard-working, decent and loyal American."

Dungey huddled with Johnson and others, and decided Gilford still did not pass muster. Dungey reported later: "The Committee after taking the affidavit under advisement and receiving legal opinion decided it was completely unacceptable because, he did not disavow any present associations with Communist fronts nor did he swear that he would not in the future affiliate himself with any such organizations."

Johnson decided to make a move of his own. During a business trip to New York City, he visited the offices of the Metropolitan Opera Company. It would be the first of many calls he would make on show-business establishments that had offended him. Johnson restated the complaint about Gilford in "Die Fledermaus," adding an appeal on behalf of his daughter Eleanor.

Recalled a Met official about the meeting: "He dwelt a great deal on the emotional aspects of the position this woman was in, with her husband overseas, fighting against Communists, and we were importing Jack Gilford to Syracuse with this alleged Communistic taint."

The Met's Reginald Allen later testified that, for the sake of protecting an artistic endeavor, he resisted Johnson's appeal to fire Gilford. He said he told Johnson: "The Metropolitan Opera in casting for any given season would be guided, first, of course, by artistic standards and then by the fact that an artist would be a member in good standing of one or more unions."

Shortly afterward, Allen said, he escorted Johnson to the door and "out on Broadway."

Some critics of Johnson would view his attempt to quash an opera production as evidence he was a country rube. Louis Nizer, the famed attorney, wrote of this in his memoirs: "An opera is not a product which needs to be displayed in supermarkets." The patronizing urbanites might have been surprised to learn that Johnson's wife, Hermione, was an ardent opera fan who faced major disappointment if her husband succeeded in blocking the production's visit to Syracuse.

Although the anti-Gilford campaign didn't make headway in Manhattan, it got a big boost in Syracuse when a supportive letter arrived from HCUA Chairman John S. Wood. He enclosed a lengthy peroration on Gilford's record under the authoritative-sounding heading: "Information from the Files of the Committee on Un-American Activities, U.S. House of Representatives." Most of the data on the sheets appeared earlier and was summarized in *Red Channels*.

This official corroboration conferred legitimacy on the Syracuse civic crusaders and energized them. After conferring with lawyers, Dungey and his fellow Legionnaires drafted a "cleansing document" for Gilford to sign to certify his patriotism. The document, bearing only a faint resemblance to Gilford's earlier statement, read:

1) I am not now a member of the Communist Party, of any Communist organization or any organization cited in the Guide to Subversive Organizations and Publications and Appendix, as revised May 14, 1951, prepared and released by the House Un-American Activities Committee ...

2) I am not at present nor will I in the future support any of the cited organizations by membership, contribution, as a speaker, or as an entertainer for them, nor will I support in any manner the National Council of the Arts, Sciences and Professions.

3) Further that I do not favor and will not favor or support any of the policies of the Communist Party.

4) It will always be my effort, both as a performer and in my personal conduct to maintain my standing as a hardworking, decent and loyal American.

On November 24, Dungey displayed his handiwork to Harold Morton, the manager of Loew's Theatre. Morton said he saw no reason Gilford would not sign it, and quickly, since the company was due to open in Rochester in two days, arriving in Syracuse within the week.

Dungey left the document with Morton—but Gilford did not sign it. Wrote Dungey later: "Despite these assurances, the signed affidavit was not returned."

Dungey diligently took one more step: Early on November 28, two days before the scheduled curtain-rising of "Die Fledermaus" in Syracuse, he sent the following telegram to Morton: "Request signed affidavit from Jack Gilford be delivered to the Legion Clubhouse 123 South Clinton Street by twelve o'clock noon on November 28th 1951." The deadline passed without an answer, and *Spotlight* went to press. Wrote Dungey: "Neither this Committee nor Post 41 intends to set itself up as a judge and jury or as an agency to 'clear' such people—however as long as the record stands as above in regards of Jack Gilford it is our duty not to support or endorse him."

Accounts of what happened next varied wildly. Stefan Kanfer, writing in "A Journal of the Plague Years," would paint a dramatic picture of tension and confrontation. Wrote Kanfer: "When *Fledermaus* played Syracuse, Post No. 41 was out with signs and chants. The crowds were ugly, the attendance disappointing." Nizer would describe a crisis in Syracuse in which Reginald Allen had to hurry Upstate "to deal with the near riots which resulted from the publicized positions taken by Johnson and Post. No. 41 against the 'Fledermaus' company."

Among Syracusans, the protests over the operetta were so noisy that, years later, Johnson business manager Mary Coyne believed her boss and Dungey had succeeded in keeping it out of town. Another source even claimed Hermione Johnson expressed her disappointment to her husband in no uncertain terms: "She said, 'I waited for 30 years for an opera to come to Syracuse, and you're the one who stopped it!'"

Syracuse University professor Marguerite Fisher also was among those with a vivid memory that the Metropolitan Opera canceled the Syracuse performance. "This would have been the highest cultural achievement since Syracuse was founded in the late 18th century, and that stupid bunch of ignorant cattle kept the Metropolitan Opera from coming to Syracuse. It's terrible in a democratic society."

The reality was, "Die Fledermaus" did indeed play in Syracuse, though apparently without Marguerite Fisher, Hermione Johnson, or Mary Coyne in the audience. *The Post-Standard* even carried an opening-night review with no mention of the American Legion or the Gilford controversy, and no report of pickets or near-riots that Kanfer and Nizer would write about later.

Under the headline "Fledermaus Offering by Met Proves Superb," *Post-Standard* reviewer Thola Tabor Schenck wrote that the audience "applauded and laughed for almost three hours of solid entertainment....Jack Gilford as Frosch was applauded before even he was visible to do his inimitable pantomime and stair slides, his helpless gesturing and salute reporting in Act III. Every move or word brought gales of laughter."

In the afternoon, the *Herald-Journal* hailed the "fresh, pretentious presentation," adding that "Jack Gilford, skillful and deft comedian...is swift, agile and amusing. His timing is something to set the audience atwitter." The only reference to possible repercussions of the anti-Gilford campaign came in an oblique reference to low audience turnout.

Lillian Reiner, who was in the audience that night, decided to attend as a show of support for Gilford. "We applauded before he came on stage," she said. "It was really very nice."

Dungey salvaged some satisfaction from the smallish audience. He disposed of the matter in a subsequent issue of *Spotlight*, arguing simply: "Jack Gilford—He and Fledermaus Struck Out."

Later, under legal pressure, Johnson would claim not to remember playing a role in trying to get the Met to drop Gilford. "I don't recall objecting to him there at all," he said. "I know there was a lot of protest about him up there, but I did not enter into it, to the best of my knowledge."

EDITORIAL OFFENSIVE

By October 1951, Senator Joseph McCarthy had attracted huge pockets of ardent supporters—including Laurence Johnson and his circle. They could be counted on to make trouble for anyone who dared to attack McCarthy, champion of the civic anti-communists. *The Post-Standard* editors knew this. But they went ahead with a lead editorial that dared to lash out at the junior senator from Wisconsin.

The editorial faulted McCarthy's recent targeting of American diplomat John Carter Vincent for alleged communist ties. Previously, McCarthy had drawn publicity for bagging another U.S. diplomatic figure, Owen Lattimore, by accusing him of being a Russian spy. Vincent was to be McCarthy's "Case No. 2."

Like Lattimore, Vincent was a Far East expert. But while Lattimore was a scholar, Vincent was a career foreign-service officer, one of the wartime "China Hands" who rose to the top under FDR. During his many years in China, Vincent listened to both the communist Chou En-Lai and the nationalist Chiang Kai-shek. However, McCarthy accused Vincent of playing into the communists' hands and betraying the nationalists' claim. In testimony before McCarthy's Senate Internal Security Subcommittee, former communist Louis Budenz claimed the Communist Party had assigned Vincent to guide Vice President Henry Wallace on his controversial 1944 China tour.

The State Department denied the charges against Vincent. Vincent's State Department colleague, Bernard F. Fensterwald, called the allegations preposterous. "Vincent was an old Georgia Boy who was probably to the right of Torquemada," he said later. "He was so appalled by the whole thing that he would do virtually nothing to prepare his own defense."

By the time McCarthy's campaign was in full swing, Vincent had been reassigned to Switzerland. So, McCarthy, lacking hard evidence against him, recruited Charles E. Davis, an American journalist living in Europe. A McCarthy aide sent Davis to Switzerland to get the goods on Vincent. But Davis proved to be clumsy, unethical, and criminal. He landed in the custody of Swiss police, charged with forging a telegram to Vincent from a Swiss communist, Emile Staempfli. Davis was convicted on October 16, 1951, sentenced to time served in prison, and deported.

McCarthy distanced himself from Davis as much as he could. Still, the story made national headlines and caught the eye of *The Post-Standard*'s editors in Syracuse.

Post-Standard publisher Dick Amberg and his colleagues had never been enamored of Joe McCarthy—the man or his methods. The Vincent affair seemed to offer a golden opportunity to air their grievances against the senator. Amberg wrote the editorial, which appeared in print three days after Davis was convicted of forging the damaging letter.

The editorial opened with a broadside: "A very significant trial has just been completed in Lausanne, Switzerland, which reflects great disgrace on the United States Senate because of the membership in that body of Sen. Joseph R. McCarthy of Wisconsin."

Amberg went into particulars: "Davis testified before the Swiss Federal Court that he tried to frame Vincent on McCarthy's orders and that McCarthy, through an intermediary, paid him money for the forgery. Davis has freely confessed both to his forgery and to the infamous part played in it by McCarthy."

Then Amberg zeroed in on McCarthy:

> In a day when the prestige of the United States is questioned in many places, and when other free nations look to us for leadership in the workings of democracy, it is damning in the eyes

of all the world to see a Senator of the United States engaged in bribery and stealth of the lowest order.

The same McCarthy was the one who framed Senator Tydings of Maryland with a fake photograph showing Tydings in an alleged conversation with (communist) Earl Browder. It is the same McCarthy who accepted a fee of $10,000 from a Wisconsin contractor for allegedly writing an article on special housing, when it turned out the article had been written by an employe of the government.

Those who speak in defense of McCarthy state that he has awakened the nation to the dangers of Communism. The fact remains that McCarthy's scattershot technique, his incredible mouthings on the floor of the Senate defaming the reputations of people who then are not given a chance to defend themselves, or are unable to sue him for libel because of his cloak of congressional immunity, has not proved one treasonable act or obtained a single conviction for disloyalty. His tirades, in the words of the poet, "are full of sound and fury, signifying nothing."

Amberg then draped *The Post-Standard* in the flag:

> It is one thing to fight Communism intelligently and courageously, as The Post-Standard has done for a quarter-century. Even more important, we have tried to point out and help destroy the causes which allowed Communism to take hold in other places. McCarthy, on the other hand, through his cheating and lying, is his own worst enemy and actually does not help the cause of anti-communism in the slightest.

Amberg wrapped up his extraordinary editorial by supporting an effort languishing in the Senate to discipline McCarthy. He wrote: "McCarthy is a disgrace to the United States Senate, as the Davis case and many other incidents fully document. This newspaper hopes that the Benton resolution to unseat McCarthy will be passed by an overwhelming vote and McCarthy removed once and for all from the Senate."

THE CONSEQUENCES

The editorial shocked readers. Just a month earlier, FBI director J. Edgar Hoover had praised the paper for a series exposing communism in Central New York. "Newspapers such as The Post-Standard are doing much to kindle interest so necessary to combat this evil," Hoover wrote. Now, the same paper was lashing out at Senator McCarthy, champion of the civic anti-communists.

Not surprisingly, McCarthy's supporters in Central New York reacted with anger. Frank M. Stapleton of Syracuse wrote in protest: "Until he began his two-fisted attack on the cancer of Communism, we—our nation—were gradually succumbing to this evil....With all the vigor at my command, I repeat, I protest this editorial." Another letter writer, Sally Sherman of rural Altmar in nearby Oswego County, imagined a communist conspiracy leading from *The Post-Standard* newsroom to the White House. "Did you prove that editorial about McCarthy was the truth, or did Dean Acheson or Harry's secretary send it to you?" she asked. "Davis so freely confessed that he probably was paid a huge sum of money just to discredit McCarthy."

McCarthy was livid when he read *The Post-Standard*'s editorial. To him, it confirmed his claim of a liberal press in league with the Communist *Daily Worker* newspaper and allied journalists. He vowed to retaliate.

In these years before the U.S. Supreme Court's 1964 ruling in *New York Times v. Sullivan* restricted the ability of public officials to successfully sue for defamation, press criticism of politicians was not well-protected by the First Amendment. As a lawyer and former judge, McCarthy knew *The Post-Standard*'s editorial was actionable by suggesting he engaged in unethical, if not illegal, acts.

With uncharacteristic restraint, McCarthy waited until December 12 to file a $500,000 libel action naming *The Post-Standard*, owner S.I. Newhouse and editor Robert L. Voorhees. It was the only time McCarthy ever sued a newspaper, though he got his share of darts from *The Washington Post*, the *St. Louis Post-Dispatch* and his home state paper, the *Madison Capital Times*. McCarthy, however, knew he had an excellent opportunity to use this editorial in Syracuse to score political points.

CHAPTER SIX: JOHNSON JOINS THE ANTI-COMMUNISTS

At first, *The Post-Standard* stood by its editorial. In February 1952, the paper's attorneys filed a general denial of McCarthy's complaint. McCarthy agreed to a pretrial examination in Syracuse.

When he stepped off the plane at the Syracuse airport on March 28, he was met by a delegation from American Legion Post No. 41, including John Dungey, Robert M. Latimore, and Dwight C. Dale. Post Commander John Sellin presented McCarthy with a parchment scroll inscribed: "Syracuse Post 41 Un-American Activities Committee presents this Scroll to Senator Joseph McCarthy as a token of appreciation for services rendered to his country in the fight against Communism." The Legionnaires escorted McCarthy to the post's club rooms on South Clinton Street for a reception.

McCarthy and his attorney, Warren Magee, spent much of the day in the law offices of Bond, Schoeneck & King, the firm representing *The Post-Standard*. During a freewheeling examination of the senator's record, McCarthy denied that Davis was his agent, and he refused to be drawn out on that or any other matter raised by *The Post-Standard*.

McCarthy acknowledged he had sent an advance man to Syracuse a few days earlier to scout out the local impact of the editorial. Donald A. Surine, an investigator on McCarthy's payroll, had spent two days on the Syracuse University campus, interviewing students and others to see if they had read the editorial. McCarthy volunteered that Surine had not been looking for communist subversion on campus.

The *Herald-Journal* gave good play to its rival's troubles—even though the afternoon paper was also a Newhouse property. It devoted eight full columns to McCarthy's visit, quoting or paraphrasing his rambling answers at length.

At one point, Newhouse attorney Tracy H. Ferguson asked McCarthy why he didn't leave the investigation of communist subversion to the FBI.

"I'm curious to know," Ferguson said. "Couldn't the FBI carry on without your help?"

McCarthy snapped back: "I don't think you're trying to be cute." Then he launched into a story about a suspect government employee who had been cleared by the FBI but stayed on the job until McCarthy intervened.

He also blithely dismissed a letter from Dwight Eisenhower, then running for president, defending a McCarthy target: "Well, Eisenhower's entitled to make one mistake." He added: "Keep this in mind: If these individuals were not able to fool good Americans, they wouldn't be dangerous."

McCarthy appeared to be in a relaxed mood, and Ferguson couldn't draw out any self-incriminating revelations. McCarthy left Syracuse after agreeing to return to face more questions. The next session was postponed, however, and in late April 1952, the Newhouse attorney filed a court order asking McCarthy to be more forthcoming. Ferguson claimed that during his Syracuse visit, McCarthy had been "parrying and thrusting," giving "non-responsive answers."

McCarthy returned to Syracuse on June 23, now represented by former Syracuse mayor Rolland B. Marvin. The senator was affable and confident during the hearing, now held in the Onondaga County Courthouse.

Ferguson sounded plaintive as he asked why *The Post-Standard* should be singled out for the libel attack. McCarthy replied: "I decided that, sooner or later, one of these left-wing smear articles would go so far that we'd have to teach them a lesson. Your paper went even further than the *Daily Worker* or *Compass*."

As Ferguson completed his examination before state Supreme Court Justice Jesse E. Kingsley, the attorney appeared to have made little headway.

Afterward, veterans feted McCarthy with a traditional clambake at Hinerwadel's Grove in North Syracuse. One of the guests was Laurence Johnson, who, standing with others, had his photograph taken with the most famous anti-communist of them all.

The Post-Standard case simmered until October 18, when Justice Kingsley granted McCarthy's request for a pretrial examination of newspaper owner S.I. Newhouse. But the Newhouse grilling never took place. The owner had no appetite for such a confrontation with McCarthy. Besides, S.I. Newhouse had nothing to do with writing the offending piece; his company had a hands-off policy regarding the editorials of his newspapers. He had steered a cautious course through the McCarthy Era, and he wasn't about to risk that in a losing cause.

CHAPTER SIX: Johnson Joins the Anti-communists

Newhouse was scheduled to appear on Monday, March 16, 1953. Two days before, McCarthy announced the case had been settled.

Under the agreement, *The Post-Standard* paid McCarthy $16,500 and promised a retraction. McCarthy withdrew his complaint and issued a statement, printed in *The Post-Standard*. McCarthy said:

> Because it became apparent in the course of the conversation that the publisher had not been motivated by malice and that the editorial had been based upon mis-information on which the editorial writer had relied in good faith, the settlement was a friendly one. The amount of the settlement is therefore of less importance than the clarification of the facts, which The Post-Standard has agreed to publish in its editorial columns.

The newspaper's retraction the same day admitted the earlier editorial on the Davis case had been spurious, "that Sen. McCarthy had not committed any act deserving of criticism in connection with the matter." The newspaper withdrew the charge that McCarthy had "framed" Senator Tydings. Regarding a $10,000 payoff for a housing booklet, the newspaper wrote that there was no evidence of wrongdoing. The editors said the Davis incident is what led them astray. "The nature of this testimony predisposed the writer to think adversely with respect to Sen. McCarthy and give credence to other allegations that have since been disproved," they wrote. "We are happy to make these corrections."

With that, *The Post-Standard* rejoined other newspapers that in 1953 were in tune with the chorus of anti-communists.

Despite the initial defense of his editorial, Amberg later admitted failing to read news reporting that raised reasonable doubt about McCarthy's alleged bribery and other misdeeds. "If the facts in McCarthy's favor had been given the prominence of those against him, I never would have written the editorial," he said.

Meanwhile, Johnson, Dungey, and other anti-communist activists in Syracuse could share the satisfaction of knowing the newly re-elected McCarthy had also achieved a score-settling victory right in their backyard.

CHAPTER SEVEN:
Syracuse and the McCarthy Era

By 1952, Laurence Johnson and other civic anti-communists, not just in Syracuse but in many places across the country, approached their mission with almost religious fervor. They were certain they had embarked on a "great crusade," believing national redemption was at hand, as historian and author Thomas C. Reeves would later sum up their worldview.

The anti-communist fears often bordered on paranoia. A story in the *New York Mirror* reported that a passerby saw two men waving red flags from a rowboat in the East River, so he called the police. Four radio cars and a police launch responded. Were they enemy agents waiting to infiltrate? No, the *Mirror* said. "The men were Consolidated Edison workers signaling to surveyors on shore, preparatory to the laying of a cable."

Other newspaper stories focused on Red-hunting in the New York educational system—in colleges, and in secondary and elementary schools. In February 1952, Saul Moskoff, assistant corporation counsel for New York City, brought in Harvey Matusow, a young ex-communist who had been working for the Ohio Un-American Activities Commission. For ten days, Matusow interviewed teachers in a room with hidden recording devices and a one-way mirror. He then provided the board with a dozen names of "suspect" teachers and with unsubstantiated evidence he had either pried out of interviewees or drawn from his files. (He also sold New York Schools Superintendent William Jansen a $24 annual subscription to *Counterattack*.)

Eight schoolteachers and six City College professors were fired in the next few months for refusing to cooperate with the local investigation.

THE GROCER WHO SOLD McCARTHYISM

On October 3, 1952, Moskoff reported that forty-five teachers had been interrogated and seventeen had resigned; a month later, he said 193 employees were under investigation.

Around this time, Senator Joseph McCarthy and others stepped up their attacks on alleged subversives in show business and the media. After two McCarthy-backed candidates joined the Federal Communications Commission, FCC lawyers investigated Edward Lamb, a wealthy liberal lawyer who owned several radio and TV stations. At one point, FCC investigators questioned a woman who claimed Lamb was a communist. Then she confessed she didn't even know the man, explaining that the "FCC lawyers told me it was my duty to testify because Lamb's radio station could beam atom bombs from foreign countries and also beam in enemy broadcasts." The FCC's case collapsed.

In 1952, Vincent Hartnett produced a sequel to *Red Channels* called *File 13*. In this supplement and another, *File 13, Vol. II*, Hartnett added 200 names to the list of show-business people under a cloud of suspicion. He was by then firmly in the inner circle of the nation's most prominent anti-communists. He appeared several times before congressional committees, took McCarthy aide Roy Cohn to dinner at Luchow's Restaurant, and later accompanied Cohn to Queens for an address to the Catholic War Veterans.

Around the time of the McCarthy libel case, Laurence Johnson intensified his anti-communism efforts by supervising the creation of the Veterans Action Committee of Syracuse Super Markets, also known as VAC. The point man was Francis W. Neuser, a U.S. Army veteran of World War II who was Johnson's fruit and vegetable buyer. Johnson business manager Mary Coyne remembered Neuser as a "charming man" who accompanied Johnson on his buying trips to New York City, where they often visited advertising agencies and met with other anti-communists.

The committee limited its membership to veterans, so Johnson wasn't officially part of it. However, his influence remained strong. Its members included Johnson employees who had served in World War II or the Korean War. In the early 1950s, the organization, with Johnson's supermarkets and Legion Post No. 41, became a battering ram of anti-communism, locally and nationally.

CHAPTER SEVEN: Syracuse and the McCarthy Era

PROTESTS IN SYRACUSE

On Sunday, April 27, 1952, John Dungey and others from American Legion Post No. 41 rallied outside the Astor Theater in downtown Syracuse to protest its showing of the movie "Anything Can Happen," starring *Red Channels* "listee" Jose Ferrer. The picket line started at noon, ahead of the matinee. Dungey noted later in *Spotlight*:

> It was unfortunate that a brand new theater in Syracuse...had to receive the first picket line in the city....The American Legion has talked and the movie industry have talked, but nothing, or at least very little, has been done to clean the Commies, fellow-travelers and fronters out of the picture business. It appears that the only way this can be accomplished is by hitting them in the pocketbook. When it no longer is profitable to use fronters and Commies, you can rest assured they will not be used.

However, the veterans decided to give Astor's management a break. Dungey reported:

> The American Legion withdrew their pickets after a token showing only because of the newness to Syracuse of the Astor Theatre and because after careful thought and discussion it was decided that a new business is entitled to at least one mistake and also because the following week they were showing the anti-Communist film, "My Son John."

Dungey was less forgiving in May when Loew's State Theatre in Syracuse booked Judy Holliday's film, "The Marrying Kind." Dungey and the Legion post's Un-American Activities Committee vowed to picket this same gilded theater where Jack Gilford and "Die Fledermaus" had drawn protests in 1951. Dungey noted that a "Mr. Weiner" from Columbia Pictures called him and pleaded with the Legion to reconsider. He reminded Dungey that Aldo Ray, Judy Holliday's co-star in "The Marrying Kind," was planning a promotional tour of Syracuse. Dungey was skeptical. Was this a diversionary tactic?

So, the Syracuse veterans held firm, and Dungey filed a report on the picket: "We went on the line May 16 at 6 p.m., in spite of phone calls received, that threatened trouble if we persisted in picketing...."

Dungey in 1952 also targeted Consumers Union, which was trying to sign up subscribers in Syracuse for its magazine, *Consumer Reports*. Consumers Union was founded by Arthur Kallet, who the newsletter alleged was a Communist Party member who had served on a labor advisory committee with "well-known Communists" Ben Gold and Louis Weinstock.

Spotlight observed: "There may be other Communists in this organization but we feel that Kallet is enough to make the magazine unacceptable to any right thinking persons. We ask that newsstands and magazine stands take this record into consideration the next time they are asked to sell the *Consumer Reports*."

Spotlight also objected to the very concept of a magazine that stood up for consumers and often questioned the accuracy of advertising. In collaboration with Johnson, Dungey prepared a lengthy indictment of the Consumers Union for the August 1952 issue of *Spotlight*. Citing reports from HCUA, Red-hunter J.B. Matthews, *Scribner's Magazine*, and the *Washington Religious Review*, the newsletter argued why consumerism was un-American:

> CU's most subtle propaganda is achieved through attacks on American business and praise for government controls....To discredit advertising is an important CU objective....Communists believe that to sabotage and destroy advertising, and through its destruction to undermine and help destroy the capitalist system of free enterprise, is a revolutionary tactic worthy of a great deal of attention....Its goal, it seems apparent from a study of its sponsors and officials, is not to build up one business at the expense of another, but to disparage and help destroy our system of private enterprise.

As Dungey noted, school boards in Ohio had banned *Consumer Reports* from the classroom. Cincinnati school administrators hastily erased the magazine from their list of recommended study sources. In Dayton,

CHAPTER SEVEN: Syracuse and the McCarthy Era

school librarians removed the magazine from the shelves and canceled their subscriptions.

Dungey wondered why the Syracuse schools had not done the same things. He wrote to Schools Superintendent David H. Patton on October 6, 1952, alerting him to the situation. Two days later, Patton wrote back:

> Dear Mr. Dungey,
>
> We are very grateful to you for your letter of October 6th relative to the publication, "Consumer Reports." We have checked our Principals and Librarians, individually, and have given instructions that under no circumstances is this publication to be placed on the library shelves nor permitted in the hands of pupils.
>
> We appreciate deeply your cooperation with us in our effort to guard our schools against any subversive activities. We know that you will continue to be alert in this situation and we shall welcome your help at any time.

Spotlight was delighted. "An orchid and many thanks from 6,000 Legionnaires of Onondaga County to Mr. David Patton," trumpeted the November issue. "No doubt Mr. Patton will receive calls from the left condemning him for his action. How about our readers writing or calling and tell him that you agree with his action one-hundred percent. David Patton is a real patriot."

Dungey kept *Spotlight* on other local matters, too. When the Syracuse Film Society screened the Soviet-made movie "The Stone Flower" on June 8, 1952, *Spotlight* fumed: "Wouldn't common sense tell anyone that anything produced in Russia would be full of Commie propaganda? Why did Syracuse Film Society bring this thing to town? Does it make you wonder?"

The following month, Dungey noted with disapproval that the Country Playhouse in the Syracuse suburb of Fayetteville was to offer a production of "They Knew What They Wanted," starring Kim Hunter and Art Smith, both "listed" performers. Hunter had just won a best-actress

Academy Award for her performance in "A Streetcar Named Desire." Despite Dungey's opposition, Country Playhouse hosted her performance as scheduled.

In December, a pamphlet began circulating in Syracuse with the provocative title, "You Can End the War in Korea Now," distributed by the American Peace Crusade. *Spotlight* told its readers not to trust the group:

> There are many organizations which have the name "Peace" in its title who are promoting the Communist line. Some are cited as Communist fronts, but a number on local levels or being newly formed have not been cited. Unfortunately, there are well-intentioned people who fall for these organizations and who work with them. They are all working hard to get a "cease fire" in Korea, but it must be according to the terms of Russia."

CASE STUDIES: BURROWS AND COTTEN

By late 1952, Laurence Johnson was bending broadcasters to his anti-communist will by appealing directly to their sponsors whose products also appeared on his supermarket shelves.

Until then, most sponsors had no say whatsoever about what went into the radio and TV programs, recalled Syracuse Legionnaire Carl Tarver, an anti-communist ally of Dungey. "The sponsors couldn't care less," Tarver said.

Johnson decided to make the manufacturers care. He and his allies soon targeted products that sponsored a show employing someone who had been blacklisted. Tarver later summed up their message: "All right, if all you're interested in is selling your product, then we're going to hit you where it hurts."

Johnson implemented this strategy after the popular writer and entertainer Abe Burrows appeared as a panelist on the Goodson-Todman game show "The Name's the Same" in December 1951. Burrows had a long listing in *Red Channels*. Johnson and others began sending letters of protest to the show's sponsor, the Swanson food company.

Company executive W. Clarke Swanson became alarmed, and he went to see Mark Goodson in New York City. After Goodson reassured him that all was well, Swanson agreed to let Burrows stay on the show.

Three months later, W. Clarke Swanson contacted Goodson again. Swanson had just received a telephone call from Johnson. Soon afterward, Burrows left the program and joined another panel show, "This Is Show Business." Protest letters soon poured in to that show's sponsor, the American Tobacco Company.

Called to testify before the HCUA, Burrows spoke from the heart. "This whole point of my Americanism being under suspicion is very painful to me," he said. "Not just painful economically, but painful as it is to a guy who loves his country." Burrows admitted his past associations. "In my heart, I didn't believe it." he said. "I would say I was stupid." After that admission, he was allowed to continue his remarkable show business career.

Johnson moved on to new targets. He sent a letter to C.F. Seabrook, president of the food giant Seabrook Farms. Did Seabrook know his company was sponsoring a radio detective series advancing the cause of "Stalin's little creatures"? The series was "The Private Files of Matthew Bell," starring Joseph Cotten and produced by Hiram Brown. Brown was listed in *Red Channels*, and Cotten had signed a petition supporting the Hollywood Ten in 1947.

Seabrook called Peter Hilton, president of Kastor-Hilton advertising agency, which handled the Seabrook account. Seabrook wanted to know what was wrong with the radio show.

Hilton later described in court the pressure Johnson put on the food company. "Johnson indicated that—if Seabrook was aware of what it was doing—that he, operating supermarkets in Syracuse, would see fit to boycott Seabrook Farms products and, furthermore, would make other supermarket operators aware of what he was doing and the reasons for doing it. This, naturally, perturbed Seabrook very much and he looked at me, since I had recommended the program, to determine what it was all about."

Hilton met with representatives of the Music Corporation of America, the show's production company. Cotten attended the meeting in New York, where Hilton supported canceling the show right away.

Eventually, they decided to visit Syracuse and meet with Johnson. Without delay, Cotten, Hilton, C.F. Seabrook and lawyer Leo Dorsey boarded a plane for Central New York. Hilton recalled:

> We proceeded from the airport in Syracuse to Johnson's office, which was in the rear of one of his supermarkets. When we arrived, after some very stiff formalities, since it was almost noon we adjourned to a nearby restaurant, and at that time Mr. Seabrook took the initiative and indicated to Mr. Johnson that he, personally, was very much against anything that might be tinged with communism. He cited the record of Seabrook Farms throughout the war and indicated that he would not knowingly support anything that might foster or help a known communist.
>
> On that occasion, as a peace offering and as an indication of good faith I suggested that one of the commercials of the three commercials we had on our Sunday afternoon program be devoted to an institutional message indicating the bounty of America, the need for protecting its free institutions. Mr. Johnson felt that that was a very good idea and it lessened the tension.

Cotten made a vigorous presentation, telling how he had entertained the troops during World War II and had taken part in war bond drives. He showed letters testifying to his patriotism.

Despite that, Hilton said, "He [Johnson] said that he had only the record to go by and he had to make his judgment as to who was American and who was not American by the record."

The luncheon meeting adjourned on this ambiguous note. Even though he still distrusted Cotten, Johnson couldn't let a Hollywood star leave Syracuse without capitalizing on his merchandising potential. Johnson invited Cotten and his companions to visit the grocer's supermarket. Recalled Hilton: "We stopped. We toured the supermarket, met the managers, and Joseph Cotten autographed some, gave some signatures to customers."

Even then, Johnson and his fellow activists kept the heat on. Hiram Brown said he was summoned to a meeting with Johnson and Hartnett in New York City, where the two men warned they would go on making trouble for him unless he used what they called "the right actors."

A skittish Seabrook soon decided he had no interest in sponsoring "The Private Lives of Matthew Bell" beyond the thirteen weeks guaranteed in the contract. The show was canceled, and Hilton's agency lost the half-million-dollar Seabrook account.

Johnson did keep in touch with Hilton, at one point proposing that the ad agency hire anti-communist Harvey Matusow as a copywriter. Hilton declined.

CASE STUDY: AMM-I-DENT

Johnson's next target was a familiar product at the time on American supermarket shelves: Amm-i-dent toothpaste, manufactured by the Block Drug Co. Chief executive Leonard A. Block was one of the first entrepreneurs who saw the immense benefits of television advertising. Block hired the Gray Advertising Agency to line up primetime spots for Amm-i-dent.

In the spring of 1952, Block began sponsoring "Danger," a popular new adventure series. Johnson and Francis Neuser of the Veterans Action Committee of Syracuse Super Markets watched "Danger" and were shocked to see several actors who were on at least one blacklist. By this time, Johnson was spending quite a bit of time scanning TV shows for "listed" performers.

In June 1952, Neuser issued a bulletin denouncing "Danger." It read, "Since April 15 of this year, the Block Company have used Communist Front sympathizers."

The unsigned VAC broadside adopted Johnson's pressure tactics, alluding to Amm-i-dent's competitors in the toothpaste section of his supermarkets. "Do the makers of Chlorodent, Colgate or Ipana tolerate the use of Communist Fronters in their advertising?" the flier asked. "NO!"

The VAC had also sent a protest letter directly to Leonard Block, dated May 28. When it received no reply, Johnson put his name to the cause by issuing a general call to the supermarket industry.

> The Block Drug Company has salaried and given credit to such Communist Fronters on their show "Danger" as Walter Bernstein, Martin Ritt, Salem Ludwig, Joshua Shelley, Lee Grant. Is it necessary to use these Communist Fronters to sell toothpaste or any other cosmetic or beauty aids? Does the Colgate-Palmolive-Peet Company use Communist Fronters to sell Colgate Toothpaste? Do Lever Brothers find it necessary to employ people who give aid and comfort to a foreign power in order to promote their toothpaste Chlorodent? What do you advise?

Even then, the Syracuse anti-communists were not making headway with Block. In August, John Dungey took up the cause in *Spotlight*. He added another "Danger" cast member, Clifford Carpenter, to the list of suspects, describing him as a "Communist May Day Parader." He asked his readers: "Is it necessary to use such talent to sell…(Amm-i-dent) when over 17,000 American boys have been killed in Korea?…Write Mr. Melvin (sic) Block, Pres. Block Drug Co., 257 Cornelison Ave., Jersey City, N.J. and ask if we should help the Communist conspiracy by buying Ammident, part of whose profits go to pay salaries of Commie fronters."

Johnson made a trip to Madison Avenue and visited the Gray Advertising Agency. By his own account, his meeting with account executive Samuel Dalsimer was unsatisfactory. Johnson later said Dalsimer "was very blunt with me…practically told me to mind my own business, which, of course, he had a perfect right to do."

Johnson then added another weapon to his anti-communism arsenal. If he couldn't win over the sponsor or the national advertiser, he would take the message directly to supermarket customers.

CHAPTER SEVEN: Syracuse and the McCarthy Era

He discussed this new strategy with Harvey Matusow, who was by now a close ally. "Johnson told me that in order for the blacklist to be really effective he felt it needed the merchandising approach—one which could hurt the sponsor in the pocketbook. He knew that a few crank letters sent to a sponsor would not do the job," Matusow recalled.

Rather than refuse to sell an offending product in his stores, Johnson initially decided to put up two counter displays, one with the product and one with a competitor. Over one, the sign might read: "Our boys are dying in Korea; the manufacturer of this product employs Communist-fronters." The sign over the competitive product would say something like: "They do not employ Communist-fronters."

Johnson's daughter Marilyn Giancola would have vivid memories of the displays shaming products that advertised on TV shows with "suspicious characters." The display would suggest buying the offending product was akin to funding the communist enemy. "The sign would say something like: 'Do You Want to Buy Guns to Shoot Your Boys in Korea?'"

According to Mary Coyne, when signs sprouted in the stores, customers seemed puzzled, perhaps indicating the message wasn't as effective as directly pressuring the manufacturer. "Of course, that would confuse the customers," she said of the signs. "Take the average John coming in. He didn't know what this was about." Coyne added that only a few customers asked her about the signs.

Years later, Johnson claimed this kind of in-store shaming strategy was only carried out on rare occasions, if at all. Johnson denied that his stores set up such displays over Amm-i-dent.

Records from 1952 showed he did make a "poll" offer during the summer in a letter to Leonard Block written under the banner of the VAC:

> If you plan to continue the use of Communist Front talent, wouldn't it be a good idea if…we could work out a questionnaire to be given to the people who buy from our cosmetic displays. A questionnaire could be drafted reading, for instance, as follows: "Do You want Any Part of Your Purchase Price of Ammident to be Used to Hire Communist Fronters? YES

(box). NO (box). Indicate your choice by X in the appropriate box."

We are sending this letter to you by registered mail because our earlier correspondence to you on May 28th evidently went astray since no answer has been forthcoming.

The letter showed that Johnson had no problem summoning the clout of the VAC when he needed it.

He did so again in October 1952 when he wrote again to Leonard Block. He reminded the manufacturer that no action had been taken to purge the subversive elements from the cast and crew of the "Danger" TV series, adding: "I passed this information on to the Veterans Action Committee of Syracuse Supermarkets."

Johnson then suggested that Block's advertising men should post their own sign over an Amm-i-dent display, explaining why the company sponsored "Communist Fronters."

In a letter to retailers, Johnson wrote:

Are the directors of the Columbia Broadcasting Company and President Frank Stanton trying to push Communist Fronters under the guise of advertising toothpaste? Why do they continually embarrass Block Drug Company by injecting Stalin's little creatures into CBS's owned show named "Danger," sponsored by Ammident?...Is this the kind of testimonial for honesty and integrity we should expect of the Columbia Broadcasting Company?

In a letter to Stanton, Johnson proposed polling his own customers with the following question: "Do you want any part of your purchase price of any products advertised on the Columbia Broadcasting System to be used to hire Communist Fronters? YES (box). NO (box)."

Knowing very well the outcome of such a loaded question, Johnson said he would abide by the results of this survey. "If the American public decides in his favor we will surely acknowledge our error." This letter, too, was sent under the auspices of the VAC.

CHAPTER SEVEN: Syracuse and the McCarthy Era

In 1952, Johnson ended yet another letter to Leonard Block with a not-too-veiled threat: The VAC would wait a few days for a reply to this letter, then would send copies to the U.S. Chamber of Commerce, the Americanism Committee at American Legion headquarters in Indianapolis, the Sons of the American Revolution, the Catholic War Veterans, the Super Market Institute in Chicago, and others.

"Danger" continued to air on CBS until 1955 when Block withdrew as a sponsor and, shortly afterward, CBS canceled the show.

By then, Johnson had grown impatient with shaming manufacturers with polls and displays while still selling their goods. So, he began sweeping offending products off his shelves, leaving messages about communists and communist sympathizers to explain their absence.

Former clerk Robert Giarrusso recalled one such sign placed on an empty shelf: "I No Longer Carry Royal Crown Cola Because They Hired So-and-So....I Will Resume This Product When So-and-So Is No Longer Employed."

Giarrusso overheard Johnson on the phone telling the bottler, "Okay, would you send a truck over, please, and pick up all your Royal Crown? They can load it up (from storage), or they can pick it up from the front of the store."

In boycott actions like this, fellow anti-communist Harvey Matusow noted later, Johnson took steps the grocer thought would protect himself legally. "In order to free himself from any libel charges, Johnson, with the help of *Counterattack*, prepared kits of documented proof to substantiate his charges," Matusow said. "The kits included photostats from the *Daily Worker*, as well as excerpts from the congressional committee reports."

What Johnson failed to see then was a need to also protect himself from Harvey Matusow.

CHAPTER EIGHT:
Harvey Matusow's Odyssey

Just as Laurence Johnson was enjoying success after success in 1952, so were his anti-communist allies. Vincent Hartnett was testifying at government hearings; Francis Neuser and the Veterans Action Committee were exercising their new clout; and John Dungey's *Spotlight* kept Legion Post No. 41 on the front lines.

Into this burgeoning movement stepped a young man who would spin through Johnson's life like a dervish: Harvey Matusow. Short, dark, with piercing brown eyes and a gentle, disarming manner, Matusow was only twenty-six when he first met Johnson, who saw in him a bright young ex-GI trying to make it as a writer. Johnson welcomed Matusow as an energetic ally who had earned credibility as an informer for the FBI while a member of the Communist Party. After leaving the party, he appeared at congressional hearings and named hundreds of alleged communists. Matusow's whirlwind journey took him to the Ohio anti-communist establishment, and on to joining Roy Cohn, Senator McCarthy, and others in the big leagues.

THE EVOLUTION OF HARVEY MATUSOW

Matusow grew up in the Bronx in the 1930s, where he would run errands for his father, who operated Uncle Herman's Luncheonette. Young Harvey would scamper next door to the labor theater to get rolls of nickels from the box office for his father's pinball machines. Show people started calling him Kid Nickels.

He said he must have seen sixty performances of "Pins and Needles," the leftist musical revue that became a four-year sensation, the longest-running musical of its time on Broadway. "Many of the people who were connected with the show are today blacklisted as progressives," Matusow wrote in 1955. "The show had its political connotations, progressive and reflecting the times, the effects of the depression and the spirited upsurge of the New Deal."

Matusow said he grew up with an inferiority complex. He never seemed able to measure up to his big brother, Danny. Whatever Harvey tried to do, he said, "Danny could do it better."

So, Harvey Matusow learned to fake it. "I tried too hard, and I pushed, bluffing my way through, being loud and glib, pretending that I could do but not proving it," he said.

The younger Matusow was fifteen when the Japanese attacked Pearl Harbor. Danny enlisted in the U.S. Army Air Forces, but Harvey had to wait until 1943, when he volunteered for the infantry.

On September 10, 1944, Sergeant Daniel B. Matusow was killed when the Germans shot down his bomber plane over Nuremberg. It would be two years before the Army confirmed his death. By then, Harvey had witnessed history on May 7, 1945, when he stood in a courtyard as the German general staff arrived at U.S. headquarters in Reims, France, to surrender to General Eisenhower.

Discharged from the Army in 1946, Matusow began to drift. He missed the camaraderie of the service. A friend introduced him to a group called American Youth for Democracy, where he met socialists and communists. He particularly felt drawn to the communists and their sense of belonging and strength of purpose. He joined the New York communists, becoming a member of the Tompkins Square section in 1947. "I thought that these young people were fighting for things I wanted," Matusow wrote. "I hated discrimination and I didn't like to see people pushed around." He also found fellowship during the summer at Camp Unity, where there were communist speeches in the morning and communist songfests at night.

In his two years with the Communist Party, Matusow was an indefatigable worker, at least by party standards. In 1948, he said, he sold an

CHAPTER EIGHT: Harvey Matusow's Odyssey

Harvey Matusow is interviewed on March 15, 1955, by WBAP-TV in Fort Worth, Texas. (University of North Texas Libraries photo)

"unheard-of" 326 subscriptions to the *Sunday Worker*. His reward was a trip to Puerto Rico, courtesy of the Communist Party.

Matusow said he eventually grew tired of the communists. He complained later about the "absolutist attitude" of his comrades and their "mechanical approach" to people. Their ideological critiques felt like "attacks upon me." There was another element of Matusow's conversion narrative he did not mention: his demotion after the party chapter accused him of "white chauvinism" for taking a job with a collection agency in Harlem.

In February 1950, he contacted the FBI, which made Matusow an undercover informant at a salary of $70 a week, equivalent to about $900 at the time this book is being published in 2024.

On May Day 1950, Matusow pleaded a war injury to get out of marching with the Tompkins Square Communists. Instead, he spent the day on the curb snapping pictures for the FBI. Matusow remembered being struck by his own duplicity. "I stood there for hours watching rank after rank carrying posters and banners proclaiming slogans which I claimed to believe in....Each of the 144 clicks of my shutter caught the face of a friend. Most of them recognized me and waved as I took their pictures. 'Send us a copy,' some of them shouted."

In July 1950, Matusow went to Taos, New Mexico, and stayed at the San Cristobal Valley Ranch, a left-wing watering hole, where he collected more evidence for the FBI.

Back in New York that November, the Communist Party uncovered his FBI connection and promptly expelled him. The *Daily Worker* of January 16, 1951, accused him of being an "enemy agent," calling him "H. Matisow" throughout its report. The editors added a slap at Matusow's party work, saying he "was also found to have engaged in irregularities and misrepresentations during a press drive." The story went on to say that he "is now operating in New York City since his recent return from the Southwest. Matisow is in his middle twenties, medium height, plump, white, has a round face, black hair and eyes."

After that, with the help of the FBI, Matusow enlisted in the U.S. Air Force, where he was sent to Wright-Patterson Air Force Base in Dayton, Ohio. There, Matusow became friends with Martha Edmiston, who handled public relations for the air base. She and her husband, John, were active anti-communists, and they took a liking to Matusow. After he was discharged from the Air Force, they introduced him to Donald T. Appell, an investigator for the HCUA. The Edmistons had once testified before the committee. They asked: Why not Matusow, too?

After traveling to Washington and appearing before the committee, Matusow gained entree into the fraternity of top anti-communists. The Edmistons also made overtures on his behalf to the Ohio legislature's Un-American Activities Committee, which put Matusow on the payroll as a research assistant.

On a trip to New York City early in 1952, Matusow met Roy Cohn, beginning a year-long professional relationship with him and his boss, Senator McCarthy. Matusow was a tireless witness, testifying for the HCUA, the Senate Internal Security Subcommittee (SISS), and the New York Board of Education. After Matusow appeared in the second round

CHAPTER EIGHT: Harvey Matusow's Odyssey

of Smith Act trials on Foley Square, federal judge Edward J. Dimock said his testimony was key to the conviction of two defendants—Alexander Trachtenberg and George Black Charney.

In 1952, *American Legion Magazine* paid Matusow $600 to write "Reds in Khaki," an expose of subversion in the military services, which appeared in its October issue.

He also did paid work for McCarthy's re-election campaign. Matusow barnstormed from Washington, D.C., to Great Falls, Montana, inveighing against the communist threat from within. In Illinois, he gave a speech lashing out at G. Bromley Oxnam, the Methodist bishop of Washington, D.C., and co-president of the World Council of Churches.

Matusow spent Thanksgiving 1952 with J.B. Matthews, the prominent Red-hunter. Matusow was invited to sign Matthews' coffee table, a symbolic gesture showing he had really arrived at the inner circle.

At about this time, Matusow met wealthy divorcee Arvilla Bentley, who, like Matusow, had testified against former communist associates. She became infatuated with the young crusader, and they took a trip together to Miami and Nassau. Matusow and Bentley married in March 1953.

By then, Matusow had become friends with Ted Kirkpatrick, Vincent Hartnett, and Laurence Johnson.

JOHNSON AND MATUSOW

When Matusow and Johnson first met at the New York City offices of *Counterattack*, the young anti-communist found the white-haired entrepreneur was already one of his fans. Some of the headlines Matusow made in 1952 had caught the eye of Johnson.

"He had heard of me through newspaper stories about my frequent testimony," Matusow recalled in the 1980s. "Like a mother hen, he took me under his wing and guided me in the role of blacklisting. I don't know if it was my youth and energy that impressed Johnson. Anyway, I became his semi-official liaison man in New York. He showed a great deal of pride in me and, when he was in New York, he proudly displayed me as his protege."

Matusow soon accompanied Johnson as he made the rounds of various advertising agencies. Johnson also introduced the young anti-communist to people connected with the Super Market Institute, praising Matusow as competent to judge the qualifications of actors and actresses.

Matusow, decades later, suggested a parallel between Johnson's anti-communist merchandising and the gonzo tactics of Abbie Hoffman and Jerry Rubin of the Yippie Left in the 1960s.

"He was like a pre-Abbie Hoffman of the right," he said of Johnson. "Remember Hoffman's book, 'Steal This Book'? Johnson would put signs up in his supermarket attacking products. Tactically, is it any different than the things that Hoffman and Rubin did with the same unconventional shock value? There's very little difference between the right and the left. They're both selling a product."

Matusow displayed a capacity for ideological dirty tricks in one anti-communist campaign that involved Yankees baseball catcher Yogi Berra. Matusow's colleagues at *Counterattack* learned Berra was scheduled to appear in August 1952 on "All Star Summer Revue," a variety show airing on NBC. Also lined up as a guest was Jack Gilford, who had raised the ire of the Syracuse anti-communists when he came to town with the cast of "Die Fledermaus."

Matusow and *Counterattack* editor Frank McNamara talked things over in New York City. They knew that, since Gilford had a contract, it would be difficult for NBC to drop him. Perhaps someone could pressure Yankees management to yank Berra off the show.

Matusow wrote later how he designated himself the point man for the mission. He called the Yankee office, claiming to be a loyal fan and a patriotic American.

"'I've supported the Yankees for years," he said over the phone, "and I think it would be a very wrong thing for Berra to be on a show which added prestige to a known communist-fronter like Gilford."

His call won a pledge from Jack Farrell, a public relations man with the club, that "something would be done about it."

Not content with this vague reply, Matusow said, he called Farrell sixteen more times, each time pretending to be different persons—"a voice technique I had developed through my hobby of working with puppets."

CHAPTER EIGHT: Harvey Matusow's Odyssey

By the seventeenth call, the exasperated Yankees representative informed Matusow that Berra would definitely not appear on the show with Gilford.

According to Matusow, Farrell finally said, "Look mister, you really don't have to get so excited. I don't think Yogi Berra knows the difference between communism and communion."

Farrell met with TV executives and delivered his ultimatum: It would have to be Berra or Gilford, not both. Gilford got the axe. It appeared that the network found an escape clause in its contract with Gilford, and the show went on without him.

After the matter was settled, Farrell issued a statement reflecting the Yankees' stance: "We have a firm policy that no Yankee player can take part in any public appearance, radio, TV or whatever it is, with persons who have been identified by authorized agencies as members of Communist-front organizations. That's our policy and we're going to stick to it."

Matusow said the men at *Counterattack* were gratified and amused by his ingenious tactics, as was the Syracuse contingent. In the August 1952 issue of *Spotlight*, John Dungey reprinted Hearst journalist Howard Rushmore's laudatory column praising the Yankees' decision.

That month, Matusow also traveled to Syracuse at Johnson's invitation to speak at a meeting of the Veterans Action Committee. His topic: the case of Elizabeth Gurley Flynn, the communist labor leader and co-founder of the ACLU, who was being prosecuted in a Smith Act trial underway in New York City. Matusow recalled that a receptive audience of 400 heard his speech.

In succeeding months, Matusow would visit Syracuse up to a dozen times. He would check into a hotel, then call Johnson and arrange to meet for dinner. "He was sort of paternal. We had a kind of father-son relationship," Matusow said. "I'd call him up if I had some problem I wanted to talk about, he was very good in that sense, he was warm and friendly. It wasn't strictly business."

Johnson and Matusow also shared a love of history and Americana. The younger man said he remembered relaxing at Johnson's Broad Street house, surrounded by his remarkable antique collection.

"We would talk historically. Sometimes we'd just sit and talk about the Civil War for a whole evening. Or we might talk about Millard Fillmore's administration. Or some other aspect of American history. And he would relate history to today, see patterns, examine the country as historians might. He had a good focus on American history from his viewpoint.

"We might go over his old campaign button collection. And from that we'd take off on tangents of history. He'd use them as props for triggering little trivia stories.

"I remember one of his favorite campaign buttons was a little silver pig, and you'd pick the pig up, and you looked in the backside of the pig, and there is a little picture of William Jennings Bryan. And on the thing it said: 'Our Next President.' It was a very rare political campaign thing —this little silver pig, you know, in a pig's ass he is our next president! Johnson was sharp enough to get that kind of political campaign button."

Despite his admiration for the supermarket owner, Matusow said, he saw Johnson as easy to manipulate. "He was a naive guy—naive in that any street kid in the Bronx could con him. He was an idealist. He was a romantic. He did believe in his country; I can't knock him for that. He was patriotic. I was not so much conning him but using him. And he was using me. And it was a mutually beneficial arrangement."

CASE STUDY: "SCHLITZ PLAYHOUSE"

In September 1952, Johnson heard that leftist actor Frank Silvera would perform on a segment of CBS-TV's "Schlitz Playhouse of Stars." Johnson sent a telegram to Schlitz Brewing Company executive Erwin C. Uihlein with the ominous question: "Are you using Communist-fronters like Frank Silvera on Schlitz Playhouse on Sept. 12?"

Johnson's telegram alarmed Uihlein, who referred the matter to Lennen & Mitchell, the advertising agency handling the Schlitz account. By this time, Johnson and his colleagues were going all out, notifying manufacturers, ad agencies and the networks of their displeasure over Silvera. It could have been a Lennen & Mitchell executive, speaking anonymously to author John Cogley several years later, who described the rat-a-tat-tat efficiency of the Syracuse activists: "At one o'clock I got a telegram signed

CHAPTER EIGHT: Harvey Matusow's Odyssey

by Larry Johnson. At two o'clock a telegram arrived signed by the Syracuse American Legion post. At three o'clock there was a wire from the Veterans Action Committee of Syracuse Super Markets."

Uihlein received word that the veterans in Syracuse had banned Schlitz beer from the ice lockers in Legion post social rooms. Beer retailers would be informed of the situation and asked to send in their protests as well.

Francis C. Barton Jr., vice president and general manager of Lennen & Mitchell, moved swiftly to calm the waters. He called Johnson, who happened to be in New York City at his home-away-from-home, the Hampshire House on Central Park South. Johnson invited Barton to dine with him, then asked Harvey Matusow to join them. Barton later testified as to what happened at that memorable meal:

> Mr. Johnson made a long patriotic speech about communists and what they were doing and how we should fight them and they shouldn't be appearing on programs where they were before the public.
>
> I assured him that we were just as patriotic as he was, and that we and our client had no more desire to have communists on our show than he did, or any other good American did, but the question was, who were communists? We had no knowledge in this field. He claimed that he did have knowledge and that a lot of other people had knowledge, and if we would take the trouble, make the effort, we could gain such knowledge and know who was and who wasn't.
>
> Then he raised the specific issue with regard to certain programs that he knew about, he said, where he had gotten the cast lists somehow, and claimed certain people were communists, and he wanted those programs off the air.

Barton said he explained to Johnson and Matusow that each episode of "Schlitz Playhouse" cost about $10,000 to produce, and that the Syracuse protest was putting this considerable investment at risk. Matusow remembered Johnson replying: "You can't use the film already produced

....I don't care if you do lose $10,000 by not showing it; you shouldn't have hired those people in the first place."

When Barton continued to resist, Johnson reportedly lost his temper. "He got fairly angry with me and started to pound the table and raise his voice sufficiently to attract attention around the dining room," Barton said. "Then he calmed down."

Matusow suggested a compromise: The show would go on as scheduled, but Silvera's name would be erased from the show's credits. And all future cast lists for "Schlitz Playhouse" were to be pre-screened for suspect performers. John Gibbs, the new producer, would have a clause in his contract forcing him to absorb the $10,000 loss if controversial names cropped up in future shows and forced their cancellation.

After agreeing to all this, according to Matusow, Barton turned to Johnson and asked: "But where can we obtain the information needed to compile our clearance list?"

Johnson smiled, nodded toward his protege, and replied: "What about Harvey?"

Johnson suggested that the agency employ Matusow as a consultant, saying that his friend could set up the clearance list. "Barton agreed and I was hired," Matusow recalled.

Matusow's assignment was to direct Barton toward back issues of *Counterattack* and to compile a list of thousands of performers, scriptwriters, and other show people. Matusow showed the Madison Avenue ad agency how to set up a rudimentary card index file, and he recommended that they employ the services of *Counterattack* editors at ABC Inc. for future clearance work.

Matusow received $150 from Lennen & Mitchell for his efforts.

MORE CASE STUDIES

In February 1952, Dungey complained in *Spotlight* that actor Elliott Sullivan had recently appeared with Kim Hunter and Lloyd Bridges on NBC's "Robert Montgomery Presents." Sullivan, identified by former comrades as a communist, had refused to cooperate with the HCUA, was cited for contempt of Congress, and listed in *Red Channels*.

Dungey noted the show was sponsored by Johnson Wax and by the American Tobacco Company, makers of Lucky Strike.

Post 41 and its Un-American Activities Committee "appreciate that Mr. Montgomery is a good anti-communist and a busy man," Dungey wrote. However, he added with a flourish reminiscent of Johnson's lexicon, "The Committee has had correspondence with some of the individuals involved in the casting of this show and has been assured that to the best of their ability the above incident will not happen again. More power to you and a hardy 'pat on the back' to you, more such action and we could clear our television and motion picture screens of 'Stalin's little creatures.'"

The campaign against Sullivan did not end there. Johnson wrote to Matusow a few months later, asking for more information about the actor. "This morning, I received a note which said that Elliott Sullivan would be on the Goodyear 'Playhouse' on Sunday, August 17. Can you tell me anything about Sullivan other than what appears in Martin Berkeley's testimony?" (Movie and television screenwriter Berkeley had collaborated with HCUA, identifying numerous Hollywood artists as communists or sympathizers.) It was not long before the campaign against Sullivan doomed his U.S. job opportunities. He would spend most of the 1950s working in England.

In 1952, Vincent Hartnett began three years of employment with the Borden Co. as a "clearance consultant." Dungey's *Spotlight* had already targeted David Pressman, director of the Borden-sponsored TV series "Treasury Men in Action." Dungey also complained about actors John Randolph, Robert Donnelly, Will Lee, Alan Manson, Stephen Schnabel, and Joshua Shelley. Branding the series "blatant CP propaganda plays," Dungey asked: "Why is it necessary for Borden to use such talent?"

The March issue of *Spotlight* featured a "Monthly Box Score" with the announcement that Pressman was "off Pall Mall's TV show 'Big Story' ...(and) also according to letters from the Borden Co. is off 'T-Men in Action.'"

Also, in March 1952, *Spotlight* zeroed in on Lever Brothers, makers of Lux Toilet Soap, Rinso laundry soap, and Spry vegetable shortening. Dungey criticized the company for allowing Lloyd Gough to appear March 2 on "Lux Video Theatre." *Spotlight* took the opportunity to critique "Big Town," another teleplay sponsored by Lever Brothers that concerned foreign infiltration in the United States. Though it "purported to be Anti-Communist," *Spotlight* said, it was the work of writers "conditioned by Communist propaganda." It added:

> Even though it was obvious that the story was about Communist agents brought into this country from Russia NOT ONCE during the entire performance was the word Communist mentioned but instead they were called "those people" and "them people"....Isn't it about time we took off the "kid" gloves and began (calling) a Commie a Commie?....How can this same Lever Bros. hire an actor such as Gough on one hand and yet run a purported anti-Communist play but fail to call the "little Creatures" Communist?

In May, *Spotlight* sounded the alarm over NBC-TV's "The Kate Smith Hour." Under the headline, "Gone to Sleep?", Dungey's newsletter complained about Smith hosting Adolf Dehn on her 4 p.m. show, although the Legionnaire encouraged readers not to blame Smith.

"Who let Kate Smith down?" was the *Spotlight* rallying cry. "Did not Kate Smith, the advertising agency handling the show, or the sponsors of the show know that Adolf Dehn has a Communist front record dating back to 1932?...When are sponsors and advertising agencies going to WAKE UP and STOP promoting the Dehns', the Hollidays' and the Pressmans'?"

On June 18, Johnson wrote to Frederick Weisman at Hunt Foods, sponsor of the Smith show. Johnson passed along criticism along the lines of what appeared in *Spotlight*. Johnson claimed that sales of Hunt products in his supermarkets were declining. Hunt subsequently canceled its sponsorship of Kate Smith.

Other entertainment figures targeted by *Spotlight* during 1952 included playwright Edward Chodorov ("named as a Communist Party member"), playwright Clifford Odets ("named in Hollywood testimony"), screenwriter Guy Endore ("named by Martin Berkeley"), actress Uta Hagen ("active for a number of years in various Communist-fronts"), actor Jose

CHAPTER EIGHT: Harvey Matusow's Odyssey

Ferrer ("notorious fronter"), actor Art Smith ("belonging to...the Communist Party"), and the writing quartet of Muriel Draper, Howard Fast, Sam Jaffe, and John Howard Lawson ("American sponsors, World Conference for Peace in Paris").

Under the classification of "all have Communist front records" were actors Lou Gilbert, Anthony Quinn, Marlon Brando, and Frank Silvera. Cited as members of the "Commie Fronters Team" were actors Adelaide Bean, Lee J. Cobb, Ruth Gordon, Howard Wierum, and Martin Ritt.

Spotlight used its "Monthly Box Score" to keep an informal tally of its campaigns. From February 1952:

> OUTS: The Weavers—Fineto.
>
> Jack Gilford—He & Fledermaus Struck Out.
>
> Philip Loeb (Jake on Goldbergs)—Done for good we hope.
>
> AT BAT: Artie Shaw—Radio Station WOLF still using his record—How come?
>
> Jose Ferrer—Maybe we should not see his new Motion Picture & how come the big LIFE Mag. spread?
>
> Judy Holliday—Ditto above regarding her new picture.
>
> George S. Kaufman—what about him and Sam Levenson on LUCKY STRIKES TV show "This Is Show Business"?

The editors added this postscript: "Too many others—space will not permit listing in this Newsletter."

On occasion, *Spotlight* praised what it called the "Loyal American Team," listing show people who "should be supported at the box office!" The list included Abbott and Costello, Gene Autry, Adolphe Menjou, Kate Smith, Veronica Lake, Mary Astor, Jack Carson, Red Skelton, Bing Crosby, Don Ameche, Richard Arlen, Fay Bainter, Warner Baxter, Ward Bond, Joe E. Brown, Vinton Ainsworth, and Walter Geaza. In one copy of *Spotlight*, the entry for Lloyd Nolan, originally listed on the "Loyal Americans" roster, had been crossed out in ballpoint—an amendment showing either how easily mistakes could be published or how quickly a name could slip out of favor.

THE GROCER WHO SOLD McCARTHYISM

When the anti-communist feature film "My Son John" was released in May 1952, *Spotlight* published a warm endorsement of its stars Helen Hayes, Van Heflin, Robert Walker, and Dean Jagger. "It is a great pleasure to know that such pictures do come out of Hollywood," the newsletter said, "when all too often the film industry persists in using talent of questionable loyalty."

CHAPTER NINE:
Out-merchandising the Competition

SYRACUSE University's Marguerite Fisher was teaching an evening class in "Modern Political Thought" in 1952 when a somewhat older student kept asking questions she thought made no sense. "It appeared soon to me and to the other students in the class that he knew nothing at all about the background of what I was trying to discuss," she said later. "It would be like me registering for a course in nuclear physics. It was like a third-grader asking questions in a graduate course."

A mutual acquaintance soon informed her that the student was John Dungey, editor of *Spotlight* and chairman of Legion Post 41's Un-American Activities Committee. Fisher heard that Dungey, suspecting her of preaching the Communist Party line, enrolled to see for himself.

"His objective was only to take the course without my knowing and get some evidence," she said. "I imagine he thought I'd come right out and advocate going out and overthrowing the government, or something equally silly."

Believing she was being set up, she delighted in thinking up comments she knew he would recognize as being aimed at him. "One thing I said: I was terribly glad the American Legion was taking an interest in my book and my course, because it proved something I didn't think was true—it proved they could read. And up to this time I didn't think they could. And he sat there, he was so dumb he didn't know how to parry my insults."

Dungey, presumably frustrated, stopped attending class before the end of the term, she said.

Fisher wasn't the only one on campus to cross swords with the Syracuse anti-communist activists. In the spring of 1952, the Syracuse University student newspaper, *The Daily Orange*, began aiming barbs at the American Legion. An editorial and letters to the editor linked the Legion with "fascism." As evidence, the editors cited Dungey's committee and its blacklisting campaigns against Judy Holliday and Artie Shaw.

Stung by a *Daily Orange* letter headlined "Legion Post Dangerous" on April 29, 1952, Dungey responded in a *Spotlight* editorial with a defense of the anti-communists:

> Why is it that the minute anyone attempts to fight Communism or Communists in this country, whether it be the American Legion, Senator McCarthy, the McCarran Committee or anyone else, they are immediately called fascists? Why is it that groups fighting the Ku Klux Klan or groups fighting against racial prejudice and bigotry are not called fascists? Don't the misinformed students at Syracuse University know that they are playing right into the hands of the Communists?

Then came Dungey's inevitable counterattack:

> Why is it, that all of a sudden some students at the University are worried about what the American Legion is doing to expose Communists and Communist-fronters?...Is it because they are so closely allied to the entertainment field or are there students and organizations on the Hill which could not afford to be exposed to the light of publicity?...We do not mean to imply that there are Communists at Syracuse University, but we do believe that there is a small group of uninformed or misinformed students there who had better wake up!

JUDGING THE JUDGES

One of the first books to deplore McCarthy Era blacklisting arrived in mid-1952. "The Judges and the Judged," by journalist Merle Miller, looked at the motivations of accusers, and it examined the ordeals of

CHAPTER NINE: Out-merchandising the Competition

blacklisted performers such as Jean Muir and John Garfield. The book also suggested that civic anti-communists hunting for people who were un-American were themselves acting in an un-American way:

> (There) is the very basic question of whether or not any private citizen has the right to investigate another and, equally important, to cut off his livelihood because of his failure to sign a loyalty oath or statement. Such methods have heretofore always been considered morally indefensible in a democratic society where, unless those words have lost all meaning, men must continue to be allowed to think and speak and write as they wish without being required to attest they are "loyal" to freedom.

The book's interviews with ad executives, actors, and producers were all off the record in their complaints about blacklisting. "Everyone was frightened," Miller recalled decades later. "It seems odd to think about such dense civilian fear in America, but there it was. Everyone (who opposed blacklisting) refused to talk or would not speak for attribution. Only the blacklisters were brave."

Within show-business unions, the stiffest opposition to the anti-communists in 1952 came from the Radio Writers Guild and from the Television Authority, affiliated with the American Federation of Labor. By the end of the year, the Senate Internal Security Subcommittee had subpoenaed Radio Writers Guild leaders, and Senator James Eastland had attacked "pro-communists" in the guild who he claimed "indirectly controlled" the contents of most radio scripts.

The television writers union met in New York City to discuss the case of actor Philip Loeb. Members approved a resolution, 259 to 63, opposing his blacklisting, The vote outraged Johnson and his colleagues. Dungey suggested that blacklisting wasn't the evil practice its critics claimed but rather involved "ousting of Commies, near commies, pro-commies and other leftist riff-raff from fancy pay spots on radio and TV."

Spotlight then called for a full-scale government probe of show-business unions:

> Phone, wire or write your Congressman and Senator arguing an immediate investigation…into the entire field with particular attention given to the Radio Writers Guild, Equity and Television Authority… If you don't protest—nobody else will do it for you. Public protests and real mass pressure removed such offensive "uninvited guests" as Muriel Draper, Philip Loeb, and others from the privacy of your homes. The real cleanup has only been started—let's finish the job.

Blacklisting came under attack again in September 1952 with Saul Carson's article in the left-wing *Sunday Compass*. Carson sketched the outlines of an anti-communist network that included Laurence Johnson, Syracuse Legion Post 41 and *Spotlight;* James P. O'Neil and *American Legion Magazine* based in Indianapolis; the Catholic War Veterans; and Jewish War Veterans. Columnists Victor Riesel, George Sokolsky, and other leading anti-communists rounded out Carson's list.

In *Spotlight*, Dungey responded on behalf of the Legion post:

> We do not mind being on their list to be smeared but we would like to have a little truth connected with it. You would think from reading the Compass that Mr. Johnson directed our operation. Let me say right here and now that we have our own staff of researchers and if our findings are such that action should be taken, we act independently. If Mr. Johnson or any other organization who are fighting Communists needs an assist on any phase of the fight and our facts match theirs, they receive our support….
>
> Furthermore, when Saul Carson says that anyone other than Post 41 publishes our newsletter called Spotlight that is also a distortion of the truth. This newsletter started with funds from Post 41 and now is supported by some paid subscribers, Post 41, Onondaga County Legion and Voiture 359 of the Forty and Eight. Six thousand Legionnaires and *Voyageurs Militaire* have not and will not take any dictates as to what goes into their Spotlight.

CHAPTER NINE: Out-merchandising the Competition

Having defended the Legion's autonomy, *Spotlight* paid tribute to Johnson, who it said "has spent time and money apprising Business firms of the way income finds its way into Stalin's Fifth Column by having on their sponsored programs party members or front supporters...Most firms were only too glad to cooperate when given the facts." It added:

> Mr. Johnson has the intestinal fortitude and foresight that more men in business should have. He rewards the firms who will not hire Commies or pro-Commies on their programs by special advertising and displays. Those who will continue to hire "Stalin's Little Creatures" get no special attention.
>
> The Communists are out there to hurt Johnson's business and reputation because he has enlisted other wholesalers and retailers in the fight all around the country. None of them want their money going to help the Communist cause and therein lies the reason for the smear in the Compass.

Dungey couldn't resist a final barb: "As of November 3, 1952, The Daily Compass went out of business. Could it be that too many people had their numbers? Good riddance!"

MUTUAL ADMIRATION SOCIETY

Whether the anti-communist groups were a malevolent cabal, as Saul Carson charged, or an autonomous, spontaneous group of civic activists, as Dungey claimed, they clearly were bound by their common mission.

That mission was tested, though, after Ted Kirkpatrick stated in *Sponsor*, a radio and TV trade paper, that he and his colleagues had not felt a need to do a fact check with the accused before listing them in *Red Channels*. "We've never said the 'facts' in *Red Channels* were correct or incorrect. We've just reported from the public records," Kirkpatrick said. After his admission, dozens of newspapers ran articles and editorials critical of the fairness of the anti-communists.

The U.S. Chamber of Commerce quickly rose to the defense of *Red Channels* in the business group's annual report entitled "Communism, Where Do We Stand Today?"

"Much furor and considerable unfair reporting has occurred over this publication [Red Channels]," the report said. "The attack...in certain circles, made much of the alleged unsubstantiated mass of rumor and gossip, which it was alleged to contain." Such an attack, the Chamber of Commerce continued, "was plain bad reporting. Listings of 'front' connections were factual, with the source indicated."

Another article defending *Red Channels* appeared in *The Sign*, a lay Catholic magazine published in Union City, New Jersey, that circulated in Holy Name societies, Knights of Columbus councils, and Catholic War Veterans posts, among other places. Under the byline of Arnold Foreman, the June 1952 article claimed *Red Channels* had been attacked in 166 U.S. newspapers and labeled a "smear pamphlet" or worse. The writer went on to praise the men from *Counterattack*, singling out Vincent Hartnett for his "firsthand knowledge of certain Communist activities in program production."

Only later was it revealed that Arnold Foreman was Hartnett writing with a pseudonym. When asked about this in 1982, Hartnett appeared temporarily at a loss. Then he offered the following explanation: Back in the 1940s, while he was writing for the Lord agency, he had done some freelance writing on the side. Hartnett said the Reverend Ralph Gorman, editor of *The Sign*, recommended the pseudonym on the grounds that the writing touched on controversial subjects that could put Hartnett's full-time job at risk.

But Hartnett was no longer working for Lord in 1952 when he used the Arnold Foreman pseudonym. Why the disguise?

"I had no objection to having my name on it," Hartnett said. "Father Gorman...said that I had written so many articles for *The Sign* magazine (as Vincent Hartnett) it would appear that, well, you know, they were buying too many from one person."

All of this, however, doesn't explain or excuse the obvious duplicity of Hartnett hiding his identity while praising himself and his colleagues.

While Hartnett, Johnson, and their fellow activists were shrewd in using the resources at their disposal, they could never have played their roles so effectively without the cooperation of many within the broadcast industry. Johnson's astute merchandising of anti-communism succeeded

CHAPTER NINE: Out-merchandising the Competition

because of zealous accommodation by industry executives who feared losing profits. One anonymous executive captured the capitalistic logic of the era when he explained to blacklisting researcher Cogley why men like Johnson were needed watchdogs on industry hiring practices. "If we don't screen out controversial people," he said, "we will be hurting the sales of the product we are trying to sell. Therefore, not to screen would be unbusinesslike and violate the trust of stockholders."

Joseph Cotten's visit to Johnson's supermarket in 1951 was one example of that accommodation. Another occurred in 1952 when Stuart Peabody, vice president of the Borden Co., made the trip to Central New York to present a trophy to the Syracuse anti-communists. Peabody wrote afterward to Johnson: "Dear Larry, I want to tell you again how grateful I am for the time and help you gave me on Tuesday. It is no exaggeration to say that my eyes have been opened as a result of your cooperation."

Later, Proctor & Gamble's Howard J. Morgens sent Johnson a note telling him his visit to Syracuse had been "pleasant and instructive." Morgens defended his company's record, while stressing the need for continued vigilance. "We honestly feel that we also have been taking effective action in this field," he wrote. "In any case, as a result of our contacts with you and your associates, our operating methods are being re-examined and will be tightened wherever possible. If you have any further suggestions to make about our radio and TV talent, I'd consider it a personal favor to hear from you directly."

Another visitor was Charles Irving, who produced and directed the popular CBS-TV soap opera "Search for Tomorrow." The Syracuse activists had complained to the network and its sponsor, Proctor & Gamble, that Irving had been linked to communist fronts and to the May Day parades of 1946 and 1948.

In 1953, he flew to Syracuse to meet with Dungey and others from Legion Post No. 41's Un-American Activities Committee. Irving showed them a statement he had written, admitting his past associations and affirming his patriotism. Dungey demurred. "We accepted Charles Irving's statement at face value," he noted later in *Spotlight*. "But it should be pointed out that no one has the power to clear anyone. Irving made his own record and it is up to him to unmake it."

Irving had written a speech he hoped to deliver to the Legionnaires in Syracuse. He didn't get a chance, but Dungey agreed to publish excerpts in *Spotlight*.

Despite their threat to his livelihood, Irving had nothing but good to say about the anti-communists:

> Thanks to the American Legion, and to a few like-minded bodies, the process of exposing and dealing with the threat was made much easier. A light was kept burning, (offering) a course back. The period when we thought we had to fight for America through a series of foreign-inspired organizations, such as those with which I was myself associated, and from which I am now in no uncertain manner completely and irrevocably disassociated—namely the National Council of the Arts, Sciences and Professions, and the organizations that in a self-named public spirit, sought sponsorship and participation in such activities as the May Day Parade, Stop Censorship and so on, is clearly over.

Irving would continue working, though his listed credits would not resume until four years later, in 1957.

For his anti-communist efforts, Johnson received powerful testimonials in congratulatory letters from influential sponsors. Wrote the president of General Ice Cream Corporation: "I think it is wonderful that you have taken this interest in ferreting Communists out of our entertainment industry. I wish there were more people like you." A vice president of Kraft Foods echoed those sentiments: "It is indeed heartening to know that you are continuing your crusade....I sincerely hope you keep up the good work."

As the networks and advertising agencies set up their screening and clearance operations to weed out communists, the sponsors responded similarly.

As early as 1950, General Foods adopted an advertising policy to avoid "material and personalities which, in its judgment, are controversial."

CHAPTER NINE: Out-merchandising the Competition

General Electric distributed a booklet to all employees entitled "What to Do About Communism."

Niagara Mohawk Power Corp., the Syracuse-based utility company, launched an internal publicity campaign, setting up magazine racks in its offices and power plants carrying pamphlets with titles like "The Red Front in the United States."

In Chicago, Paul S. Dougherty, president of the Metal Coating Corp., announced his company would not buy products from any sponsor on radio or TV whose shows employed communists or sympathizers. Dougherty wrote to Dungey: "Business must fight Communism, for business controls the thoughts of more people, and is more influential to a greater number."

John M. Fox, president of Minute Maid Corp., came close to adopting the rhetorical techniques of Johnson and the Syracuse activists in pressuring broadcasters. He explained his company's policies in a letter to Joseph H. McConnell, president of NBC:

> I have become increasingly disturbed about the reports that the television and radio industries, along with many other of the country's vital nerve centers, are being successfully invaded by Communist Sympathizers. The dangers of this invasion to everything that we hold dear in America are too obvious for comment. In fact, the mere thought that Minute Maid advertising dollars could be lining the pockets, unwittingly to be sure, of these people has been giving me nightmares lately.
>
> Accordingly, Minute Maid has adopted a policy, effective immediately, of insisting that we be advised well in advance of the names of all people, guest stars, and production functionaries as well, who are scheduled to partake or assist in radio and television performances that we sponsor. It will be our purpose to screen these programs as effectively as possible in order to assure ourselves that only Patriotic Americans are receiving the benefit of our advertising expenditures.
>
> Furthermore, if it can be demonstrated to the satisfaction of our people that a Communistic fellow traveler has slipped

through your own investigative network, we will promptly call the situation to your attention. I am sure you are as keenly interested as we are in taking a firm stand against this dangerous threat.

Fox concluded with a recognition that this approach could hurt the wrongly accused:

> I have no sympathy for "witch hunting" or "blacklisting," but I have less sympathy for blithely assuming that all of the evidence which has been dug up by the various federal investigative committees is an exaggeration. We have no intention to pillory innocent people, but we certainly will take most seriously true evidence and facts that are available.

ON THE STUMP

During the 1952 presidential campaign, as the anti-communists were on the rise, their political standard-bearers in the Republican Party painted the opposition as traitors to democracy and servants of Moscow. The circle of suspicion extended far beyond the Truman administration, encompassing the civil service, the military, trade unions, defense contractors, teachers, journalists, librarians, and, of course, those employed in show business.

Renegade ex-communist Harvey Matusow joined Senator McCarthy's campaign during the summer of 1952 and was dispatched to Wisconsin. Later, Matusow made campaign swings through other states, including Montana, where anti-communist strategists had targeted liberal Senator Mike Mansfield for defeat. The popular Mansfield, however, went on to win re-election in a hectic contest in which Matusow only played a bit part.

In speeches during his exuberant road trips through Utah, Idaho, and Washington State, Matusow's charges grew bolder and bolder. He began painting lurid scenarios of communism subverting virtually every institution of American life. His targets were so indiscriminate that a reporter

CHAPTER NINE: Out-merchandising the Competition

covering his speech to students at a Great Falls, Montana, high school observed: "His appearance was sponsored by the American Legion—one of the few organizations that he did not accuse of being Communist-infected."

Matusow warned his audiences about Reds in government, radio and television, the press, the movies, even in church. Every major college had at least one communist on the faculty, he declared. He said there were 500 dues-paying communists in New York City high schools, and others in Los Angeles, San Francisco, Milwaukee—"and maybe in Great Falls." He claimed that to get a job in radio in New York City "you must be a member of the Communist Party." Among "Red-infiltrated" institutions he cited were CBS, the Boy Scouts, the YWCA, the USO, and most religious denominations, except the Catholic Church and the Mormons.

Matusow zeroed in on the New York City media establishment with the kind of reckless specificity used by Senator McCarthy. "The Sunday section of *The New York Times* alone has 126 dues-paying communists," Matusow told a student audience in Great Falls. "On the editorial and research staffs of *Time* and *Life* magazines are seventy-six hard-core Reds. The New York bureau of The Associated Press has twenty-five."

Matusow repeated his charges to an audience of adults later that day in the Great Falls municipal auditorium.

Of course, the media giants accused of employing armies of communists denied Matusow's accusations. However, in 1952, as Election Day came and went, very few were willing to vigorously stand up to Matusow and his fellow anti-communists.

In 1953, world events further emboldened the anti-communists as the Soviet Union became submerged in the mysterious death of Joseph Stalin and the succession of Nikita Khrushchev, and as the USSR answered the Americans with its own H-bomb in August.

Despite the seriousness of the anti-communist mission, their efforts in the United States often sparked elements of farce.

Civic leaders in Moscow, Idaho, took the time to forward an indignant resolution to the Soviet Embassy in Washington, D.C.: "Whereas the citizens of Moscow, Idaho, believe they have a prior and superior right to the name....Be it resolved that the city officials of Moscow, USSR be requested to change their name from Moscow to some other name that will not by association embarrass the citizens of Moscow, USA."

In New York City, *Women's Wear Daily* offered, in apparent sincerity, a preview of fashions for the nuclear age. "Atomic bomb attacks on our cities would place new responsibilities upon the lingerie industry at every level," the publication noted. "Strapless and sleeveless designs will have to be eliminated as well as designs with tight-fitting front sections. At least one scientist thinks slips with loose, made-in panties would be needed to afford the fullest protection."

Around this time, authorities in New York City canceled the annual May Day parade. While this was a blow to the communists, it also hampered civic anti-communist activists like Harvey Matusow and Vincent Hartnett, for whom the parade was a valuable source for gathering data. Instead of roaming the fringes of the parade, snapping photos and taking notes, Hartnett attended an Americanism Day rally in Elmhurst, New York, where the Queens County American Legion was honoring him, along with Roy Cohn and special guest William Jansen, the New York City schools superintendent. That month, the HCUA had begun probing alleged communist infiltration of schools in New York City. On September 24, the New York State Board of Regents became the first state education agency in the nation to bar Communist Party members from employment in public schools.

Robert Hutchins of the nonprofit Fund for the Republic complained to *Look* magazine that anti-communists were harming the ability of teachers to do their jobs. "Education is impossible in many parts of the United States today because free inquiry and free discussion are impossible," Hutchins said. "In these communities, the teacher of economics, history or political science cannot teach. Even the teacher of literature must be careful. Didn't a member of Indiana's Text Book Commission call Robin Hood subversive?"

Founded in 1951 by the Ford Foundation to promote civil liberties, the fund already had angered the anti-communist movement with its left-leaning studies, "Digest of the Public Record of Communism," "The Draftee and Internal Security" and "Case Studies in Personnel Security."

CHAPTER NINE: Out-merchandising the Competition

NUMBERS MOUNTING

Growing numbers of civil servants, diplomats, social workers, trade unionists and show people felt the sting of anti-communist attacks in 1953. The Attorney General's List of Subversive Organizations now totaled 254 groups. Congressional committees were compiling indices of more names that would lead to more suspicion and ostracism. Blacklisted employees were leaving government employment in droves, if not through resignation, then by suspension or dismissal. In show business, at least 250 people had become unemployable by 1953 because of loyalty investigations and screening.

If losing a job wasn't enough to fear, the government's June 19 electrocution of Julius and Ethel Rosenberg for espionage showed how far the country would go to crush communism in its midst.

Senator McCarthy, newly re-elected, entered 1953 as the powerful chairman of the Permanent Subcommittee on Investigations of the Senate Committee on Government Operations. He would use this platform over the next two years as an institutional guerrilla operation, apart from but allied with the Senate Internal Security Subcommittee.

In 1953, a Gallup poll recorded a 50 percent favorable rating for the Wisconsin senator, with 21 percent holding an unfavorable view and 21 percent undecided. In September, comedian Bob Hope was on a visit to England when asked what he thought of McCarthy. Hope reportedly replied that he rejected the term "McCarthyism" in favor of "Americanism," adding that he felt McCarthy was correct 99 percent of the time.

Early in 1953, Roy Cohn and his young aide, G. David Schine, toured overseas libraries in Europe on behalf of McCarthy in an investigation of the U.S. Information Agency and the Voice of America. Although they were mocked by European journalists, Cohn and Schine returned to claim that, on USIA library shelves, they had discovered 30,000 books by communists.

In August 1953, McCarthy decided to take on the U.S. Army. By October, he was holding hearings on alleged communist infiltration at the Army Signal Corps radar center in Fort Monmouth, New Jersey. The senator zeroed in on an Army dentist, Irving Peress, who recently had

THE GROCER WHO SOLD McCARTHYISM

Senator Joseph McCarthy, center, with counsel Roy M. Cohn, left, and aide G. David Schine during a hearing of the U.S. House Committee on Un-American Activities on August 23, 1953. (*Los Angeles Times*/UCLA Library Special Collections photo)

received a routine promotion to the rank of major, despite his affiliation with the American Labor Party, a target of the anti-communists.

Calling General Ralph W. Zwicker to testify, McCarthy demanded, "Who promoted Peress?" Army Secretary Robert T. Stevens afterward objected to having high-ranking Army personnel "browbeaten or humiliated." Eisenhower press secretary James C. Hagerty added that the president supported Stevens' remarks: "On behalf of the president, he has seen the statement. He approves and endorses it 100 percent." The White House maneuver was a rare example of Eisenhower deploying presidential prestige against McCarthy. The senator laughed off Stevens' criticism, vowing to continue his military probe.

General Electric's anti-communist public relations campaign had earned the approval of John Dungey and Legion Post No. 41's *Spotlight* newsletter. But the major defense contractor did not escape the

CHAPTER NINE: Out-merchandising the Competition

steely glare of Senator McCarthy after *The Saturday Evening Post* raised alarms in October 1953 with an article and editorial about the threat of communist subversion in GE plants in Schenectady, New York, and Lynn, Massachusetts. In November, McCarthy convened hearings in Boston and Albany on communist infiltration of the electrical workers unions serving GE.

Company executives moved swiftly to limit the damage. On December 9, GE President Ralph J. Cordiner announced a new companywide loyalty policy: Any employees who invoked the Fifth Amendment against self-incrimination when asked about their affiliations would receive a ninety-day suspension, followed by dismissal if the questions remained unanswered. Among the 28 employees subsequently suspended were two Syracuse GE workers, James I. Jones Jr. and Edwin R. Wagner.

MISTAKES WERE MADE

In their zeal to publish names, the anti-communists often got sloppy. Johnson alerted Hartnett to a mistake in the case of Marvin Miller, branded by Hartnett as a left-wing actor but who actually was a dues-paying member of the ultra-conservative Motion Picture Alliance for the Preservation of American Ideals. Hartnett relented, but not without grumbling to Johnson, saying that he had "no responsibility to go out looking for these things when an individual has created by his own public activity an unfavorable record."

Everett Sloane, who starred in "Citizen Kane" and had been a regular performer in film and television, was puzzled when he suddenly found his career going nowhere. Then he learned about a scriptwriter and former Communist Party member named Allan E. Sloane who was listed in *Red Channels*. Concluding that a case of mistaken identity was hurting his own job opportunities, Everett Sloane set out to clear his name. He went to the United Nations, where he did some radio writing, and got a copy of a memo from the U.S. secretary of state to the U.N. secretary general verifying an FBI background check had been completed. "After a full field investigation," the document read, "it has been determined that there is no reasonable doubt as to the loyalty of Everett Sloane to the government of the United States."

However, when Everett Sloane took this to Hartnett's colleague Paul Milton, the anti-communist wasn't persuaded to issue a statement clearing the actor. "I take this (FBI) document with a grain of salt," Milton said. "We...have different standards of clearance than the United States government's agencies. We are a little more stringent. We feel they are a little too lenient."

Similarly, when Madeline Lee, a radio actress specializing in baby noises, was listed in *Red Channels*, three other performers suffered from misidentification. One of them shared her name, Madeline Lee; a second, Camilla Ashland, looked like the blacklisted actress; a third, Madeline Pierce, shared not only the first name, but also the baby-gurgling specialty.

Hollywood writer Sheridan Gibney was blacklisted after movie mogul Jack Warner erroneously labeled him a communist. Gibney's career remained damaged, even after Warner issued a retraction.

The actress Martha Scott also had her career interrupted by the anti-communists, even though her only offense was to share the same last name as *Red Channels* "listee" Hazel Scott.

In a report on blacklisting in 1956, researcher John Cogley told of an unnamed actor who had to devote four years to the task of proving that he did not serve with the partisans in the Abraham Lincoln Brigade during the Spanish Civil War.

These scattered cases of mistaken identity should have raised doubts about the anti-communists' methods. But in the paranoid atmosphere of the early 1950s, the doubters were ineffective and often self-defeating. The anti-communists seemed immune, lawsuit-proof, and protected from the consequences of their recklessness by an accommodating establishment, acquiescent media, and indifferent public.

CAMPAIGNING ONWARD

When it came to the latest anti-communist campaign targeting entertainers, Laurence Johnson almost always seemed to be at center stage, or,

CHAPTER NINE: Out-merchandising the Competition

at the very least, waiting in the wings. In June 1953, when young anti-communist Matthew Cvetic visited Syracuse, he met with Johnson and allies from the Veterans Action Committee of Syracuse Super Markets and Legion Post 41.

By then, the national TV networks were picking up the anti-communists' signal loud and clear. Reaping tremendous dividends from the exploding popularity of television, the last thing broadcasters wanted was controversy. As more and more sponsors were drawn to this potent new medium, profits soared—and programmers grew even more cautious.

Hartnett often found new ways to profit financially on these fears. He penned an article, "They've Moved in on TV," which appeared in the January 1953 edition of *American Legion Magazine*. Before going to press, Hartnett and Johnson contacted Borden and other companies receiving negative mentions in the article. Stuart Peabody, who handled advertising for Borden, immediately offered to hire Hartnett as a "talent consultant" to screen names of performers appearing on shows sponsored by Borden.

Ethically, Hartnett should have refused the job as a journalistic conflict of interest. Instead, he accepted, and then doubled down by modifying the article to put his new employer in a more positive light. Hartnett had the magazine add an italicized note to the article stating that Borden, in particular, had a practice "not only of providing splendid entertainment but also of making positive contributions to Americanism. For this they deserve the support of all patriotic Americans."

Years later, Hartnett would claim that he had no idea at the time that Johnson had pressed Borden to give him the consulting job.

Originally, Hartnett was paid twenty dollars for each name he checked. As his volume increased, Hartnett lowered his rate to five dollars per new name, two dollars for subsequent checks. Eventually Borden paid him a flat retainer.

Others who hired Hartnett as a clearance consultant soon included Lever Brothers, Young & Rubicam advertising agency, the Kudner advertising agency, and the American Broadcasting Company.

CAMPUS SIDESHOW

Syracuse University in the McCarthy Era found itself embroiled in some of the same anti-communism attacks that targeted college campuses across the country. On May 28, 1953, Abe Gelbart, a math professor at SU, testified before the HCUA, repeatedly invoking the Fifth Amendment when asked about his communist affiliations.

Gelbart managed to hang on to his professorship. William Tolley, Syracuse University chancellor at the time, years later recalled: "Gelbart was not a communist, but he told me that he couldn't clear himself and would have to take the Fifth. I said: 'Take it.'" Tolley noted that some other faculty at SU had been Communist Party members, but no one was fired over it.

Another threat to SU occurred when Harold Stassen, who was serving in the Eisenhower administration, arrived on campus to speak at commencement. Meeting with Tolley, he mentioned the problem of communist infiltration of university faculties.

"He told me he wanted to send someone up to see me," Tolley said. "A few days later the man came to me, showed me his dossier."

At the top of the list of suspects was Paul Appleby, dean of the Maxwell School. Appleby had raised suspicions through his New Deal associations with the likes of Henry Wallace.

"You won't get defense money until he's off your faculty," the Stassen aide warned Tolley.

"That's all right," the chancellor said he replied. "I like him. I hired him. He has a good philosophy. He has close associations, but he's not a communist. I'm not going to fire him."

As it turned out, the threat of losing defense contracts never amounted to much, and Tolley said he never even told Appleby about the confrontation.

Faculty members on other campuses did not fare as well as Gelbart and Appleby. Of forty-three students or faculty who took the Fifth before the SISS and HCUA, as of July 1953, fourteen had been fired, four resigned, four were suspended, four were deemed special cases, and fourteen had cases pending. Only three won permission to stay on campus.

CHAPTER NINE: Out-merchandising the Competition

ANTI-COMMUNIST THEATER

In Syracuse, Sam Gilman, the manager of Loew's State Theatre, got hold of the 1951 documentary "The Hoaxters." Distributed by MGM, it purported to be a condensation of two million feet of film in a blunt expose of communism from 1917 to the present. Gilman began screening the film once a week at his theater on South Salina Street. Every week, theatergoers were treated to grim footage narrated by celebrities like Marilyn Erskine, Howard Keel, George Murphy, Walter Pidgeon, Barry Sullivan, Robert Taylor, and James Whitmore.

The Syracuse anti-communists gave the film, which was nominated in 1952 for an Academy Award for Best Documentary Feature, a ringing endorsement. Dungey wrote in *Spotlight*:

> For younger members of the audience, "The Hoaxters" will present for the first time a panoramic history of Communism, its insidious methods of operation and infiltration, and the deadly parallel between the aggressive Communism of today with the forces of evil which only recently threatened the world ....Legionnaires of Onondaga County should give Sam and Loew's State support in this production of MGM.

Dungey was back on offense in September 1953 when Syracuse's Midtown Theatre screened Charlie Chaplin's "Limelight." Dungey complained in *Spotlight*: "Mr. Chaplin has seen fit to help the Communist conspiracy continuously....Does the Midtown Theatre deserve the support of Legionnaires?" Letters went out to the downtown theater, encouraging it and its customers to boycott Chaplin's new film. "This request was made because Legionnaires, who have served their country well in three wars, did not want money going to help the Communist cause," Dungey wrote.

As it turned out, the film's box-office success overcame its star's notoriety. The Midtown held over "Limelight" for an extra week.

The Legionnaires had more success singling out a couple of blacklisted actors scheduled for live theater dates in Syracuse. When word went out that Albert Dekker was to appear at the Astor Theatre on September 29, the Legionnaires printed up a broadside citing his record. A meeting was arranged between Legion Post 41's Un-American Activities Committee and Ted Isaacs, the Astor's advertising representative. Dungey reported later: "He was very courteous and at no time was it ever suggested to him that Dekker should be removed from the cast." However, the Astor dropped Dekker, buying out his contract to make certain he did not appear in Syracuse. The theater management and the Onondaga County Veterans Council issued a joint statement applauding the theater's action and admiring the Legion's "fairness."

Dungey soon learned the same Astor Theatre had booked actor Lloyd Bridges to appear in a show called "Dead Pigeon" in December. On November 15, the Legion sent a letter to the Astor asking if Bridges was still scheduled to perform. A few days later, the theater's manager announced that "Dead Pigeon" had been canceled. Dungey called the theater on November 19, and reported afterward that the manager told him the Astor had received an anonymous letter complaining about booking Bridges. The manager also claimed there was an organized campaign of harassment. Dungey denied his group was behind it:

> The American Legion is against any campaign that uses anonymous letter-writing or telephone calls. It is not in accord with the American way of fair play. The American Legion never will condone such tactics....When the American Legion protests the appearance of any individual it does not attempt to tell anyone what to do. The facts are brought before the public and they can make their own choice.

The Legion's claims of acting in a purely informational way was straight from the Laurence Johnson playbook of plausible deniability.

Johnson himself would employ it in 1953 when he helped to put the squeeze on a sponsor of one of actor Burt Lancaster's television appearances: Colgate toothpaste. That October, Johnson alerted Colgate-Palmolive-Peet Co. President Joseph McConnell to Lancaster's record of being a communist sympathizer because the actor had signed a letter supporting the Hollywood Ten.

CHAPTER NINE: Out-merchandising the Competition

Later, Colgate endured the same pressure tactics over Lancaster from John W. Neff of Neff's Markets, an influential groceryman who admired Johnson's anti-communist merchandising.

Johnson later claimed he couldn't remember urging Neff to join the campaign. But in a letter to McConnell, Neff had acknowledged the aid of Johnson and the Onondaga County Veterans Council, and he ended with a trademark Johnson flourish: Unless Colgate took steps to curtail Lancaster's TV appearances, "Neff's will be forced to advise Mr. and Mrs. Shopper that (with) every purchase they make of a Colgate-Palmolive-Peet Company product, they are helping to put extra money into the pockets of, or add to the prestige of, Communists or Communist-front causes."

Despite the threats, Lancaster's career thrived in the 1950s and beyond.

In December 1953, Johnson took on Swanson again over the TV panel show "The Name's the Same." This time, the food company's offense was to sponsor a show with Judy Holliday as a celebrity guest. Johnson wrote to the company with another of his loaded "polls," this one suggesting that two displays of Swanson products be set up in his store: one by Swanson, the other by a local patriotic organization. In one display, Swanson would defend its sponsorship of Holliday. In the other, the anti-communists would state their case against the actress and urge customers not to buy products that help to support "Stalin's little creatures."

Johnson noted he had just the group for the job: Legion Post No. 41. "Mr. Dungey and his committee wishes a test to be made on the Judy Holliday-Swanson affair," Johnson wrote, "and the case to be taken not only to the people who are buying Swanson products, but also those people Swanson's are urging through their advertising to be Swanson customers."

Johnson later would say that neither Legion Post 41 nor any other group went so far as to set up an anti-communist display over Swanson products in his supermarkets. Johnson also played down the economic threat to Swanson posed by his proposal. "I think the letter speaks for itself," he said.

The message definitely got through in 1953. An attorney for Swanson telephoned Johnson at once, making it clear that company was not interested in conducting the type of suggested poll, and that it did not want to be in conflict with the American Legion.

C.S. Swanson wrote to Johnson on January 8, 1954, assuring him that the food giant would cooperate with the anti-communist agenda "100 percent" in its advertising. Swanson attorney Cecil A. Johnson also sent a letter to William H. Harris at the American Legion's National Americanism Commission in Indianapolis, congratulating Laurence Johnson and Dungey for alerting Swanson to the communist threat. Judy Holliday did not reappear on the Swanson-sponsored TV program.

Meanwhile, Kim Hunter, the Oscar winner who had become virtually unemployable in 1953, through her agent appealed to Hartnett and another influential clearance expert, Roy Brewer, of the Motion Picture Alliance. Brewer told her agent that, to clear Hunter, "an affidavit would be necessary that would be acceptable to Mr. Hartnett."

Hartnett advised Hunter to review her communist-front record scrupulously and to put out a statement repudiating her former associations and reaffirming her loyalty. Hartnett also said he would review her record for a fee of $200.

Brewer, meanwhile, offered to coach the actress on how to clear herself. The process was to continue until 1955.

SPOTLIGHT ON 1953

Dungey and the staff of *Spotlight* in 1953 stepped up their attacks on figures in the media and show business. One target was Syd Hoff, the cartoonist whose work appeared in *Parade Magazine* and *The Saturday Evening Post*. The newsletter reported in April that he had also drawn for the *Daily Worker, People's World* "and other Communist publications" under the pseudonym "A. Redfield."

In May, Spotlight noted that choreographer Jerome Robbins had named names in testimony before the HCUA. Dungey furnished an annotated list that included Madeline Lee, wife of Jack Gilford. "We protested Gilford in the opera 'Die Fledermaus' Nov. 1951," Dungey noted.

CHAPTER NINE: Out-merchandising the Competition

In June, *Spotlight* lamented the recent elections in Actors Equity, the show business union. While blacklisted performers Kim Hunter and Joseph Anthony had been voted onto the union council, it noted, only two actors from the anti-communist slate had been chosen: Thomas Mitchell and Lois Wilson. "This election showed the apathy and lack of understanding of Communism which is prevalent today," *Spotlight* said. "Had the good people of Equity listened to the facts, and had they taken an interest in the election, the union would be in a strong position to counteract the Communists, and therefore could have contributed much to fighting this menace throughout the United States."

In September, *Spotlight* celebrated the culmination of a longstanding campaign against The Weavers. "We get this piece of information from *The Hollywood Reporter* of July 31, 1953: 'The Weavers dissolved as a singing group and Decca bought off their contract. Goodnight, Irene...'"

Other show-business targets of *Spotlight* during 1953 included Karen Morley, Howard Fast, William L. Patterson, Danny Kaye, Carey McWilliams, Patricia Neal, Beatrice Straight, Arthur Kennedy, Sam Moore, Walter Bernstein, Alexander Scourby, and Eli Wallach.

Spotlight also took aim at local alleged communist activities in 1953.

In February, Dungey and his veterans alerted the community to a couple of publications being circulated by the Syracuse and Onondaga County chapter of the American Labor Party, one under the banner "National Guardian." Both advocated left-wing causes, such as support for Roosevelt Ward Jr., a Labor Youth League leader sentenced to three years in prison for refusing to comply with his induction order. *Spotlight* wondered: "How much time, effort and money are we in Syracuse (who want to see pure Americanism survive) spending to counteract this diluted American thinking? There is much to be done before Communism is no longer a threat."

In April, *Spotlight* targeted the Labor Youth League's local chapter, whose members had been spotted passing out pamphlets outside the GE plant on Electronics Parkway just north of Syracuse. The pamphlets publicized Pope Pius XII's plea for mercy in the case of the soon-to-be-executed spies Julius and Ethel Rosenberg. "Communist propaganda," was *Spotlight*'s assessment of the pamphlets.

THE GROCER WHO SOLD McCARTHYISM

The veterans also took to task Syracuse Women for Peace, which had held a public screening of the film "A Time for Greatness," a critical analysis of U.S. Cold War policies. *Spotlight* called it a "propaganda movie," and the newsletter noted with satisfaction that attendance was sparse at St. Michael's National Club, a Slavic social organization.

FEEBLE PROTESTS

Opponents of the anti-communists were hampered in 1953 by their own caution and by the general public's willingness to tolerate blacklisting. The critiques of these "anti-anti-communists" ranged from timid to exaggerated, but none of it seemed to matter. The public wasn't listening.

One of the strongest rebuttals to the anti-communists came from an ad hoc group formed by blacklisted show-business people. They included Millard Lampell, Walter Bernstein, and Sam Moore, who began publishing a newsletter, *Facts About the Blacklist*. The first issue featured an article with a passionate and highly opinionated attack on Laurence Johnson, his methods, and those of the veterans in Syracuse working with him:

> For the astounding fact is that Johnson cannot appreciably hurt a sponsor's sales. He represents no sizable section of the public. He has met with little success and much hostility in his attempt to draw other merchants into this kind of intimidation. If ignored, all he can summon up are a few letters, many of them with the same postmark, mailed at the same time and containing identical phrases.
>
> Johnson represents no one but himself, his friends, and some of the clerks in his employ, whom he has organized into an impressive letter head called "The Veterans Action Committee of Syracuse Super Markets."
>
> And yet this man terrorizes a major American industry.

Johnson and his allies shrugged off the criticism. In *Spotlight*, John Dungey wrote that the staff of *Facts About the Blacklist* had communist and "front" records. Dungey noted that Bernstein had held office in the

CHAPTER NINE: Out-merchandising the Competition

American Legion's Duncan Paris Post, which "had its charter revoked by National Headquarters of the American Legion because it was Communist-controlled."

Many years later, Vincent Hartnett said the critics of anti-communists singled out Johnson and others in Syracuse because they were "the most determined, dogged, persistent."

"Other groups throughout the country didn't have the continuity of operation that the Syracuse groups did," he said. "I don't think they felt as keenly about it as the Syracuse groups did.

"Away from the metropolitan area, you had this different atmosphere, of not being willing to tolerate anything that even smelled of un-Americanism; so that they had a different rationale than other large organizations like the national American Legion would have. In the heartland of the country, they had the pulse of the people."

Another damning take on blacklisting appeared in January 1953, when the *New York Post* ran a six-part series by reporter Oliver Pilat entitled "Blacklist—The Panic in Radio-TV." Two parts presented an expose of Johnson, the Syracuse veterans, and *Red Channels*.

It was an attack much in the style of *Facts About the Blacklist*. Pilat's lead paragraph: "Laurence A. Johnson is a collector. He used to collect such things as grocery-store Americana, cigar store Indians, mechanical toys and piggy banks. You might say he now collects human scalps." Pilat documented how "this stocky, 63-year-old Syracuse business man exercises something approaching a veto over employment in the $2,000,000,000 radio and TV industry."

Pilat reported on his visit to Johnson's "airless cubbyhole" office in Syracuse, where the reporter apparently learned about collecting Americana but little else. Pilat quoted some sources anonymously and he claimed that Johnson was unpopular in Syracuse—at least among radio station owners and "intellectuals on campus and in town." He added:

> Johnson thinks of himself as a patriot. Others may suggest that the motives behind his devious effort may include an unconscious wish to throw his weight around, to rub shoulders with the glamorous and the great on terms of superiority, and thus anoint his own ego.

Pilat asked Johnson whether it was right for him to set himself up as judge, jury, and executioner.

Johnson's reply: "As for morality, the shepherd protects the lamb from the wolf, the lamb hails him as a benefactor but the wolf denounces him as the destroyer of his liberties. That's from Lincoln, and I may not be quoting it right."

"Clearly enough," Pilat wrote, "Johnson thought of himself as the shepherd, but what about those who had reason to fear the sharpness of his teeth?"

Far from refuting Johnson's charges or exposing flaws in his techniques, the series elevated Johnson's status as a champion of anti-communism. The rambling account's failure to substantiate most of its allegations blunted the force of Pilat's expose.

In his series, Pilat had tried to persuade readers that Johnson was a reckless, unqualified fanatic. But the overwhelming public reaction was to defend Johnson and his allies.

In the February 9 issue of *Food Field Reporter*, the editors wrote:

> Laurence A. Johnson, the well-known supermarket operator, was recently the subject of a newspaper attack....Mr. Johnson, with great persistence, and with the help of other operators including the most important chain personalities, has been devoting himself to ferreting out the alleged reds and pinks in the entertainment field. Manufacturers have been persuaded to drop this kind of citizen from their radio and TV programs ....Apparently the campaign has been more successful than has been commonly known.
>
> The Post is outraged because the "innocent" have been driven from their lucrative posts into a position of diminished earnings. Now, we are in no position to judge the merits of The Post's vehement contention that many talented young artists have been wronged, and as a matter of fact, judging from the internal evidence in the articles, The Post isn't either. Perhaps the articles are an example of objective reporting. If they are,

CHAPTER NINE: Out-merchandising the Competition

then we are at a bit of a loss to figure out how the many innuendos and gibes fit into this classification. Mr. Johnson is called a "collector of scalps" and even an illness of some time back is cited along with other things to give the impression Mr. Johnson is a terrible person.

On the other hand, the artists are given—without presentation of any special evidence—a clear bill of health. What we spell out of it all is that the man who is acting from patriotic motives is billed the scoundrel, and those accused of aiding the enemy are absolved of all blame, regardless of whether this is actually the true state or not.

Under a subhead, "Opportunity Missed," the editors of the food industry magazine added a suggestion to the *New York Post*:

It seems to us The Post has missed the opportunity for an act of great public service. It should have investigated the artists and in a series of articles shown where Mr. Johnson was wrong ….The Post also appears to have no realization that concourse with Soviet philosophy is considered the unforgivable sin of this generation, and like all sin it must be paid for with an expiation that to some seems too great a price. Sometimes, we have no doubt, the innocent are caught with the others. None wishes that. But our suspicions are aroused when the fear of injustice is greater than our zeal against the Russian portion. In the lack of any clarification of the situation, the suspicion remains that the artists now appearing white, may appear so because their eagerness for red has been diminished by a failing supply of green.

The sentence about an "eagerness for red" and "a failing supply of green" must have tickled Johnson's love of colorful phrases, because he included the article as one of the few anti-communist artifacts in his scrapbooks.

In an August 1953 article in *American Legion Magazine*, conservative columnist Victor Lasky also defended the anti-communists' scruples.

THE GROCER WHO SOLD McCARTHYISM

While he lamented honest mistakes in reporting on communist infiltration or in congressional testimony, that didn't blunt the validity of the overall effort. Speaking of *Red Channels*, Lasky wrote:

> This booklet is one of the most important anti-Communist source books yet; if not evaluated properly, the material it contains can do harm to the anti-Communist cause. In the words of the foreword to *Red Channels*, "Every safeguard must be used to protect innocents and genuine liberals from being unjustly labeled." In more than three years since *Red Channels'* publication, a score or so of those listed have made their pro-American position clear. They should not be punished for past stupidities.

Lasky concluded by recommending that anyone contemplating action against someone listed in *Red Channels* should first contact its publisher, *Counterattack*.

As 1953 ended, most Americans seemed to agree with the tactics of the anti-communists, including Senator McCarthy. He and his allies in the HCUA and SISS, together with Johnson, Hartnett, Syracuse veterans, and the men from *Counterattack* in New York City, had success after success in one of the most remarkable political pressure campaigns in American history.

Yet, in their zeal, the anti-communists seemed unconcerned with how they flirted with defamation and libel. Their denunciations had devastating consequences for careers and livelihoods, often involving unsubstantiated charges. Yet the anti-communists seemed emboldened by the fact they had gotten far without serious consequences. The few lawsuits were brushed aside, not so much because of flaws in the plaintiffs' cases, but because the tenor of the times permeated the courtroom.

So, as 1954 began, the anti-communists grew ever bolder.

THE BIRTH OF AWARE INC.

Flush with their success, Johnson and his allies had decided in 1953 they needed to form a group specifically to monitor the entertainment media. Thus, Aware Inc. was born.

CHAPTER NINE: Out-merchandising the Competition

A moving force behind Aware's founding was Godfrey P. Schmidt, a Fordham law professor who also was an attorney for New York Cardinal Francis Spellman, an anti-communist of long standing. Schmidt read children's stories on the radio, thus qualifying for membership in the American Federation of Television and Radio Artists (AFTRA), the show business union previously known as AFRA.

At a December 3, 1953, press conference at the Gotham Hotel in New York City, Schmidt made his pitch for why the group was necessary: "American entertainment-communications, employing hundreds of thousands, providing access to millions, has been and is a prime target of the international conspiracy. It seeks to use the field as a source of funds for the Communist Party and its satellites and is a lever to influence public opinion in the direction of collaboration with communism."

The officers of Aware were Schmidt as president; actor Ned Weaver as first vice president; Paul Milton, the radio and television writer formerly employed with Vincent Hartnett at the Lord agency, as second vice president; actor Richard Keith as treasurer; and Jeanne Somerville as secretary. The first board of directors included Howard Hotchner, William Neil, William Keene, Bob Novak, Jim Shean, Leigh Whipper, Wynn Wright, Vinton Hayworth, V.L. Chalif, and Vincent Hartnett.

Laurence Johnson joined Aware and actively participated in its meetings and projects, but characteristically, he avoided any official leadership role.

The Aware board adopted a ten-point program. Its authors stressed their purpose was not to "smash" individuals but to eliminate the communist conspiracy. A news release listed Aware's marching orders for 1954:

1. Planned public relations to inform the public of AWARE's purpose.

2. Distribution of material on the nature of the Communist conspiracy; its activities; and the duty of those in the entertainment field to fight back.

3. Study of publications on Communism; issuance of reading lists and notice to members of government publications.

4. Monitoring and investigation of Communist influences in all the various aspects of entertainment; distribution of facts on the organization and individuals employing Communists and fellow travelers and denying employment to non-Communists.

5. Compilation of factual material on Communist activity within the industry for the use of members, AWARE committees, etc.

6. Dissemination of facts on specific controversies arising in the industry from time to time. Public presentation of AWARE's stand.

7. Suggesting anti-Communist authorities for guest appearances on forum programs in radio and television, before organizations, etc.

8. Liaison with other anti-Communist groups both within and without the industry.

9. Study of legislation respecting Communism and development of opposition or support as required.

10. Issuance of studies exposing the misused slogans of the Communist conspiracy such as "thought control," "blacklisting," "private political beliefs," "guilt by association," and others.

From the start, Aware was in the big leagues of the anti-communist movement, feting Roy Cohn in a gala at the Waldorf and socializing with Senator McCarthy. Over the next two years, Aware's membership would approach 350.

MATUSOW FALLS APART

For young anti-communist Harvey Matusow, the decision in May 1953 to testify before Joseph McCarthy's Senate panel was supposed to be a no-brainer. McCarthy's questions concerned a subject in which Matusow supposedly was an expert—communist infiltration of the New York media. Matusow had spoken in his cross-country campaign tour about subversives at *Time, Life,* The Associated Press, and *The New York Times.*

But by asking Matusow to testify, McCarthy had inadvertently put his young aide on the spot. Matusow was now under oath as he was asked to confirm the wild charges he had made in Great Falls, Montana, and elsewhere during the 1952 campaign for McCarthy.

Before the subcommittee, after Matusow acknowledged his expertise, McCarthy said: "I would like to have you, if you will, supply us in executive session with the names of all the communists, those known to you as communists who have infiltrated the various news media whether it is radio, newspapers, or television. I know that will be quite a monumental task so we will not set any defined date, but you can get that for us at your convenience."

Matusow responded vaguely: "I will discuss that with Mr. Cohn after the session."

As he explained later, Matusow stalled because he had no basis for the charges; he had no list of communists in the media. "My answer was the only way I could get out of it," Matusow said. "I did not say yes, nor did I say no. I just said I would discuss it with Roy Cohn—an answer which I knew would take the heat off McCarthy and leave the impression that I was a reliable witness who could fulfill the task."

Following his close call before McCarthy's subcommittee, Matusow began to rethink and regret his anti-communist efforts. He would claim he had developed deep remorse for the false information that had damaged so many careers. "McCarthy's request for a list of Communist newspapermen, and the ensuing events, started me toward my eventual break with the McCarthy forces," he wrote later in his book "False Witness."

His professional reassessment came at a time of personal turmoil in his life. In August 1953, his brief marriage to Arvilla Bentley was dissolved. Matusow wrote in his diary: "I look back at my short life and find that I cannot count the dishonesties, for they are too many....Like a jet plane as it nears the sound barrier, I was building up to where I was ready to break that barrier, but something went wrong. I crashed."

He said he wrote to Senator McCarthy to explain his own actions. In his letter, Matusow condemned himself as someone who would do anything for a buck, and added a philosophical summing up:

> Next month I will be twenty-seven. Twenty-seven years of being a coward and being dishonest. I have gone through life hurting the things I love and believe in. Being dishonest with them for I was afraid that if I were honest I would be hurt by them. I was wrong....
>
> I don't want to go near politics ever again. And I never want to be part of the Communist question, pro or con. It might be that you look at this as the coward's way out, but if I am to go on as an honest—honest with myself—human being I have to use saltpeter in my living. I have to tone down my temptations which made me dishonest....I don't know which course I'll take. I still wish there were a middle ground.

Matusow said he received no reply from McCarthy.

In September 1953, Matusow left New York for Sante Fe, New Mexico, aiming to start over in a part of the country that had soothed and inspired him earlier. Driving from Reno to Las Vegas, he was overcome with despair. "I made up my mind that I would hit the accelerator of that car, and as I watched the speedometer climb, 90, 95, 100, I said to myself, I'll just keep this car on the road and at the first turn I come to, I won't turn."

Suddenly, a rabbit crossed the road in his path. As he heard the thud of the animal's body hitting the car, Matusow woke from his melancholy with a will to live and a determination to make amends for his past.

CHAPTER TEN:
McCarthyism Beyond McCarthy
(1954-1955)

IN 1954, it would not be Harvey Matusow's misgivings that would pose the first significant challenge to Senator McCarthy. That would come from CBS, which yielded to the urging of broadcast journalist Edward R. Murrow and producer Fred Friendly to allow them to assemble a program with damning footage of McCarthy in action.

On the March 9 edition of Murrow's "See It Now," the TV audience from coast to coast saw unrelenting footage of the pugnacious, squinting McCarthy as he bullied an official with the parent agency for Voice of America, scoffed at President Eisenhower, and hectored General Ralph W. Zwicker and Army Secretary Robert T. Stevens. Murrow ended the broadcast by facing the viewers head-on, unsmiling, beagle eyes wide, offering his take on McCarthyism:

> No one familiar with the history of this country can deny that congressional committees are useful....(But) the line between investigation and persecuting is a very fine one, and the junior senator from Wisconsin has stepped over it repeatedly. His primary achievement has been in confusing the public mind as between (the) internal and external threat of communism ....He didn't create this situation of fear; he merely exploited it, and rather successfully. Cassius was right: "The fault, dear Brutus, is not in our stars but in ourselves."

Murrow's broadcast was a watershed event. While it did not cause McCarthy to change his ways, it did lift the hopes of those who believed as Murrow did but dared not speak out—or who didn't have their own platform to make such views heard.

In the *New York World-Telegram,* Harriet Van Horne wrote that those who "regard the senator as the scourge...went to bed with the feeling that Mr. Murrow had permitted...McCarthy to hang himself."

The *New York Journal-American* heard from a flood of readers criticizing the broadcast, but calls and telegrams to CBS and its affiliates reportedly ran ten-to-one in favor of Murrow.

The day after the McCarthy broadcast, as Friendly waited to hear from the senator (he had been offered equal time for a response), the CBS producer had a surprise visitor: Harvey Matusow.

The way Friendly recalled it later, Matusow was having an identity crisis. "He came into my office, closed the door and said that he was impressed with Murrow's broadcast and wanted to help us 'get McCarthy.' He said he had a lot of secret information, that he had 'the goods' on the senator, and that he would like to help us."

Friendly added: "I told him that I did not think we were interested in what he had to offer."

Two days after the "See It Now" broadcast, TV cameras recorded another dramatic scene in the Senate Caucus Room as McCarthy browbeat Annie Lee Moss, a Black woman who had lost her job as a code machine operator in the Pentagon after another McCarthy witness identified her as a former Communist Party member. When it started to look like the committee had the wrong person, that she knew nothing about classified codes or communism, McCarthy abruptly excused himself from the hearing room, leaving his counsel, Roy Cohn, to clean up the mess.

Before the day ended, Senator John McClellan, a Democratic committee member from Arkansas, gave a little speech, interrupted by frequent applause. "I don't like to try people by hearsay evidence," he said. "It's not sworn testimony. It's convicting people by rumor and hearsay and innuendo."

McCarthy eventually took up Murrow's offer of equal broadcast time on CBS to respond. In his April 6 response, McCarthy chose to attack Murrow rather than defend his own behavior highlighted in the broadcast.

CHAPTER TEN: McCarthyism Beyond McCarthy (1954-1955)

"Now, ordinarily I would not take time out from the important work at hand to answer Murrow," McCarthy said. "However, in this case I feel justified in doing so because Murrow is a symbol, the leader and the cleverest of the jackal pack which is always found at the throat of anyone who dares to expose individual communists and traitors."

He dredged up Murrow's participation in the Moscow summer school of 1935. (True enough. Murrow had served as an adviser to the international institute that Stalin had praised for providing "the socialist motherland with educated, cultured, and active warriors for communism.") McCarthy also attempted to link Murrow to the sins of Stalin and the "loss" of China. He noted that the *Daily Worker* had made a favorable reference to "See It Now" in its TV listings, as did blacklisted individuals Owen Lattimore and Harold Laski.

CBS stood by Murrow, and President Eisenhower, in a news conference, made a point afterward of referring to Murrow as "my friend."

In a subsequent "See It Now," Murrow defended himself against McCarthy's charges. However, an internal CBS survey showed 33 percent of respondents thought McCarthy had succeeded in raising legitimate questions whether Murrow had pro-communist leanings.

For the time being, McCarthyism was still packing plenty of power.

McCARTHY VS. THE ARMY

Senator McCarthy had more to contend with in March 1954 than a feisty CBS broadcaster. The press was making much of McCarthy's and Cohn's flouting of military protocol in seeking special treatment for their assistant, G. David Schine, who had been inducted into the Army the year before.

A furious McCarthy alleged the Army was holding Schine "hostage" in exchange for an end to McCarthy's Army probe. Army Secretary Stevens said the charge was "utterly untrue."

The matter came to a head in what became known as the Army-McCarthy hearings, called to sort out the conflicting stories. Up to then, McCarthy had enjoyed the television spotlight and how it amplified his claims, true or not. However, these televised hearings in the Senate Caucus Room between April 22 and June 17, 1954, were different: McCarthy was not fully in charge of his own subcommittee; his primary role was as a witness. The hearings opened with an acting chairman, South Dakota Republican Senator Karl Mundt, a close ally of McCarthy.

As the committee attempted to gain clarity on the Schine affair, McCarthy went again on the offensive, trying to keep the focus on alleged transgressions by Army personnel, including Stevens.

Army counsel Joseph Welch, a courtly, bow-tied Boston attorney, had his hands full as McCarthy and his counsel grilled the Army secretary.

Then McCarthy blundered. A photo was introduced of the Army secretary and Schine standing alone together, presumably an attempt by McCarthy to show the young serviceman didn't need his help to enjoy privileged status. When Welch claimed the original was a group photo, McCarthy accused him of "lying." Cohn and Schine insisted that no one was edited out.

But then Welch produced a wider version of the picture, revealing that Stevens and Schine had been photographed with two others. To their critics, this proved that McCarthy and Cohn were "cropping" evidence to make their case.

Welch called it a "doctored photo" and asked if a "Pixie" had produced it, apparently a reference to a model of camera. When McCarthy gamely asked Welch to define "pixie," Welch grinned and replied, eyes glittering, that "a pixie is a close relative of a fairy. Have I enlightened you?"

Welch's quip might have passed as a light moment, but it was nothing of the sort, according to author Richard Gid Powers. In Welch's "fairy" remark, McCarthy might accurately have concluded it was a sly reference to Cohn being gay. McCarthy believed he had a deal with Welch not to refer to Cohn's closeted homosexuality, which many believed included infatuation with his handsome protégé Schine. In exchange, McCarthy would not mention Frederick G. Fisher, Welch's young law associate who once belonged to the National Lawyers Guild, which had been listed as a communist front.

The hearings continued. On June 9, Welch pressed Cohn as to why, if he and McCarthy had information about communist subversion at the

CHAPTER TEN: McCarthyism Beyond McCarthy (1954-1955)

Army base in Fort Monmouth, they kept it in their files for months without telling anyone, including the Army secretary. "And you didn't tug at his lapel and say, 'Mr. Secretary, I know something about Monmouth that won't let me sleep nights?'"

McCarthy had had enough. He jumped up and spoke into the TV cameras: "In view of Mr. Welch's request that the information be given ...I think we should tell him that he has in his law firm a young man named Fisher whom he recommended, incidentally, to do work on this committee, who has been for a number of years a member of an organization which was named—oh, years and years ago—the legal bulwark of the Communist Party...."

As McCarthy spoke, Welch listened in white-faced anger. Cohn sat slumped in his chair, shaking his head. Finally, Senator Mundt broke in to observe that, to his knowledge, Welch had never recommended Fisher to the committee.

Then Welch took over. "Senator McCarthy," he began, his voice shaking, his image flickering on TV screens across the nation. "Until this moment, Senator, I think I never really gauged your cruelty or your recklessness."

Welch explained that Fisher worked for him, and that he had been considered for the team working for the Army. But when Fisher told Welch of his prior association with the National Lawyers Guild, Welch said, the decision was made to keep him off the case.

"Little did I dream that you could be so reckless and so cruel as to do an injury to that lad," Welch said in the hushed hearing room. "If it were in my power to forgive you for your reckless cruelty, I would do so. I like to think I'm a gentle man, but your forgiveness will have to come from someone other than me."

In the hearing room, McCarthy attempted to regain the moral high ground. He complained that Welch had been "baiting Mr. Cohn here for hours," and that the senator only wanted to put the matter of Fisher on the record.

Welch interrupted: "Senator, may we not drop this? We know he belonged to the Lawyers Guild....Let us not assassinate this lad further,

Senator; you've done enough. Have you no sense of decency, sir? At long last, have you left no sense of decency?"

When the senator attempted another question, Welch added, "Mr. McCarthy, I will not discuss this further with you. You have sat within six feet of me and could have asked me about Fred Fisher. You have seen fit to bring it out. And if there is a God in heaven it will do neither you nor your cause any good. I will not discuss it further."

He then directed the chairman to call the next witness.

After the applause died in the caucus room, Senator Mundt called a five-minute recess. McCarthy looked around at his unsmiling audience, spread his hands palm upward and wondered aloud: "What did I do wrong?"

It is difficult to separate the showmanship from the genuine outrage in Welch's eloquence. Few of those in his national TV audience knew that Fisher's record was already public knowledge, even reported in *The New York Times*. Fisher did not suffer professionally. He remained an attorney with Welch's law firm, Hale & Dorr, and later was made a partner.

However, for many Americans watching on television, this tussle marked the moment when they finally had enough of McCarthy's careless and conniving ways. One poll right after the hearings showed more Americans disapproved of McCarthy than approved of him.

THE AFTERMATH

In Syracuse, *The Post-Standard* editors, still smarting from McCarthy's libel suit the previous year, lamented in a May 4 editorial that the televised hearings were mainly contrary to the national interest. "The Washington Circus," as they called it, unnecessarily dragged the Army through the dirt.

"Perhaps its only advantage," the freshly emboldened editors continued, "is that it has given the nation a chance to see Joe McCarthy stripped of any pretense of sincere anti-communism, shown up as the wily, essentially selfish and self-seeking politician that he is."

This was strong stuff for many in Syracuse. On May 9, *The Post-Standard* printed nine letters from local readers, all of them either defending the Wisconsin senator or criticizing the editorial.

CHAPTER TEN: McCarthyism Beyond McCarthy (1954-1955)

"As far as I can see," Florence T. Hopkins wrote, "he has conducted himself with honor, trying to get the truth out of those who were obstructing justice."

Janet F. Moe objected to a headline suggesting that McCarthy "yelled." "Thanks to television, I was at the hearing too," she wrote, "and he did not 'yell.' He did rise and speak his protest with feeling."

Anne Hueber worried that the hearings were interfering with Senator McCarthy's mission. "The Communists are positively pleased that Mr. McCarthy's work of investigation is stopped," she wrote. She suggested she could not count on *The Post-Standard*'s coverage: "I have taken to getting my information from factual reports." One such report, she said, was "The Red Plot Against America," a novel by HCUA counsel Robert Stripling.

Also on May 9, *The Post-Standard* carried a syndicated editorial cartoon titled "Joy in the Red Fox Den." It depicted the Army-McCarthy hearings as a full-scale dogfight observed by a quartet of gleeful foxes labeled U.S. Reds, Saboteur, Spy, and Fellow Traveler.

In another editorial, the editors stressed their own strong anti-communism, distinguishing it from McCarthy's tactics and making the point that the senator himself was to blame for distracting the dogs from the pursuit of the foxes of subversion. The editors wrote:

> While we have never believed that McCarthy was a sincere anti-Communist, we have nevertheless felt that the many very obvious good results of McCarthy and McCarthyism outweighed the many very obvious bad features of the man and the adjective describing his activity.
>
> Today, this view needs reappraisal, and it is receiving it, in this newspaper and in many others, including even The Chicago Tribune, and most important of all, with the people themselves, as the polls show.
>
> In the earlier days from 1950 to the end of 1953, McCarthy did a great service for America in awakening this nation from the "red-herring" apathy toward Communism....His accomplishments are more in the general than in the specific, however.

> He has not convicted one Communist of anything. Of the 35 suspended at Fort Monmouth, many have been cleared and returned to work and other files are being examined. None was a Communist, and none took the Fifth Amendment.
>
> Many branded by him in the headlines, like Annie Lee Moss of Washington, turned out to be nothing more than a case of completely mistaken identity....The bad of McCarthy now outweighs the good, he has tried to arrogate to himself the powers of prosecutor, judge and juror. He has pulled the prestige of the nation to shocking depths, at a time when prestige is so vital a factor to us in these days of peril....From here on, unless the leopard changes his spots, the country has arrived at its own assessment of the man, and we shall, when this is over, hear less and less of him in the future.

In July, stung by letters and phone calls criticizing their coverage of the senator, *The Post-Standard* editors published a score sheet of "pro" and "anti" McCarthy headlines in the paper since the beginning of the Army-McCarthy hearings. There were eleven "anti-McCarthy" headlines, thirteen that seemed "pro-McCarthy," and seventeen others they termed neutral. "It is time to lay this phony issue to rest," the editors wrote. "The Post-Standard has been entirely fair...."

By then, "McCarthyism" had firmly entered the American lexicon as a pejorative. The American College Dictionary listed the term with the following definitions: "(1) Public accusation of disloyalty...unsupported by truth, (2) Unfairness in investigative technique."

At the end of August, Senator Mundt and his subcommittee issued a split decision on the Army-McCarthy hearings. McCarthy himself was cleared of misconduct. However, even the Republicans concluded the senator had failed to rein in his staff (i.e. Cohn) in seeking favors for Schine. All of McCarthy's counterchages against the Army were dismissed. The Democrats insisted that "Sen. McCarthy and Mr. Cohn merit severe criticism."

By November, with the U.S. Senate considering disciplinary action against the unrepentant McCarthy, his supporters gathered in Madison Square Garden for a "God Bless McCarthy" rally during which one

CHAPTER TEN: McCarthyism Beyond McCarthy (1954-1955)

speaker called for solidarity in the "long and perhaps bloody fight" against the "hidden force" of communist subversion.

Noting this kind of pressure on the U.S. Senate not to censure McCarthy, the editors of *Spotlight* in Syracuse took aim at his critics. "We wonder now if the many 'liberal' commentators and newspapers will be shouting about the intimidation of the Senate," the newsletter observed. "These papers never did complain about the Communists picketing Congress or the White House."

On December 2, the Senate reached its decision. Having considered a list of charges against McCarthy, it chose "condemnation," a lesser rebuke than censure. The final vote was 67 to 22. Although the punishment was relatively mild, it permanently undercut McCarthy's power in Congress.

In Syracuse, the editors of *Spotlight* refused to acknowledge McCarthy had been discredited. They headlined their lead editorial of the January 1955 issue "Congratulations on a Job Well Done," and managed to turn McCarthy's departure from the investigating subcommittee into a hero's farewell. "To you, Senator Joseph R. McCarthy, our sincere thanks and congratulations on the magnificent job done as chairman of the Permanent Senate Investigations subcommittee," the newsletter continued. "We hope that the next chairman will do as well."

The editorial concluded with a couple of well-wishes that turned out to be wide of the mark. "Keep your right up in order to counter the jabs from the left and good luck and good health. We will be hearing from you again."

Not long afterward, McCarthy's health deteriorated amid his heavy drinking; he seldom made headlines again. He died in 1957 at age forty-eight of symptoms related to chronic alcoholism.

THE AWARD GOES TO ...

Even as McCarthy was facing a reckoning in the Senate for his tactics, other anti-communist activists took pains to pat each other on the back. The Onondaga County American Legion presented its Americanism medal to Alfred Kohlberg, the entrepreneur and financier who helped *Counterattack* and Aware Inc. get started. Kohlberg visited Syracuse for the occasion on March 11, 1954, and gave a talk entitled "Foreign Policy: Shield the Republic?" *Spotlight*'s editors noted Kohlberg was being recognized because of his "untiring and patriotic work in the fight to keep the United States American and free from foreign influence...."

On April 10, in honor of the thirty-fifth anniversary of American Legion Post No. 41 in Syracuse, *The Post-Standard* printed an editorial tribute: "With the current emphasis on Communism and its plans for world conquest, the mission of those agencies which fight Communism intelligently by positive Americanism programs becomes more important than ever."

The Stanley Pennock Post 2893 of the Veterans of Foreign Wars in the Syracuse suburb of Solvay awarded Laurence Johnson its citizenship medal on April 18. *The Post-Standard* covered the event, noting that Johnson was honored "in recognition of his fight against Communism."

On April 30, *Post-Standard* reporter Luther "Gus" Bliven received a special citation and the Citizenship Medal from the Onondaga County American Legion's Un-American Activities Committee for his series, "Communism in Central New York." Noted the editors of *Spotlight*: "He placed the facts before the public after tireless research. There is a great need for factual reporting. Recognition by the Legion is one recompense for the effort involved."

On May 25, Johnson received the Americanism Citation from the Catholic War Veterans.

Johnson enjoyed another moment in the spotlight on July 28 when he was introduced during a New York City testimonial dinner for Roy Cohn, by then the ex-counsel for McCarthy's subcommittee. Attendance at the affair on a sweltering Wednesday evening was 2,000. ("Another 6,000 were turned away," *Spotlight* reported in September.) Sharing the accolades were Westbrook Pegler, J.B. Matthews, Louis Budenz and Victor Lasky. Tributes for Cohn came from Aware Inc. President Godfrey Schmidt, Senator McCarthy, and conservative author William F. Buckley Jr. "Sen. McCarthy received an especially long accolade," *Spotlight* noted, before turning to the guest of honor. "Visibly affected by the tributes paid him, Roy Cohn rose to respond, the most important point in his speech was that he will continue his fight against atheistic Communism...."

CHAPTER TEN: McCarthyism Beyond McCarthy (1954-1955)

In the fall of 1954, Francis Neuser of the Veterans Action Committee of Syracuse Super Markets won national recognition at the VFW convention in Philadelphia. Neuser also was named New York State chairman of the VFW's Un-American Activities Committee. A news item about Neuser in the *Food Merchants Advocate* noted the close coordination among Johnson, VAC, and the American Legion:

> Neuser was instrumental in founding VAC a few years ago, an organization whose members watch television, radio and movie programs sponsored by leading food manufacturers in an effort to detect any sign of subversive talent. Members of the group work closely with the American Legion and have access to latest government reports. They claim some 300 actors and actresses known to be members of Communist-front organizations have felt the influence of VAC, when they have been "pulled off" radio or television programs sponsored by food companies. VAC makes its headquarters in one of the Johnson stores and has had the ardent support of the well-known grocer.

Spotlight, in its September issue, offered its own accolades for VAC's leader:

> Mr. Neuser's introduction to vital work against subversion was made through the efforts of Laurence A. Johnson....(VAC) has done a remarkable piece of work in bringing to the attention of radio and television sponsors the fact that Communists and Commie fronts were working on their programs and that some of the money paid them must back their un-American plans. The Veterans Action Committee has also done a terrific job in giving the facts to the consumer by speaking and letter writing and letting this final judge decide which product to buy ....Spotlight salutes Franny Neuser as a hard-working Legionnaire and for his recognition by the VFW. We are proud to have him as a member of our editorial staff.

While the Syracuse anti-communists savored their successes in 1954, they were not complacent. At American Legion Post No. 41, *Spotlight* editor Dungey launched a bylined column in September, "What's New in Red Circles." In October, he warned: "Informed sources say that the Reds are planning a new drive into radio, TV and the movies."

In December, at a two-day district convention in Syracuse, American Legion Commander Jim McHale scheduled an Anti-Subversive Seminar at Legion Post No. 41 followed by a dinner dance. Among those asked to address the gathering were Father Joseph La Manna of Schenectady, whose anti-communist work had focused on the GE plants there; Lee Pennington, national chairman of the Legion's Americanism Committee; and George S. Schuyler, the Black journalist and commentator listed by *Pageant* magazine as "one of six top anti-Communists."

History buff Johnson's influence on *Spotlight* was apparent in the November 1954 issue, which included the headline: "Commie Fronters and Named Communists Show Up In 'Folklore' and 'New York History'." The subhead read: "Official Publications of New York State Historical Assoc. and Its affiliate The Farmers Museum use Pete Seeger and Morris U. Schappes as Feature Writers."

The article shared a long letter sent to two dozen directors and officers of the state Historical Association by Robert P. Flood, chairman of the Onondaga County American Legion's Un-American Activities Committee, complaining about the alleged communist and pro-communist records of Seeger, Schappes and a third individual, Les Rice, profiled in a *New York Folklore Quarterly* article. "We are presenting these facts to you with the thought that many of you might like to comment on this situation for our American Legion publication Spotlight," Flood wrote.

This pressure campaign met with little success. In January 1955, *Spotlight* editors noted that "only two people of the twenty-two who were warned of the conditions in their organizations bothered to answer the letters sent them." They noted further that December's issue of *Folklore* contained an article by scholar B.A. Botkin, one of at least seven blacklisted people associated with the publication. In March 1955, Dungey used his newsletter column to urge readers to complain to the president of the New York Folklore Society.

CHAPTER TEN: McCarthyism Beyond McCarthy (1954-1955)

JOHNSON'S NEW PRIORITY

Johnson's anti-communist anger would eventually target dozens of products, according to Mary Coyne, his business manager. She said Johnson hired a secretary to handle the paperwork and other chores connected to the wide-ranging correspondence and projects related to his anti-communist work.

As Johnson deployed his anti-communism strategies with undiminished zeal, this work began to interfere with efficient operation of his stores, Coyne said. By the mid-1950s, Johnson was sweeping whole shelves clean of products whose manufacturers sponsored what he considered the "wrong" shows.

Product after product came under Johnson's interdict, with his employees carting them back and forth, first off the shelves and out of the store, then back, then out again when an offending actor reappeared on a radio or TV show carrying advertising by that product's manufacturer.

Coyne remembered how Johnson "blew up" once over a listed actor appearing on a show sponsored by Kraft. "Well, here was a fellow selling Kraft cheese who (Johnson decided) wasn't good enough to be an American," she said. "So what he [Johnson] did, and this was the crux of it, he'd get so upset, we had to hide the Kraft cheese."

Johnson continued to use his membership in the Super Market Institute as leverage when he called Kraft to complain. "He would say, 'I am Laurence Johnson and I resent this actor appearing for the sponsor,' and he said what he was doing about it," Coyne said. "The Kraft people just made the cheese and set the money aside for advertising. However, they paid the bill. So, they would immediately notify their (advertising) agency and say, 'Now, you just stop this!'"

Neuser and Johnson held weekly meetings with allies, working in concert with Dungey and the American Legion. There were business trips to New York City, during which Johnson, sometimes accompanied by Neuser or others, would stay at the Hampshire House or the Barbizon and go out for meetings with Hartnett, attend Aware sessions, or call on advertising agency executives—in addition to doing supermarket business, Coyne said.

Johnson's anti-communist activism had become "an obsession," eventually a higher priority for him than supermarket innovation and retail merchandising, she said. He watched television every night, Coyne said, and if he saw a program with someone he thought was a communist, he would direct employees to remove its sponsors' products from his shelves.

Coyne recalled one time when an employee asked where they would store all the products they had to remove. "He [Johnson] didn't care. He didn't want people to buy Lipton soup, or Campbell soup, or Proctor & Gamble."

Before long, Johnson's anti-communist orders began to hurt his supermarket sales. "It affected our business," Coyne said. "If your wife wants to go in and buy Lipton soup, she doesn't want to buy something else. We couldn't just push something else on display. Our normal business was to merchandise, and it got to the point where we just couldn't merchandise, because he felt so strongly."

THE STOUFFER SURVEY

In 1954, critics of Johnson and his allies grew bolder. Even the broadcasting executives showed less fear of them, especially after the Army-McCarthy hearings. NBC-TV canceled its anti-communist series, "Last Man Out," on March 28. The editors of *Spotlight* took note and advised: "CBS or ABC should be interested in this educational program." They weren't.

In May, the Emergency Civil Liberties Committee (another blacklisted group) assessed the atmosphere of paranoia and suspicion, and it issued a warning: "The threat to civil liberties in the United States today is the most serious in the history of our country."

That same month came the publication of *Facts About the Blacklist, No. 2*, edited by Walter Bernstein and Sam Moore. The tract leveled more criticism at Johnson and his allies, especially American Business Consultants Inc.

A more scientific approach came from Harvard Professor Samuel A. Stouffer, whose team of scholars and researchers gathered information for a landmark study of American attitudes toward the communist threat.

CHAPTER TEN: McCarthyism Beyond McCarthy (1954-1955)

Under the auspices of the Fund for the Republic, itself a target of the anti-communists, Stouffer spent $125,000 and sent 530 interviewers to visit 8,800 homes and make 15,000 phone calls. The broad questions Stouffer wanted answered included: How tolerant are Americans of communists and other non-conformists, and are attitudes toward both related? Is there a genuine national crisis of anxiety over the Red menace? What do people fear or distrust most about communism? Are people concerned about risking liberties in order to crack down on the alleged communist conspiracies?

For his unprecedented survey, Stouffer reached out to "local community leaders," concentrating on 123 cities with populations of 150,000 or less. Syracuse's population was about 220,000 at the time, so it would not be included. But had Syracuse been surveyed, the researchers would not have interviewed Laurence Johnson because they focused on formal civic leaders. Johnson belonged to the Kiwanis Club, the Onondaga Historical Association, Liederkranz, and Sons of the American Revolution. He was also a member of Aware Inc. and was a *Spotlight* contributor, but his leadership role in local civic groups and the anti-communist establishment was, by choice, an informal one.

Stouffer's report, published in 1955 in a volume entitled "Communism, Conformity and Civil Liberties" suggested that fear of communism among Americans wasn't as extreme as some supposed.

At the same time, hardly anyone surveyed expressed sympathy for communist doctrines: Seventy-seven percent said communists should lose their citizenship. Ninety-four percent opposed hiring atheists to teach in college. Sixty-four percent supported wiretapping to gather evidence against communists. Seventy-three percent said they would report suspicious neighbors or acquaintances to the FBI as possible subversives. Fifty-one percent favored jailing communists.

However, when survey respondents were asked if an employer should fire workers whose loyalty has been questioned but who swore they were not communists, the overwhelming majority answered no.

Respondents also were asked if they would follow the advice of someone in their community who suggested they stop buying a particular brand of soap because the manufacturer advertised on a radio show with a particular singer. Ninety-two percent of community leaders said no, as did eighty-three percent of a national cross-section of respondents.

What about boycotting a brand of soap because it was being advertised on a show with a *communist* radio singer? In the national sample, thirty-six percent said they would go along with the boycott, while fifty-six percent still said they would not "stop buying that soap." That response suggested that, even if a network refused to fire a communist actor, even if the sponsor refused to drop the show, and even if Johnson led a boycott, most consumers would still buy the product.

The last finding would once again prompt the question: Was Johnson's threat far less potent than broadcasters and advertisers believed? If so, it would rank as one of the most overblown yet effective bluffs in merchandising history.

HARVEY MATUSOW'S DEFECTION

Anti-communist activist Harvey Matusow had spent the fall of 1953 seriously overweight and brooding after flirting with suicide during his drive west. He managed to find work at radio station KTRC-AM in Santa Fe, New Mexico, which was geographically and spiritually about as far as he could get from Laurence Johnson and the Aware activists back East. However, he couldn't escape the past completely; the local paper learned Matusow was working in town, and it printed an article under the headline, "Commie Hunting Harvey Matusow Takes Job with Radio Station." A false rumor was even circulating that he was in Sante Fe to work undercover for Senator McCarthy.

In the fall, Matusow agreed to testify before the federal Subversive Activities Control Board in Washington, D.C. It was investigating the Labor Youth League, of which Matusow had been a charter member. He returned to the SACB to testify against the Council on American-Soviet Friendship and the Veterans of the Abraham Lincoln Brigade.

"When I was first contacted, I hedged, not committing myself," Matusow said later. "But I appeared before the…(SACB) and justified my testimony by saying to myself, I will have nothing to do with the congressional hearings."

CHAPTER TEN: McCarthyism Beyond McCarthy (1954-1955)

Matusow moved to Washington but declined an invitation to appear again before the SACB, this time concerning the Jefferson School, a communist-led adult education program in New York City.

In February 1954, he received a letter from Charles F. Herring, the U.S. attorney in Austin, Texas, thanking him for his testimony in helping to convict Clinton E. Jencks, the labor organizer and dashing young president of the International Union of Mine, Mill and Smelter Workers in New Mexico. Jencks was found guilty of violating the Taft-Hartley Act by falsifying an affidavit vowing he wasn't a communist. What Herring didn't know is that Matusow had invented testimony at the trial of Jencks.

Now suffering pangs of guilt, Matusow said, he went to see G. Bromley Oxnam, the outspoken Methodist bishop in Washington, D.C. Matusow asked for help in undoing the harm he had done to innocent people. Oxnam took Matusow's plea seriously in a very personal way since the bishop himself had been a victim of accusations by Matusow and others of having communist sympathies.

Before long, Matusow was subpoenaed by the HCUA, which asked him about Bishop Oxnam's public revelations of their private meeting, including Matusow's confession to Oxnam of lying before congressional committees.

"I hemmed and hawed, giving evasive answers," Matusow said. "Did Bishop Oxnam lie? I was asked. And all I could answer was, 'I would call him a dishonest man.'"

Even so, Matusow took a further step away from his past on March 24, 1954, by signing an affidavit recanting the allegations of communist infiltration that he had leveled at *Time* magazine in 1952.

During the remainder of 1954, Matusow strengthened his resolve to abandon anti-communism. Matusow met with two lawyers, Nathan Witt and John T. McTernan, both acknowledged communists. Witt, who had represented Clinton Jencks, heard about Matusow's change of heart and thought the young man could help his client. Matusow agreed to cooperate.

Pro-Soviet publicist Albert E. Kahn offered Matusow a book deal to detail his false testimony. Between October and the end of 1954, Matusow,

Witt, and Kahn held up to a dozen tape-recorded conversations. Then Matusow started putting it all into a book.

There was no looking back at that point. On January 20, 1955, Matusow signed an affidavit recanting his testimony against Jencks. He signed another on January 31, taking back his testimony against twelve communists convicted in the Smith Act trials in New York City in 1952. He also claimed that Roy Cohn coached him on his false testimony.

Matusow's 250-page book was published in February. In a play on ex-communist Whittaker Chambers' 1952 memoir, "Witness," Matusow titled his book "False Witness."

Matusow's past allies and foes swiftly reacted to his public defection from anti-communism. Fellow informer Herbert Philbrick wrote in the *New York Herald-Tribune* that Matusow was nothing more than a money-grubbing publicity seeker. Bella V. Dodd, a New York City labor organizer, said he was "acting the part of a communist plant."

The anti-communist activists in Syracuse also reassessed their erstwhile ally. With disdain reserved for the traitor in their midst, John Dungey and the editors of *Spotlight* headlined their story, "Harvey Matusow: Renegade Communist." They wrote:

> Matusow has the singular distinction of being a double turncoat. He reported with great glee and exact detail on his knowledge of the Communist conspiracy. Now, with equal relish, he says all that was lies to involve people in the unsavory stew he was creating. His motive in the first place was supposed disillusionment with the evils of Communism, his present motives are obscure but seem to hinge on the proceeds of a book or becoming an actor.
>
> It is dubious that this man can do much harm to the anti-communist cause....It is to be hoped that Matusow will never make a cent out of the curiosity of people who want to read his book for the sensational aspects. Let the fronters and fellow travelers buy it and support him in his degradation.

Based on Matusow's affidavit, the Smith Act defendants filed a motion for a new trial. At hearings on the motion in federal court in February,

CHAPTER TEN: McCarthyism Beyond McCarthy (1954-1955)

Matusow drew Laurence Johnson into this new controversy. Matusow said Johnson kept "his own blacklist," and he also told of Johnson's threats to boycott products of sponsors of the "Schlitz Playhouse of Stars" in 1952. Matusow also revealed the grocer's efforts to get Matusow hired by the Lennen & Mitchell advertising agency "to draw up a blacklist for its guidance" in connection with the "Playhouse" and its sponsors.

News coverage of Matusow's testimony carried denials from the advertising firm—then renamed Lennen & Newell—that there had ever been a relationship, or even a meeting, between the agency and Johnson.

When newspapers hit the streets carrying the story of Matusow's betrayal of anti-communists, Johnson was in Chicago on a business trip. A reporter for *The Post-Standard* reached him the evening he returned to Syracuse. Johnson claimed he had played no part in any conferences involving Matusow's hiring. He also denied carrying out any lobbying on Matusow's behalf, although Johnson's denial came with considerable vagueness: "I had nothing to do with any setup like that." Pressed further, Johnson said he recalled having met Matusow at a large gathering in New York City. The reporter continued: "Mr. Johnson stated flatly that at no time did he, Matusow and a Lennen & Newell Agency official ever meet to discuss the Schlitz program or the agency's hiring of Matusow to prepare a blacklist."

As for his efforts to keep communists off the air, Johnson told the newspaper, "I never published any blacklist." The Syracuse supermarket operator also misleadingly insisted that he had "never refused to handle" any product and that "we have never boycotted anything."

Top law enforcement officials were openly skeptical of Matusow's recantations. U.S. Attorney General Herbert Brownell argued that Matusow's recantation was "part of a concerted drive to discredit government witnesses, the security program, and ultimately our sense of justice." He claimed Matusow had not been lying in his earlier testimony—that, instead, he was lying now in claiming that he had lied earlier.

A federal grand jury began scrutinizing whether Matusow's recantation was itself a communist plot. However, no one could prove anyone had brainwashed Matusow into writing "False Witness."

Matusow was called to El Paso, Texas, where he appeared before federal judge Robert E. Thomason, who sentenced him to three years in prison for contempt of court—not for Matusow's testimony in the Jencks case but for the affidavit contradicting his past testimony. Like Brownell, Thomason decided to believe Matusow was lying now, not then.

"You deliberately and maliciously and designedly schemed to obstruct justice and cause the filing of an affidavit that obtained this hearing on a motion for a new trial," Thomason said at sentencing. "You attempted to obstruct justice to put aside the conviction of Clinton Jencks to further your personal ends."

Matusow appealed, and Judge Thomason's contempt sentence was reversed.

As for Clinton Jencks, the U.S. Supreme Court threw out his conviction, too.

By April 1955, federal judge Edward J. Dimock had agreed to new trials for Alexander Trachtenberg and George Black Charney, two of the Smith Act defendants convicted based, in part, on Matusow's now-recanted testimony. Both were convicted again, creating further confusion over Matusow's credibility.

On July 13, 1955, a federal grand jury indicted Matusow, charging him with six counts of perjury for lying on the witness stand.

That November, the Syracuse anti-communists took one last shot at Matusow. In his *Spotlight* column, Dungey argued that the record should stand since Matusow was the only one who had changed his testimony, and since he was a discredited witness. Dungey added:

> Harvey Matusow threw a pall of doubt over the testimony given by him and others who testified against the Reds. The Left quickly picked up the cry that you could not believe the Anti-Communists.
>
> The truth always will come to the fore. Here it is, short and simple. The answer is that the 194 persons named by Matusow in testimony were given the opportunity by the House Committee on Un-American Activities to deny, explain or admit

CHAPTER TEN: McCarthyism Beyond McCarthy (1954-1955)

Communist party membership as pointed out by Harvey Matusow. Not one of the 194 have contacted the committee and appeared voluntarily to deny membership.

Until that time when any one of those named by Matusow take advantage of the HUAC invitation we as Legionnaires must in conscience say "that Matusow's testimony is on the record and stands unrefuted even by him."

By the time of his ten-day trial in September 1956, Matusow had slimmed to 150 pounds—due to a strenuous diet, he explained, along with a healthier outlook. His erstwhile ally Roy Cohn, now building a lucrative law practice in New York City, denied allegations under oath that he had encouraged Matusow to lie. He said if he had known how unreliable Matusow was, he would never have allowed him to testify in the Smith Act trials. Seemingly heedless of his own fate, Matusow in open court referred to himself as a "vicious liar," admitting at one point, "I don't even trust myself."

On September 26, he was convicted of five counts of perjury. According to one report, Matusow "slumped in his chair and brought his hand to his eyes as he heard the verdict." Judge John F.X. McGohey sentenced Matusow to five years in prison. Matusow had a statement ready: "Harvey Matusow is dead as far as I'm concerned....He died a year or a year and a half ago. I took his body. Morally, I have to accept what is coming to me. I will never have to be ashamed of anything I do from this day forward."

In Syracuse, there was no indication that McCarthy's comeuppance or Matusow's recantations gave Laurence Johnson and his allies any second thoughts about their anti-communist crusade.

CHAPTER ELEVEN:
The Crest of the Anti-communist Wave

THE Cold War lost some of its chill in 1955. The Soviet Union recognized democratic West Germany and withdrew the last of its occupation troops from Austria. Soviet leadership was even denouncing Stalin's reign of terror and calling for peaceful coexistence with the West.

But the Soviet Union also tightened its grip on parts of Europe. On May 14, it signed a treaty of mutual assistance in which Poland, Albania, Bulgaria, Czechoslovakia, Hungary, Romania, and East Germany officially became Warsaw Pact nations behind the Iron Curtain, in thrall to the vast USSR.

In July, President Eisenhower met his Soviet counterpart Khrushchev in Geneva. It was a summit meeting heavier on symbolism than substance, though it bothered the editors of *Spotlight* in Syracuse enough to warn "The Geneva Spirit" had "lulled many Americans into a false sense of security." The editors continued:

> The goal of Communism is the same. Only the methods of attainment of world conquest by the Communists have changed. The Soviet agents in this country are vigorously pressing for the end of our security system.
>
> Unless Americans wake up and demand the truth from the local press we will be free no longer....(This) is not the outlook fifty years hence but in ten, maybe fifteen years, at the most.

At home in the mid-1950s, though, most Americans seemed more intent on grabbing their share of the good life than worrying about communism. Even some anti-communists, buoyed by their successes, believed their job was done. Concrete evidence was plentiful: The Smith, Taft-Hartley, and McCarran laws were in the books; loyalty programs were in place on the federal, state, and local levels, and it seemed anyone with a hint of a communist past had trouble finding work in television, radio or movies, let alone in government or in schools.

"In the late 1950s and the early 1960s there wasn't the same threat, the same danger for internal communism as there was in the early 1950s," Vincent Hartnett said later. "I think by 1955 the entertainment industry was thoroughly alerted to this, and the trade unions also."

By one estimate, anti-communist campaigns had removed 106 writers, thirty-six actors, eleven directors, and various other show-business talent from employment, for a total of 214 persons. Still, the anti-communist activists saw more work to do. In 1955, Hartnett and Jack Wren, the "clearance" man for Batten, Barton, Durstine & Osborn, were calling each other at least twice a month.

Years later, television producer David Susskind offered a snapshot of this outside clearance for his anthology show, "Appointment with Adventure." Between April 1955 and March 1956, Susskind submitted as many as 5,000 names for clearance through the advertising agency Young & Rubicam, which forwarded names to Hartnett. Within 48 hours, the names would come back as approved or rejected. Susskind said the rejection rate for this show was 33 percent, "perhaps a little higher."

The process played out in secrecy, Susskind said. "Because of the necessity of political clearance," he said, "we always booked actors on what we called a hold....Then I would put the names in for clearance. When they came back rejected...it was stipulated that I was never to tell any rejectee why he was rejected."

The Borden Co. grew so fearful of sponsoring communist performers that it put together a "whitelist" of 150 previously cleared actors and actresses, which Susskind said Young & Rubicam submitted to him for use on another show, "Justice."

Aware President Godfrey Schmidt defended his organization's methods, saying it had to name names to be effective—even if, on occasion, it got some of the details wrong. In the January 1955 issue of *Spotlight*, he wrote:

CHAPTER ELEVEN: The Crest of the Anti-communist Wave

(The) most ineffectual method of fighting Communism is to talk in endless generalities about it....Of course we will make mistakes from time to time!...Well, if we let such fears make cowards of us, the Communists will multiply and rejoice....We will be like the man who stayed in bed because he was afraid, if he went out, he would run risks.

This is a mistake which AWARE does not propose to commit. From time to time AWARE will not hesitate to point the finger at individuals who upon the basis of fact and cogent evidence are aiding Communist infiltration into the field of entertainment-communications. Communist germs, like microbes, are carried by real, flesh-and-blood people. These we must convert or stop.

Aware was anxious to demonstrate that, while it was determined to act, it was not unforgiving. The group provided its version of a penitent's manual in early 1955, a pamphlet exhaustively entitled *The Road Back (Self-Clearance): A Provisional Statement of View on the Problem of the Communist and Communist-Helper in Entertainment Communications Who Seeks to Clear Himself.*

The manual began with a biblical quotation: "That they should have a change of heart and mind, performing deeds fitting this change. (Acts 26:20)."

It then proceeded to offer a dozen steps individuals could take to clear themselves, including a "full and frank disclosure" of all connections with subversive elements; a voluntary and cooperative interview with the Federal Bureau of Investigation; and a written offer to cooperate with the Committee on Un-American Activities of the House of Representatives.

CONTINUED VIGILANCE IN SYRACUSE

On February 19, 1955, Francis Neuser, under the letterhead of the Veterans Action Committee of Syracuse Super Markets, wrote to John Kraft of Kraft Foods to complain about the scheduled appearances of Ossie Davis and Rex Ingram on an upcoming television movie "The Emperor Jones" by the Kraft Television Theatre. He enclosed records linking both actors to blacklisted groups and to lobbying on behalf of spies Julius and Ethel Rosenberg. "Would you be kind enough to check with your advertising department as well as your advertising agency to ascertain whether or not the Ossie Davis who is scheduled to appear is the same Ossie Davis indicated in the enclosed material?" Neuser asked. "And is the Rex Ingram, who is also scheduled to appear, the same Rex Ingram indicated...?"

Kraft did not reply to Neuser's letter, and the show aired as scheduled.

On June 15, *New York Herald-Tribune* columnist John Crosby, while commenting on the battle over blacklisting in AFTRA, the show-business union, spoke up for Kraft and took on Johnson and the anti-communist merchandising effort. "Some sponsors, notably Kraft, Philco and Goodyear (all NBC shows), have shown great courage in telling the blacklisters to go chase themselves," Crosby wrote. He criticized Borden and other sponsors that cooperated with Hartnett and his colleagues.

Dungey quickly wrote a reply, which he dispatched to the *Herald-Tribune* on June 28. "What Mr. Crosby is trying to say in his column is that we, the American public, have no right to protest as far as entertainers who have helped the Communist cause are concerned," Dungey wrote. "We have every right to say who we want to bring into our homes by means of the air waves."

Later in his letter, Dungey adopted Johnson's technique of suggesting a "poll" to decide which side is right:

> We offer Mr. Crosby a challenge. We have here in Syracuse a group of supermarkets which are willing to take this problem to their customers and let them settle it. After all the customers buy Kraft products and they certainly have the right to know where their money is going....Will you join us in conducting this poll? Let us just ask the customer if they want any part of their purchase price of a product, in this instance Kraft's to go to help pay the salary and enhance the prestige of talent who have in any way aided the Communist cause and have not as yet made honest efforts to undo the help given to this conspiracy whether knowingly or not.

CHAPTER ELEVEN: The Crest of the Anti-communist Wave

On July 12, Crosby tartly replied to Dungey's letter:

> I know far more about actors than you do or anyone else in Syracuse Post 41 of the American Legion....I was not trying to say in my column that the American public had no right to protest about entertainers who have helped the Communist cause. But there are very, very few of them. The vast majority of actors who have been blacklisted have done nothing more heinous than to contribute their talents or their money to causes—many of them noble—in which they believed....To deprive an actor of his living for something he couldn't possibly know about...is unjust, is un-American, and is pretty close to being criminal—if it isn't criminal.
>
> If you people knew what you were talking about, you would still be far exceeding your authority. The Communist conspiracy is a matter for the FBI, not for you....You don't know how the theater operates, or how theatrical people operate, or how they think. If there is a Communist conspiracy in the entertainment world, it's buried so far underground that you and your supermarket boss in Syracuse would be the last to find out about it.
>
> Meanwhile, Mr. Schmidt's and Mr. Hartnett's methods for detecting Communists are so childish they must be affording the Party a hearty laugh.

The editors of *Spotlight*, who reprinted Crosby's letter verbatim, added this postscript: "We leave it up to our readers to determine if John Crosby really answered our letter."

In August, *Spotlight* criticized the University Methodist Church in Syracuse for permitting the Syracuse Peace Council to hold a meeting at which a recording entitled "The Investigator" was played. The radio play, scripted and performed by "listee" Reuben Ship, parodied Senator McCarthy and the congressional committees targeting alleged communists. The Canadian-born Ship had been kicked out of the United States in 1953 after being identified as a Communist Party member and refusing to answer the HCUA's questions.

"It is estimated that the work of this deported Communist may gross better than $500,000 in sales," *Spotlight* claimed. "We urge all of our readers to alert all recording shops and other stores as to what help they give the C.P. if they sell this piece of Communist propaganda."

Toward the end of 1955, Syracuse anti-communists took aim at a scheduled public forum called the "Freedom Agenda" held at the Onondaga County Public Library. The event was organized as part of a national campaign sponsored in part by the liberal Fund for the Republic, that fact alone making it suspect in the eyes of the anti-communists.

The forum drew sponsorship from a score of civic leaders, including Schools Superintendent Dr. Paul Miller, Rhea Eckel ("prominent Syracuse club woman and civic leader," *Spotlight* said); and local broadcaster E.R. "Curly" Vadeboncoeur, one of Johnson's friends. *Spotlight* called the event a "fear forum" and a "strange gathering." After describing materials designated for the forum, the writers concluded:

> Even with this slight background, it is obvious that the conclusions reached by the study groups, if based on the texts, the authors' tendencies and the recommended readings will be: Congressional committees, loyalty programs, antisubversive legislation are today's threat to our civil liberties; that Americans have more to fear from Anti-Communism than from Communism....
>
> We feel that this program with its slanted texts, one-sidedness and real lack of America's traditions of fair play and hear both sides is but a hollow mockery of what they purport to strengthen: Freedom.

The editors sent copies of their critique to the sponsors of the Freedom Agenda program, along with form letters requesting their views. In the next issue of *Spotlight*, it printed a mix of responses.

Schools Superintendent Miller wrote: "It appears that...we have arrived at slightly different conclusions....I assure you that, as a sponsor, I shall

CHAPTER ELEVEN: THE CREST OF THE ANTI-COMMUNIST WAVE

watch very carefully all developments in the field of education so that they do not take on any characteristics which would affect our national security."

Wrote Rhea Eckel: "I consider it a worthy project, since its main purpose is to stimulate interest in and discussion of the principles contained in our Constitution and Bill of Rights."

While Miller, Eckel and others remained loyal to the Freedom Agenda forum, some wavered. Wrote W.E. McClusky: "I am not a sponsor of the Freedom Agenda. My name no longer appears upon that list."

Raymond J.H. Kennedy of Le Moyne College in Syracuse wrote that his name appeared "through an error," and that "I sent a letter to Mrs. Jacob E. Eckel advising her to remove my name from the list of sponsors."

Melanie A. Kreuzer, president of the Syracuse Common Council, sent Dungey a copy of her letter to Eckel: "I believe that as a public official, I have the…obligation to the citizens of Syracuse whom I represent, to be currently and adequately informed about the activities of any community group with which I am identified. Therefore, it is my considered judgment that I should not be a sponsor and ask you to withdraw my name from the Freedom Agenda Forums."

RIDING HIGH

In 1955, when NBC wanted to make sure a top performer was free of troublesome associations, it asked for two testimonial letters: one from the Anti-Defamation League and one from the president of Aware Inc., Godfrey P. Schmidt.

Sponsors, advertisers, and broadcasters were well-tamed by then, routinely refusing to hire anyone who might upset the heartland. Industry sources told the *New York Post* of "an increasing reluctance recently on the part of advertising agencies to use performers or material which 'won't sell toothpaste in Alabama.'"

By this time, Aware, with its membership mailing list of 2,285, had expanded its targets to include those silent on communism. It was an argument pretty much along the lines of the maxim: If you're not part of the solution, you're part of the problem. Beware of "dangerous neutralism," Aware warned in one of its publications. "No one can be neutral before the Communist challenge and peril....Its threat to our civilization demands that people stand up and be counted."

In Syracuse, Jim McHale of the American Legion brought speakers to town to boost the cause. Roy Cohn drew a crowd to Central High School for a speech about the American flag. On March 23, former FBI undercover agent Herbert Philbrick, whose experiences inspired the TV drama "I Led Three Lives," spoke in Syracuse at a program sponsored by Laurence Johnson's Kiwanis Club. Conservative actor Ronald Reagan visited the Syracuse Legionnaires at Dungey's invitation. Johnson covered Reagan's expenses, and the future U.S. president waived his fee.

On April 12, Legion Post No. 41 honored Johnson's daughter Eleanor Buchanan, whose talks to local groups and monitoring of broadcasts in 1951 had helped inspire her dad's entry into anti-communist activism. She received the Legion's Americanism medal and a citation reading in part: "We recognize the fact that if it were not for Eleanor Buchanan and her awareness of the communist conspiracy and discovering a way to combat it we would not have as effective an anti-communist movement here in Syracuse today."

Before the end of 1955, the National Association of Retail Grocers gave the anti-communist efforts of Johnson and his allies an endorsement at its annual convention, passing the following resolution:

> WHEREAS, this country is now threatened by Communism both from foreign and from domestic sources;
>
> Communism is the greatest and most terrible evil the world ever faced since the beginning of time;
>
> The liberties of the people of the country and its institutions of freedom are the prime target of the insidious Communist doctrine;
>
> For some time many people have been diligently working to prevent any Communistic influence from operating in the field of radio and television;

CHAPTER ELEVEN: The Crest of the Anti-communist Wave

It is particularly important that this effort go forward since public opinion is influenced greatly by radio and television, and we know that Communists and their supporters are constantly working to use radio and television facilities to preach and spread their evil doctrine;

BE IT RESOLVED: That the National Association of Retail Grocers in their 56th annual convention do hereby call on sponsors of radio and television programs and their agencies to exercise constant vigilance against infiltration of their programs by Communists and other subversive forces.

In October 1955, *The Post-Standard* published a photo of Laurence Johnson congratulating Dungey during a testimonial dinner honoring the *Spotlight* editor for his anti-subversive efforts. The caption noted that Johnson was the evening's main speaker, a testament in itself to his star power in anti-communist circles.

Just four months later, Johnson sold his chain of stores to Victory Supermarkets, losing the business platform that had provided his activism so much credibility and leverage.

Although out of the grocery business, Laurence Johnson did not immediately abandon his anti-communist efforts. He and his allies decided in early 1956 to target a major entertainment union and one of its most esteemed members, the charismatic storyteller and radio host John Henry Faulk.

CHAPTER TWELVE:
Enter John Henry Faulk

During 1955, the anti-communists had devoted considerable energy to keeping the leadership of the American Federation of Television and Radio Artists from falling into the hands of a faction that opposed blacklisting. One of the faction's most outspoken members was John Henry Faulk, who for several years entertained listeners of WCBS-AM in New York City.

Faulk campaigned that fall for election as AFTRA's second vice president on a slate that included comedic actor Orson Bean for first vice president and newsman Charles Collingwood for president.

During the summer, Faulk talked a lot about the union as he gathered with friends and colleagues at his summer place on New York's Fire Island, where he entertained them with gamey versions of the folksy tales and cracker-barrel wit that were making him famous in show business.

"On Friday and Saturday nights," Bean wrote later in an essay for the *National Review*, "groups of actors, writers and broadcasting people who summered on Fire Island would gather at Johnny's house, drawn by his magnetic personality like ants to jam. Mrs. Faulk would scurry about serving drinks, their tanned and beautiful children would clamor to be allowed to stay up a little longer, the goat would frolic and the guests would bask in the healthy American wonder of it all."

Along with anecdotes and shaggy-dog stories, Faulk increasingly spoke out against the anti-communist faction in AFTRA. Night after night that summer on Fire Island, Bean said, Faulk held forth on the evils of the blacklist.

THE GROCER WHO SOLD McCARTHYISM

Talk-show host John Henry Faulk interviews a guest July 8, 1952, on CBS radio. (CBS photo)

Bean recalled Faulk telling him, "Honey, don't kid yourself. These people are fascists and dangerous. They'll sit there grinnin' like an egg-suckin' dawg, all friendly-like, but they'll kill you and they'll kill the country.'"

This warning would soon be viewed as tragically prophetic. On September 1, 1955, Philip Loeb, the popular father of "The Goldbergs" who had been unemployable after he was blacklisted, took an overdose of pills and died in the Hotel Taft in New York City.

Even before Loeb's death, Faulk was certain that most in AFTRA opposed Aware and its tactics, which made him increasingly frustrated over the union leadership's acquiescence to Aware's agenda. Faulk wrote later: "Instead of heeding the obvious desire of the membership to curb Aware's influence and oppose the blacklisting of union members, the board of directors started mumbling that the vote to condemn Aware was part and parcel of a Communist plot."

Faulk decided the best way to counteract the board's passivity was to

CHAPTER TWELVE: Enter John Henry Faulk

seek a board seat himself in the December 1955 election. Faulk joined the self-described Middle-of-the-Road slate, which included Aware opponents Garry Moore, Faye Emerson and Janice Rule, as well as Collingwood and Bean.

On election day, Faulk and the other Middlers startled many when they won twenty-seven of thirty-five seats on AFTRA's New York local board.

The Communist *Daily Worker* crowed a bit too optimistically that the AFTRA election "marks the end of Aware Inc.'s influence and interference in the affairs of the union." It called the vote one of the "cultural highlights of the closing year."

Faulk continued to stress that he and his colleagues were not sympathetic to communism in any way. The members of the slate "were chosen for their opposition to communism as well as their opposition to Aware," he explained. He also stressed the positive agenda of the new board members: "The first interest of a union's officers should be employment of members, not blacklisting them."

Until thrust into prominence as an AFTRA officer, Faulk's name had not surfaced on the blacklists compiled by the anti-communists. However, shortly before the election, Hartnett had visited the New York Public Library to scan HCUA documents and look up back issues of the *Daily Worker* while compiling information on Faulk and other Middlers. Hartnett then wrote to the HCUA, sending along data on Faulk. Hartnett also approached sponsors and advertising agencies, pointing out to the Kudner Agency and Young & Rubicam that Faulk might have "a significant communist-front record."

In January 1956, as Faulk took office, Hartnett called Lt. Thomas Crain of the New York Police Department. Years later, Hartnett was asked the purpose of that call. Was it about Faulk?

"I think I did tell him certain information I had about Mr. Faulk," Hartnett answered.

Hartnett was on familiar terms with Crain; they had collaborated dozens of times, going back to the 1940s when Hartnett was writing episodes for the radio series "Gang Busters." In recent years, Hartnett shared with him allegations against show people.

Hartnett's chief interest in early 1956 was John Henry Faulk.

PUBLICATION 16

The pamphlet that appeared February 10, 1956, looked innocuous on the surface. It even had a bland title: *Aware Publication 16: News Supplement to Membership Bulletin*. This was not strictly an issue of *Counterattack*, the Aware newsletter, although the anti-communist pamphlet contained the customary list of names of people in show business and their alleged communist-front links.

As in a previous Aware bulletin, *Publication 12*, there also was a focus on AFTRA and its new leaders, including Collingwood and Bean. Aware's Hartnett and Milton said they were not claiming the leadership was communist. "The identified Communists in the N.Y. AFTRA local were shrewd enough not to run their own slate in the December election," they wrote.

Then Hartnett and Milton turned their attention to Faulk, the new union leadership's most outspoken critic of blacklisting. Referring to Faulk's avowal that he and his Middlers colleagues opposed communism, the authors observed: "In most cases, this may well be true. But how about Faulk himself? What is his public record?"

Drawing on press clippings and other sources, Hartnett and Milton listed seven items they suggested implicated Faulk:

- According to the Daily Worker of April 22, 1946, "Jack Faulk" was to appear at Club 65, 13 Astor Place, N.Y.C. —a favorite site of pro-Communist affairs.

- According to the Daily Worker of April 17, 1947, "Johnny Faulk" was to appear as an entertainer at the opening of "Headline Cabaret", sponsored by Stage for Action (officially designated a Communist front). The late Philip Loeb was billed as emcee.

- According to the Daily Worker of April 5, 1948, "John Faulk" contributed cabaret material to "Show-Time for Wallace" revues staged by the Progressive Citizens of America (officially designated a Communist front) in

CHAPTER TWELVE: Enter John Henry Faulk

support of Henry A. Wallace's candidacy for the presidency of the U.S. Although Wallace was the officially designated candidate of the CP, by no means all his supporters were Communists or pro-Communists. What is in question here is support of any candidate given through a Communist-front setup.

- A program dated April 25, 1946 named "John Faulk" as a scheduled entertainer (with identified Communist Earl Robinson and two non-Communists) under the auspices of the Independent Citizens Committee of the Arts, Sciences and Professions (officially designated a Communist front, and predecessor of the Progressive Citizens of America).

- Vol. 3, Nos. 1 & 2, of the Bulletin of People's Songs (officially designated a Communist front) named Faulk as one who had sent greetings to People's Songs on its second anniversary.

- "Johnny Faulk" was listed in a circular as an entertainer or speaker (with Paul Robeson and two others) to appear at "Spotlight on Wallace" to be held in Room 200 of the Jefferson School of Social Science on February 16, 1948. The Jefferson School has been found by the Federal Government to be what it is, the official training school of the Communist conspiracy in New York.

- "John H. Faulk" was a U.S. Sponsor of the American Continental Congress for Peace, staged in Mexico City, September 5-10, 1949, as shown by the official "call." The Congress was later described by the HCUA as "another phase in the Communist world 'peace' campaign, aimed at consolidating anti-American forces throughout the Western Hemisphere."

THE GROCER WHO SOLD McCARTHYISM

The Aware bulletin's report on Faulk concluded with a skeptical question: "Will John Henry Faulk, an AFTRA VP, discharge his responsibility to enforce the AFTRA constitutional amendment and National Rule against Communists and those who defy the Congress when asked if they are communists?"

THE WORD SPREADS

On Sunday, February 12, two days after the issue date of the Aware bulletin, the phone rang in Faulk's Manhattan apartment. It was Val Adams, who reported on radio and television for *The New York Times*. He told Faulk about *Publication 16* and asked for a comment. Faulk later recalled he mustered a bravado reply as fire alarms went off in his head.

The next day, Faulk got hold of a copy of the bulletin, reading it in a taxi as he crossed town. "It was a cleverly constructed piece of work," he wrote later. "The way it had positioned my name in sentences with 'Communist Party' and 'Communist front,' its use of phrases like 'officially designated a Communist front,' and its skillful mixing of half-truth and falsehood suggested the work of a hand skilled at innuendo." He continued:

> I sat pondering the matter as the cab moved slowly through the mid-morning Manhattan traffic. I had a vague, uncomfortable feeling of guilt. But I had done nothing wrong. Why should I feel guilty? I realized at that moment that I was going through the frustrations and anxieties that had been experienced by countless other performers when they had found their names linked with subversion by AWARE.

Collingwood was able to brush off the Aware bulletin and remain unscathed. Hartnett and Milton didn't have much on the AFTRA president other than to report that he had once sent a critical letter to the HCUA.

The bulletin targeted Orson Bean for an appearance August 19, 1955, at Carnegie Hall where the brilliant young comic had performed a satirical sendup of HCUA at a rally for AFTRA members facing congressional probes. Hartnett and Milton noted that a rally sponsor, the Emergency

CHAPTER TWELVE: Enter John Henry Faulk

Targeted by anti-communists were, from left, actors Joseph Cotten, Kim Hunter, Orson Bean, and Judy Holliday, seen in 1950s publicity photos.

Civil Liberties Committee, was "described by the U.S. Senate Internal Security Committee as a Communist front 'to defend the cases of Communist lawbreakers.' It has also been attacked as a Communist-tainted organization by the American Committee for Cultural Freedom."

The entry puzzled Bean, he wrote later. Did his association with this rally mean that he was subversive?

He also was worried because of the bulletin's linkage of him to Faulk, who was cited with a long list of alleged misdeeds. Bean recalled running over to Faulk's office at CBS to ask him about them.

"It isn't true, is it, Johnny? You didn't appear at those places, did you?" Bean asked.

"'Oh, honey, what does it matter?" Faulk replied. "Don't you see those people are fascists? If they didn't have something on us, they'd have made something up."

Bean stood, his mouth agape, in Faulk's office, staring at him. "I could feel my ears burning," Bean wrote later. "I wanted to cry or hit him in the face or shake him. Instead, I just walked out of his office and went home."

Despite the flimsy evidence against him, Bean's work in show business dried up almost immediately. "Overnight, from being the hot young comic at CBS television, I stopped working. Just stopped," he wrote. "I saw actors cross the street to avoid having to say hello to me. I was even snubbed by the doorman at CBS. The money stopped coming in, the glory was gone and my career as a television comic seemed like a memory."

The day the Aware bulletin was issued, Bean said, television variety-show host Ed Sullivan called him.

"Orson," Sullivan asked, "have you heard about the Aware bulletin?"

"What do you mean?" Bean said, later recalling that he felt the blood drain from his face.

"They've cited you in their issue that came out today and I'm afraid the bookings are out," Sullivan said. "In fact I won't be able to use you on the show at all anymore."

Bean recalled Sullivan then told him: "Incidentally, if you tell anyone I said this, I'll have to deny it."

With a name and face blacklisted, Bean turned to commercial voiceovers where he could perform in relative anonymity until the storm blew over. As it turned out, the damage to his career was temporary. He soon was back performing as himself on TV. Even Sullivan eventually relented and invited him back, regardless of what the sponsors said.

Unlike Bean, Faulk saw no immediate damage from *Publication 16*. Faulk was firmly established with CBS on radio and was poised to become a major television figure. His yearly income was climbing rapidly toward the $35,000 mark (equivalent to over $400,000 in 2024). For Faulk, it was conceivable that, within a couple of years, his annual income could reach the heights of TV stars such as Steve Allen, Bud Collyer, and Bill Cullen, reportedly pulling in upwards of $100,000.

Aware initially mailed 2,285 copies of *Publication 16*. In addition to Aware members, the bulletin went to radio and television executives; advertising agencies and sponsors like Colgate-Palmolive and General Foods; the National Grocers' Association; leading newspaper columnists; and government agencies, including the HCUA, the Justice Department and its FBI (J. Edgar Hoover got his own copy). Other recipients included police departments, book publishers, theater producers, motion picture companies, and even the Daughters of the American Revolution.

On March 31, 1956, the Syracuse anti-communists went into action to enforce *Publication 16*. In his capacity as chairman of the Anti-Subversive Committee of the Onondaga County American Legion, John Dungey

CHAPTER TWELVE: Enter John Henry Faulk

wrote to Harris Perlstein, president of the Pabst Brewing Co., a sponsor of Faulk's radio show:

> Dear Mr. Perlstein:
>
> These are indeed trying times not only in the field of international politics but also in the TV and radio field.
>
> For International Communism to succeed in bringing the rest of the world under the yoke of their conspiracy they must gain complete control of the air-waves. The Communists are working around the clock to accomplish this.
>
> They must also raise money to finance their operations. As an example four Communist fronts in the entertainment field raised over a million dollars for the Communist cause.
>
> The American Legion for years has realized the efforts that Communists are exerting in the field of entertainment and has gone on record not to support programs that feature Communists or individuals who have supported Communist causes.
>
> Therefore, we respectfully call to your attention one of your salesmen, John Henry Faulk, whose program comes through WCBS, New York City—5:05 to 6 p.m., Monday through Friday.
>
> We are enclosing data from publication AWARE on a John Henry Faulk and would like to know if this is the same John Henry Faulk who has this WCBS program.
>
> We of the American Legion sincerely hope that you will look into this situation and will be waiting a reply since we want to have our facts straight as to the person in question and his sponsors. We have previously brought to the attention of the public facts concerning Communism in the entertainment field as may be seen by copy of enclosed Spotlight.

Dungey was playing dumb with his request. He knew perfectly well that the CBS host was the same Faulk targeted by Aware.

Dungey sent copies of his letter to Wayne Murphy at the Legion's National Americanism Commission in Indianapolis, and one went to his Syracuse colleague Francis Neuser, head of the Veterans Action Committee of Syracuse Super Markets. Dungey also sent one to Laurence Johnson.

Years later, one of Faulk's attorneys, Paul Martinson, asked Johnson if he remembered receiving the letter from Dungey.

"I probably got it, but I didn't pay any attention to it, as I wasn't reading my mail at the time," Johnson replied.

Pressed on the matter, Johnson conceded that he received the letter at the same time others did. Johnson then added a rare spontaneous comment on Dungey's letter. "A darned good letter about Faulk," he said. "I believe that was the first time I ever received a letter from him that was a copy of letters. I just made a note of that."

Johnson also acknowledged that he got Aware mailings, including *Publication 16*. Martinson wanted to know if Johnson, while attending a cocktail party sponsored by Aware in Manhattan in January 1956, learned about the imminent release of *Publication 16*. Johnson didn't recall "anything of that nature what was talked about there."

THE TIDE STARTS TO TURN

In March 1956, the Middle-of-the-Road AFTRA leaders were still talking tough against the anti-communists, promising to take action against any show-business employer who discriminated against workers because they were blacklisted. But support among the union members was fading.

On April 11, when Faulk rose to speak in his own defense at an AFTRA meeting, the mood was hostile. Faulk had followed actor Dick Stark to the microphone. Stark had just attacked the Middle-of-the-Road faction's leadership. Faulk was surprised and unnerved by his own sudden unpopularity, which he knew was because of the Aware bulletin. He said he ended up delivering a disorganized, ineffective speech.

Faulk wrote later: "As I gazed out over the faces, I saw only cold disdain. Ed Sullivan and a hard core of our opposition were sitting in the front

CHAPTER TWELVE: Enter John Henry Faulk

rows, staring up at me with unfeigned contempt. A terrible feeling of impotent rage overcame me as I sat down."

As it happened, Laurence Johnson was in Manhattan that day to visit Madison Avenue, where he lodged his own complaints about Faulk.

Most advertising agencies then still catered to Johnson and his anti-communist allies. But at least one account executive wasn't aboard. He was Thomas Murray of the Gray Advertising Agency. When Johnson telephoned him to ask why the agency handled the accounts for Faulk sponsors Pabst beer and Hoffman Beverage Co., Murray would have none of it.

In court testimony later, Murray recalled that Johnson "said that he owned several supermarkets and had influence over a number of others in Central New York....Mr. Johnson then said that he thought it was a disgrace that our company was using a communist, John Henry Faulk, to advertise its products."

Murray replied that he had no such knowledge about Faulk.

"Well," Johnson said, "you had better get in line because a lot of people along Madison Avenue are getting in line, and the display space which the Pabst Brewing Co. has in the stores that I either own or control" was "hard-won space."

When Murray continued to resist, Johnson challenged him: How would you like it if your client were to receive a letter from an American Legion post?

Murray replied that he was a "veteran myself" and that he could not believe that an American Legion post would take part in what he considered to be an attempt at blackmail.

"Well, you will find out," Johnson said before the call ended.

When Murray reported the conversation to Gray Executive Vice President Samuel Dalsimer, his boss quickly reined him in. Dalsimer had tangled with Johnson and his allies in the Block Drug Company's Ammi-dent case in 1952. Dalsimer told Murray that it was a strategic blunder to defy Johnson and that Murray needed to fix the situation.

Murray immediately called Johnson at his hotel, seeking to make amends. Unable to reach Johnson, Murray took a cab to the hotel.

Approaching the desk clerk, he asked, "Can you help me find Mr. Larry Johnson? I have to find him."

The clerk answered: "He is standing right over there in the lobby with that other gentleman."

Murray went over and introduced himself.

"I am the Tom Murray who talked to you on the phone a while ago, Mr. Johnson, and I would like to discuss the matter with you further."

Johnson said, "After the way you spoke to me, I want nothing further to do with you."

With that, Johnson turned and left the hotel with his companion.

As Johnson had promised, the letter of protest from Legion Post No. 41 arrived at Murray's office a few days later. Murray decided he had no choice but to take it over to CBS.

By then, the campaign against Faulk was having an effect at WCBS. The same day Faulk spoke to that hostile audience at the AFTRA meeting, Libby's canceled its frozen-foods advertising account that co-sponsored Faulk's radio show.

WCBS radio's general manager, Carl Ward, met with Faulk to talk over this major setback.

"This is serious, Johnny, very serious," he said. "Libby's frozen-foods account just canceled today. It looks like you'll lose Libby's canned-vegetables account this week, too. If Johnson forces all these people off your show, you'll lose your commercial value to the station."

Faulk wrote later that he understood Ward's position. "He wasn't mad at me," Faulk said. "And he wasn't indignant at Laurence Johnson. He was upset at losing an account."

On April 13, Faulk wrote a statement affirming his patriotism and loyalty, and had it notarized. Copies of the statement went to the salesmen assigned to sell his show to the sponsors. Other show people had tried this strategy, but the anti-communists were usually unimpressed.

JOHNSON STEPS UP PRESSURE

Johnson soon appealed directly to the companies that manufactured and distributed the products advertised on Faulk's shows. Instead of calling Foote, Cone & Belding, the agency that handled the Rheingold beer

CHAPTER TWELVE: Enter John Henry Faulk

ads for the show, Johnson called Harry J. Blackburn, for 24 years manager of supermarket and chain store sales for Liebmann Breweries, makers of Rheingold.

Blackburn reported later that Johnson told him outright: "John Henry Faulk, who Rheingold is sponsoring, is a Communist." Johnson had a different recollection years later when asked about the conversation: "I told him the sources of my information, and let them make up their own minds, whether those were bona fide references."

Blackburn said he told Johnson that he must be mistaken about Faulk. Yet Blackburn was keenly aware of the commercial value of the display space he thought was at risk in Johnson's supermarkets. He passed along Johnson's claims about Faulk to the ad agency, and soon another memo terminating a Faulk sponsorship landed on desks at WCBS.

Increasingly concerned, Faulk hit on the idea of calling Lansing Shield, president of Grand Union Supermarkets in Paterson, New Jersey. Shield was both a friend and admirer of Faulk, as well as a professional acquaintance of Johnson. Shield offered to call Johnson and straighten things out. He said he was sure that, once Johnson realized a mistake had been made, Faulk's worries would be over.

Unable to reach Johnson by telephone, Shield wrote a letter to him on May 7 with a plea for Faulk. He defended Faulk as a loyal American who had insisted that only one very innocuous incident cited in the Aware bulletin was correct. Shield continued:

> It is my understanding that certain union leaders in New York of unsavory reputation are behind this move to either intimidate or discredit John Henry Faulk.
>
> I know that you would not consciously be a party to any such effort and for that reason I am calling your attention (to) this serious miscarriage of justice. Anything you can do to remedy this mistake will be greatly appreciated.

A few days later, Johnson called Shield. According to Shield, Johnson said that he knew all about Faulk, that the radio host was a very dangerous man, and that Johnson would furnish Shield proof of this in coming days.

Following this telephone call, Shield advised Faulk: "John, you had better get you the best lawyer you can find, and get this thing straightened out. It's very serious."

Johnson sent a copy of Shield's letter to Vincent Hartnett, who later recalled: "Larry…asked me what information I had about Faulk, so undoubtedly, I did either write or telephone him and tell him what I knew."

Around this time, Johnson decided to do some research of his own by visiting the newspaper division of the public library and looking up back issues of the *Daily Worker*. Then he visited Hartnett at his midtown office to talk about Faulk.

Johnson and Hartnett agreed to press on with the campaign against Faulk.

Although CBS newsman Murrow and others spoke up for Faulk, the network was finding it harder and harder to tolerate the financial hit. The cancellation of Libby's frozen-food spots represented a loss of 15 percent of Faulk's advertising revenue. Next out the door went the Nestle Company, Libby's canned foods, Diamond Crystal Salt, Nucoa, and others. Pall Mall would be gone by September. Other sponsors wavered: Ford, Sarah Lee cakes, College Inn, Stahl-Meyer meats, Coca-Cola, Kretschmer wheat germ, Piels beer, Marlboro, and White Rock Beverages.

Faulk also saw an abrupt halt to his bookings for television. But for the time being, he kept his radio job, thanks in part to the intervention of AFTRA President Collingwood. Meeting with WCBS Radio President Arthur Hull Hayes, Collingwood warned that if Faulk were dismissed, AFTRA would demand a full investigation, including a probe of the ad agencies' and sponsors' roles in the affair.

Hayes responded that he opposed blacklisting, and that he considered men like Hartnett, Dungey, and Johnson presumptuous and un-American. He assured Collingwood that Faulk would not lose his job because of the anti-communists' pressure campaign.

Even so, in June 1956, smarting over the loss of television work and unsure of his future, Faulk took Lansing Shield's advice and went searching for a lawyer.

That same month, a ground-breaking report by researcher John Cogley detailed the rampant havoc wrought by blacklisting, giving particular attention to operators such as Johnson who maneuvered behind the scenes,

CHAPTER TWELVE: ENTER JOHN HENRY FAULK

pulling the levers of power with both finesse and secrecy. The 287-page report didn't mention Faulk. But the radio host would later say he quickly "made good use" of the report in fighting Aware's allegations. Said Faulk of Cogley, "And in no instance did we find him inaccurate."

CHAPTER THIRTEEN:
The Cogley Report

On June 24, 1956, the nonprofit Fund for the Republic published a two-volume document, "Report on Blacklisting," offering a mostly unflattering look at anti-communists, including Laurence Johnson. The report by John Cogley was the most ambitious study yet of the campaigns to weed out communist influence in show business. One chapter was titled "The Syracuse Crusade"; another was "Aware Inc."

The report's revelations managed both to embolden critics of the anti-communists and to outrage supporters of Johnson and his allies.

Cogley, a former executive editor of the liberal Catholic weekly *Commonweal*, was a personal assistant to Robert Hutchins, president of the Fund for the Republic. The Fund, backed by the Ford Foundation, provided $127,000 to finance Cogley's research into the blacklists. Cogley hired ten reporters who worked for eight months to gather material, including interviews with nearly 500 people in and around show business.

His report highlighted the plight of people put out of work, careers destroyed, income lost, reputations ruined, and paranoia running rampant. It laid out the anti-communists' *modus operandi* and the impact on the industry—their use of suggestion and innuendo, unsubstantiated or unevaluated evidence, third-hand sources, misrepresentation, vague documentation, and an overall disregard for due process and scrupulous reporting.

Cogley identified Aware Inc.'s Vincent Hartnett as the point man in the show-business campaign. "Hartnett may be the most widely criticized man in the radio-TV industry," Cogley wrote, "because he is frankly in the business of exposing people with 'front records' and then, later, of

THE GROCER WHO SOLD McCARTHYISM

'clearing' them—or as the (New York) *Times* writer delicately puts it, 'advising them on how to counter pro-Communist propaganda.'"

Cogley described Johnson as "a businessman of some prominence around his hometown of Syracuse, New York." Cogley traced Johnson's anti-communism actions from their earliest days following the lead of his daughter Eleanor, who "fired a crusade that reached out far beyond Syracuse."

According to Cogley, Johnson's role was as an avenging grocer who kept merchandising strategies at the ready, providing anti-communists an economic tool to bend the will of broadcasters, who mostly gave in out of fear of controversy and losing revenue.

"His shrewd colorful merchandising has won the admiration of other store owners all over the United States," the report said. "But to the 'security officers' on Madison Avenue Johnson is a good deal more than a successful grocer. He is at once a nuisance and an asset, for he keeps a watchful eye on their hiring practices and, in doing so, bears out their common contention that blacklisting, however regrettable, is economically necessary." Cogley added:

> For in Johnson, the Madison Avenue fraternity sees a germ of reality worth a thousand opinion polls. The man from Syracuse saves the industry from looking like a punch-drunk boxer who takes a swipe at the air here and there, then staggers back from imagined blows. With Johnson in the ring, the industry spokesmen do not have to feel foolish when someone asks how real the "economic" threat is. That argument is based on pleasing "the public"; for purposes of defending blacklisting, Johnson *is* the public. He can always be cited if one asks what the industry is afraid of. In going straight to the sponsor, Johnson hits the exact nerve center.

A producer interviewed for the report said: "The hub as I know it is Johnson. There is a list in every agency and even one in this office. But the master plan is held in Syracuse because nowhere else is there so much activity."

CHAPTER THIRTEEN: The Cogley Report

Cogley noted: "Up and down Madison Avenue there are steady complaints about Johnson's interference. But the industry has never tested the grocer's power in any meaningful way. On the few occasions when he had been challenged he appears to have come off second best."

The report quoted a letter from a "corporate executive" who lamented Johnson's heavy-handed technique:

> Briefly, Mr. Johnson for several years has been taking it upon himself to put various pressures on the food manufacturers, and others using television, to force them to refrain from engaging certain individuals accused by Mr. Johnson and his group from Syracuse of being identified with the Communist movement....The only difference of opinion between Mr. Johnson and us is that we are not willing to accept his accusations or statements as sufficient reason for putting any individual on a blacklist....
>
> The facts of the matter are that Mr. Johnson is desirous of our hiring certain individuals whom he names, to tell us how to run our business....It is apparent that Johnson is not interested in our desire to work with him and cooperate—he and his group want to dictate our policies....

A "prominent producer and packager" spoke even more disparagingly about Johnson and his anti-communist allies:

> These blacklisters are crackpots. This is the McCarthy group and they get into this thing because it makes them feel good. It gives them a chance to push people around.....Big corporations scare easily. They're afraid of publicity. One complaint is enough, you know. Even program directors who haven't yet been attacked by Johnson are afraid they might be. As far as the protest letters go, I've never seen even one that wasn't inspired by these people.

In a section of the report headlined "Blacklisting Experiences," Cogley shared interviews with actors, directors, and others who found themselves suddenly out of work, often without initially knowing why.

One actor identified as "F.T." said he had performed in several major movies, and had a long background in radio and television, before discovering he had been blacklisted. The report continued:

> In the spring of 1952, *F.T.* finished a picture in Hollywood. Immediately after this, he was replaced in a forthcoming role by someone else. He had a conversation with an executive at the studio who asked him pointblank, "Are you a Communist?" *F.T.* told the executive he wasn't. The executive then told the actor that the American Legion Post #41 in Syracuse, New York, was "after" him. He mentioned a whole series of charges, and predicted a bleak prospect for future employment unless *F.T.* cleared himself....Later some films he had made prior to getting in trouble were shown on television, and there were more attacks from Syracuse.

One obvious weakness of the report—which its critics were quick to point out—was that most of the blacklisted insisted on anonymity, as did others interviewed from the networks, advertising agencies, and sponsoring companies. On the other hand, Cogley named the anti-communists, including Vincent Hartnett and Godfrey Schmidt, Aware's president, because they cooperated and agreed to be identified.

Cogley noted in a postscript that one scared producer, after speaking so bitterly, said softly: "Publicly of course I have to take an on-the-fence position. I can't make any statements."

While the anti-communists appeared to be forthright participants in the report, the critics of blacklisting, in their demand for anonymity, looked like they lacked courage or just had something to hide.

THE ACTIVISTS REGROUP

Not surprisingly, the communist *Daily Worker* in New York City endorsed the Cogley report. The paper's TV critic David Platt wrote: "The Report is an indictment of Aware Inc., Counterattack, Red Channels, the Veterans Action Committee of Syracuse Supermarkets and all the other

CHAPTER THIRTEEN: The Cogley Report

Vigilante and Blacklisting outfits and rags which have been preying upon entertainers for years."

Otherwise, the immediate media reaction to Cogley's report was largely negative. "While in no wise pro-Communist, the report cannot help but bring joy and comfort to the communists," wrote Frederick Woltman in the *New York World-Telegram and The Sun*. The anti-communist columnist himself had been cited in Cogley's report.

An editorial in Hearst's *New York Journal-American* slammed Cogley's sponsor, the Fund for the Republic, calling the report "further conclusive evidence of the anti-anti-communist slant" of that institution.

In Syracuse, *Spotlight* added to the chorus of criticism:

> Since there is no middle road, we of the American Legion have to either join in with the Fund for the Republic and the Communists and Left Wingers or with Aware, Inc., Counterattack, Veterans Action Committee and such individuals as Vincent Hartnett, L.A. Johnson, Godfrey P. Schmidt...and all the others who are, without any thought of personal financial gain or glory, effectively combatting the Communist forces in this country.

As for Laurence Johnson, he had no immediate response to the Cogley report; Johnson was vacationing in Europe with his wife, Hermione, and wasn't in Syracuse for the report's release.

Four days after the report was published, the HCUA subpoenaed Cogley to appear before the committee on July 10 for questioning. Chairman Francis Walter, a Democrat from Pennsylvania, said the hearing would attempt to find out "what the purposes of the Fund and Mr. Cogley truly are."

On the first day, Cogley was accompanied into the chamber by future presidential candidate Eugene McCarthy, then a young congressman, who threw his arm around the shoulder of the embattled scholar in a public gesture of support.

HCUA members and staff grilled Cogley for hours, making much of the backgrounds of several of his staff members: Michael Harrington, the brilliant and outspoken young socialist; Paul Jacobs, who had belonged to the Young Communist League twenty years earlier; and Dr. Marie Jahoda, a member of the Socialist Democratic Party in Austria before coming to the United States in 1945.

Cogley answered the committee's questions but refused to reveal the identities of any sources who still wanted anonymity. Perhaps anticipating the HCUA would attempt to subpoena his notes, Cogley said he had destroyed them.

Vincent Hartnett also testified at the Cogley hearings, which would be put into a report with the skeptical title "Investigation of So-Called 'Blacklisting' in Entertainment Industry—Report of the Fund for the Republic Inc." In the hearing room, Hartnett condemned the Cogley report for "dangerous slanting," adding that the researcher was "either woefully ignorant or he is a rogue." Hartnett rejected blacklisting as "a nasty term," preferring to define the practice as "honest, intelligent, reasonable and fair patriotic efforts to keep subversives out of radio and television."

Despite acknowledging earlier that he and his anti-communist allies were close to achieving their goals, Hartnett testified how prevalent the subversive influence still was in show business. "(I)n spite of all the investigations conducted by both state and congressional committees," he told the HCUA, "not more than 5 percent...of the past and present communists in the entertainment industry have been uncovered."

How did this subversive influence continue to manifest itself in the entertainment industry? In anti-American programming, Hartnett claimed. "You will find script after script in which the policeman shoots an innocent teenager, not the bad teenager," he testified. "It is always the innocent. The wrong man is identified and sent to jail. An honest official abroad is suspected of being a communist agent and the man who points the fingers at him is always a fanatic, disgruntled." Hartnett insisted that Americans were being "brainwashed" by the entertainment industry.

Witness after witness disputed Cogley's findings, impugning his loyalty and that of his co-workers and his sponsoring foundation while praising the practices Cogley criticized and calling for more.

The witness roster was a who's who of anti-communism: Woltman of the *New York World-Telegram*; James F. O'Neil, publisher of *American*

CHAPTER THIRTEEN: The Cogley Report

FROM LEFT: Aware Inc. founders Godfrey P. Schmidt and Paul R. Milton testify before the House Committee on Un-American Activities on July 13, 1956. RIGHT: Vincent W. Hartnett testifies before the committee a day earlier. (Associated Press photos)

Legion Magazine; Aware Inc.'s Paul Milton and Godfrey Schmidt; and Frank McNamara, former editor of *Counterattack*.

One notable absentee was Johnson, who once again, when it came to his anti-communism activities, avoided the microphones and cameras.

After a recess, the HCUA hearings resumed in Philadelphia, where two blacklisted actors who allowed their names in the Cogley study were called for questioning. The first, actress Gale Sondergaard, complained of "harassment," noting that she was just now engaged in a creative project after having been virtually unemployable since pleading the Fifth Amendment in 1951. The second was Jack Gilford. Still smarting from his run-ins with Johnson and the other anti-communists, he took the Fifth again.

"Everyone hates the blacklist. The whole TV industry hates the blacklist," he shouted angrily during his HCUA examination.

Later, Cogley expressed disappointment that so many who anonymously complained about the blacklist still refused to step forward when his final report could have used their testimony of support.

IN PRAISE OF LAURENCE JOHNSON

In the U.S. Senate, longtime anti-communist Karl Mundt, a Republican from South Dakota, took on the Cogley report, the Fund for the Republic, and its backer, the Ford Foundation.

On the floor of the Senate, Mundt portrayed Laurence Johnson as the real victim in the blacklisting debate. This God-fearing, taxpaying American, Mundt said, was up against the Fund for the Republic, an organization that "enjoys the tax-exempt privilege to criticize him, to attack him and to discourage customers from coming to his doors, so as to reduce the size of his economic activity." It was Johnson, Mundt said, who first determined "that none of the money spent in his stores by his customers would be used to build or extend the communist apparatus in America." The senator continued:

> So he advertised in the newspapers and by means of placards placed in his stores that, to the best of his ability, he would not spend any of his money to buy food products publicized or propagandized by communists or their agents; that whenever he heard or learned of some television show or radio broadcast or motion picture or some other advertising medium or some advertising agency which was utilizing communist talent in urging the public to eat a certain product or to drink a certain product or to chew a certain product or to mix a certain product, he would immediately discontinue handling that particular product or brand of merchandise and would not publicize it through the medium of his stores or by putting it on the counters in his stores; that he would not urge his particular customers to buy it; that, instead, he would tell the people of Syracuse, N.Y., that to the best of his ability to determine such things, he would sell in his stores only the products which were made, publicized and advertised by good Americans; that no other products would be sold in his stores.

> That took some courage…because many advertising agencies have permitted a good many communist sympathizers to creep

CHAPTER THIRTEEN: THE COGLEY REPORT

into their talent positions and into other areas of publicity. But Mr. Johnson is a courageous American who believes that patriotism, like charity, begins at home.

He believes also that, as a good American to whom the country has been good as he has expanded his activities, he has the obligation of doing what he can decently and rightfully to help discourage Communists from getting jobs in advertising agencies and to help discourage the use of communist actors and communist actresses on television and radio programs, as part of the advertising process in America. To his satisfaction, and perhaps to his surprise, his stores gained customers.

Returning to the Cogley report, Senator Mundt concluded:

So, the Ford Foundation is correct when it says that Mr. Laurence Johnson "not only lends credence to the economic argument for blacklisting" but that "generally speaking, he *is* the argument," because he continues to point out that Americans should refuse to purchase products advertised by communists. Instead of attacking him for that, however, the Ford Foundation should have praised him for it.

To the anti-communists, the hearings and Senator Mundt's very personal tribute to Johnson affirmed both the correctness of their goals and their methods to achieve them.

But in 1956, the anti-communists had a new adversary to contend with: John Henry Faulk, whose bold defiance of the blacklist would be unlike any seen before.

CHAPTER FOURTEEN:
The John Henry Faulk story

"JIMMIE Higgins" was a fictional character used by American socialist leader Eugene V. Debs to describe the human raw material of socialism in America. In the early 1900s, a young Jimmie might have grown up on the Plains, in hardscrabble country, on sagebrush prairies, or in one of the raw new cities springing up on riverbanks and around railroad depots. Jimmie, in the 1930s, would know the privations of the Great Depression firsthand. He would eke out a meager existence, working when he could. Desperation and isolation would kindle the fires of unionism in his soul.

When Debs and his fellow prophets of socialism spoke, Jimmie Higgins and his kin listened, and they were stirred to action. Seeking security and finding solidarity in the workers' movement, Jimmie gravitated toward the radical Wobblies and thence into the orbit of the Communist Party. The communists were eager to please. One of the insistent themes emanating from party headquarters on East 12th Street in New York City was the need to break down barriers between urban intellectual communists and the oppressed masses—the working poor, the unemployed, ethnic outcasts, and minorities. Jimmie responded to the Socialist Party values of tolerance, equality, and a shared mission. He and others listened to the communist leaders. When someone passed the hat, Eugene Debs would say, Jimmie "emptied the frayed pockets of his shiny black suit."

John Henry Faulk had a trace of Jimmie Higgins in him. Writing years after he battled the blacklist, Faulk described the roots of his activism:

> We have always honored a citizen who felt strongly enough
> about his country's problems to join with his neighbors, meet

and discuss how best to solve them. Once we got our right peaceably to assemble and to petition the government for a redress of grievances nailed down good and solid in the Bill of Rights of our Constitution, we started joining and we haven't slowed down since. That is, we didn't slow down until after World War II, when we were suddenly told that we had better stop this joining or we would get hauled in before a committee and made to apologize or get publicly pilloried, blacklisted. We suddenly lost our appetite for joining. And most of us quit joining. And we quit questioning and doubting. If we didn't quit, we kept quiet about it. We knew the vigilantes were riding.

FAULK'S GRASSROOTS

Faulk was born August 21, 1913, and raised in Texas. He grew up in Austin, where his father, Henry, was a well-known lawyer, a Mason, and a dedicated Methodist. Henry Faulk's long list of friends included Debs and political heavyweights Sam Rayburn and Lyndon Johnson. John Henry Faulk described his father as a man with a strong spiritual kinship to Jimmie Higgins: "He began to envisage the unlimited joy and happiness that could come to mankind through achieving a liberated mind. Yet Daddy identified so completely and affectionately with his Texas surroundings that he was not regarded as alien in the community. I suppose few of them understood what he really believed."

Faulk remembered his father warning him that "bigotry was a two-edged sword that punished the wielder as much as it did the victim." He told his son: "We've come a long way, Johnny, and we've got a long way to go. But America has the juice and power to get there."

Faulk enrolled at the University of Texas, receiving his bachelor's and master's degrees there. After graduation, Faulk was hired as an English instructor at the university, and energetically pursued an original research project: He traveled within the state as much as he could, recording and collecting the words of Black Texas preachers. Faulk learned by heart

CHAPTER FOURTEEN: THE JOHN HENRY FAULK STORY

some of the lyrical Old Testament stories—Samson and Delilah to David and Goliath.

When World War II started, Faulk was turned down for military service because of a blind eye. He joined the U.S. Merchant Marine, drawing hazardous duty on convoys. He put in a stint with the Red Cross in Egypt, and in 1944, when physical requirements for enlistment were looser, he joined the Army. He was assigned to Camp Swift in Bastrop County, Texas, where he received training as a psychiatric social worker.

Discharged in 1946, Faulk became determined to try his luck in broadcasting. He packed up his belongings and drove east to New York City. His mellifluous Texas drawl, ready wit, and easy charm got him on the air. Radio jobs soon led him to CBS, and by 1951 he had a contract.

Faulk was a natural radio host and interlocutor, putting his guests at ease and entertaining listeners with his colorful stories and gentle wit. Soon he had his own network program, "Johnny's Front Porch," and some fans compared him to humorist Will Rogers. Faulk also emceed R.J. Reynolds' radio quiz show, "Walk a Mile for a Camel." On the side, he lectured on American heritage from time to time in churches and before charitable groups.

By the mid-1950s, Faulk was poised to transition from radio personality to TV star. Faulk started out with a nine-month stint on a panel show for CBS-TV, "We Take Your Word," where he explored word derivations with Harriet Van Horne, Abe Burrows, and host John Daly.

On the talk show "Leave It to the Girls," guest panelist Faulk defended the male gender against the likes of Elsa Maxwell and Dorothy Kilgallen. In the show's final season in 1954, Faulk became the permanent male panelist. *Variety*, the show business trade magazine, gave Faulk's TV personality a rave review: "Faulk was relaxed, natural, knew how to shade his satire, and emerged so warm a personality that he should cast his iconoscopes on wider wavelengths."

Faulk also had guest slots on two panel shows for ABC, "It's News to Me" and "The Name's the Same."

By 1956, he had made hundreds of TV appearances. The future looked bright.

TWO STUDENTS OF AMERICANA

Without the nation's divide over communism, John Henry Faulk and Laurence Johnson might have become friends, or at the very least enjoyed mutual respect. Both men had roots in the same traditions. Faulk's ancestors, like Johnson's, gathered at the country store to talk politics and munch crackers around the stove.

Both men loved American folklore. Johnson was a lifelong collector of merchandising memorabilia. He assembled a respectable collection of campaign buttons and other artifacts. Faulk's interest in folklore grew in his junior year at the University of Texas when he took J. Frank Dobie's course on the life and literature of the Southwest. Dobie's scholarly articles on folklore were of the kind interesting to Johnson, whose own writing appeared in the pages of *New York Folklore Quarterly* and *The Chronicle of Early American Industries*.

Johnson and Faulk both staked a claim to a piece of America that was righteous and proud. While dedication to American values led Johnson to become a civic fighter against communism, it propelled Faulk with equal vigor to oppose tactics of the anti-communists. Each believed in his own obligation to society that transcended personal interests.

Like Johnson, Faulk was a masterful merchandiser, but in his own ways. Faulk pitched his sponsors' products on the air in the manner of Arthur Godfrey, using soft-sell and folksy charm to make the sale. Faulk devised his own merchandising gimmick, visiting retail stores to represent the sponsor at personal appearances.

The fans gathered, the products disappeared, and everyone was delighted. CBS promoted its star traveling salesman to the hilt. Merchandising director Howard Lally ordered a slick flier printed; it described a successful Faulk road trip to a Flushing supermarket on behalf of Hunt's tomato sauce.

"Arriving at 2 p.m. the photographer found that 69 of the 75 cases in the featured display had been sold to eager customers," the promotion read. "Only six cases were left for the remaining four hours of Saturday shopping. In other words, this was a merchandising effort so successful that it left no evidence for picture taking."

CHAPTER FOURTEEN: The John Henry Faulk story

Faulk's appearances made news in the same trade publications Johnson read and wrote for. "John Henry Faulk is about as persuasive a talker as they come," read one capsule sketch. "He's an authority on the language and lore of our American heritage. He developed his skill as a folk humorist while teaching at the University of Texas. He is one of the top-rated personalities among major stations in New York, and he is backed by extensive point-of-sales promotion in more than 900 metropolitan stores."

Typically, Johnson would have lionized this kind of food supersalesman. But Faulk had a streak of Jimmie Higgins in him, and Johnson was a Higgins-hunter.

The chasm grew even wider after Faulk joined the liberal faction of the American Federation of Radio Artists, which became AFTRA when TV got going.

THE UNION BATTLEFIELD

The radio union had long been an arena in the struggle between the anti-communists and the anti-anti-commmunists (labeled "pro-communists" by their critics). The anti-communists had dominated the 7,000-member union since the early years of World War II. They demonstrated their power in July 1951, just before TV workers joined the union. The AFRA board put to a vote a measure that would bar membership to anyone identified as a communist after 1945. The measure passed 2,118 to 457. After this, communists in AFTRA—and there were some—kept a low profile while continuing to exert influence within the union.

In December 1954, a slate of twenty-six AFTRA members mounted a campaign to unseat the anti-communists, who had exercised power over the New York local's board for a dozen years. The insurgents talked about ending blacklisting and urged the union to take a stand against anti-communist activism. This first skirmish ended in defeat. Anti-communist incumbents even gained support in the election of Vinton Hayworth and Bud Collyer.

The escalating struggle between AFTRA factions made for tense union meetings. Interviewed for "Report on Blacklisting," actor Leslie Barrett recalled one such gathering. "The meeting ended and I left dejected and miserable, the reason being that the tenor of these meetings is fraught with fear, distrust and acrimonious debate," he said. "There is disagreement but few if any will speak out. Why? 'Because I have a little list,' so the saying goes, and if your name is listed, you do not work."

Barrett noticed that a man he didn't know at the meeting was studying him carefully. Two days later, Barrett received a note:

> Dear Mr. Barrett:
>
> In preparing a book on the Left Theatre, I came across certain information regarding you. A photograph of the 1952 New York May Day parade shows you marching.
>
> It is always possible that people have in good faith supported certain causes and come to realize that their support was misplaced. Therefore I am writing you to ascertain if there has been any change in your position.
>
> You are, of course, under no obligation to reply to this letter. As a matter of fact, I am under no obligation to write to you. However, my aim is to be scrupulously fair and to establish the facts. If I do not hear from you, I must conclude that your marching in the 1952 May Day Parade is still an accurate index of your position and sympathies.
>
> I am enclosing a 3-cent stamp for a reply.
>
> Very truly yours, Vincent Hartnett.

As Barrett recalled it, he first checked with AFTRA and learned that Hartnett was a member in good standing and an influential leader of the anti-communist faction. Then he called the FBI and asked if Hartnett was a bona fide loyalty investigator. The bureau told him that, while they didn't endorse the work of civic activists like Hartnett, there wasn't much they could do about it—it was a free country, after all.

Barrett then called his lawyer. The attorney sent Hartnett a statement affirming Barrett's patriotism and denying his client had ever marched in a May Day parade. Hartnett's reply was prompt and curt:

CHAPTER FOURTEEN: The John Henry Faulk story

> Dear Mr. Barrett:
>
> To my surprise I received today a letter dated December 13 from Mr. Klein, a lawyer....As things stand at this point, I have not received from you any reply to my December 9th letter. I have no way of establishing that Mr. Klein is authorized to speak for you or that he has accurately transmitted to me your statement.
>
> Parenthetically, is this the same Harvey L. Klein who is listed as having signed Communist Party nominating petitions in 1939-40?
>
> Enclosed is a photograph of a group of marchers in the New York May Day Parade in 1952. The gentleman underneath the left arrow looks like you. Possibly I am mistaken. There may be some other actor in New York who closely resembles you. I have no desire to harass you.
>
> My only desire is to establish the facts. Frankly, I am disappointed up to this point. In my previous experience in similar cases, people who had nothing to hide did not pull a lawyer into the discussion. They simply and candidly denied or affirmed the evidence. I hope you will be equally candid and direct. You will find me most sympathetic and understanding.
>
> Sincerely yours, Vincent Hartnett.

Barrett quickly complied with Hartnett's request, sending him a personal letter restating his own patriotic bona fides—and now his lawyer's, too. Hartnett, apparently mollified, dropped Barrett's name from his lists. Hartnett followed up with one more note:

> Dear Mr. Barrett:
>
> I appreciate your writing me. I hope you incurred no expense by this unnecessary move of calling in a lawyer. This only muddied the waters.

Frankly, two people in radio and TV who know you thought the man pictured in the May Day Parade photo was you. Research to establish a positive identification of the man is continuing.

Sincerely yours, Vincent Hartnett.

Barrett had escaped the widening net of the anti-communists. Other AFTRA members were not as fortunate.

THE BATTLE IS JOINED

During a particularly acrimonious meeting in the spring of 1955, AFTRA debated a resolution condemning Aware Inc. and its *Publication 12*, which in late 1954 had listed the alleged communist front records of fifteen AFTRA members who had been part of the anti-blacklisting slate.

Godfrey Schmidt of Aware argued in defense of his group: "There is a clear intent expressed here in the anti-Aware resolution that another type of activity should be denominated blacklisting. That is to say, to tell the truth about candidates....The truth, ladies and gentlemen: Every single line in this (bulletin) is the unchallengeable truth, the best proof of it that none of you will dare, if you feel aggrieved, bring it to court, as you could."

Actress Lee Grant, one of the AFTRA leaders who had faced Aware before, counterattacked. "I think the fact that our board members are sitting with a man, Vincent Hartnett, who is the author of *Red Channels* and helped to put out lists is a shameful, shameful thing and should not be tolerated in our union," she said.

Actor Harold Gary addressed Schmidt: "When I learned about Americanism—and I like to think of myself as a pretty good American—I learned nobody can appoint himself as a self-constituted judge and jury of his fellow man....I don't know how long you have been an actor, Mr. Schmidt, if you are one, but I want you to know that you're playing with dynamite, and only people who are duly authorized and licensed should be permitted to play with dynamite."

CHAPTER FOURTEEN: THE JOHN HENRY FAULK STORY

Amid applause Gary continued: "An actor's career is very precariously perched. I have been an actor long enough to know that. The least bit of censure, whether justified or unjustified, can ruin him, whether it is on moral, political, or other grounds, and I think it is a horrendous thing, a criminal thing, for you to toy with other people's careers that they have given all their lives and emotions and study to."

There were some pro-Aware speeches. Radio announcer Rex Marshall said AFTRA was "indebted to a group that gives its time freely to expose elements that are dangerous to this country and to this union. I don't think you can condemn a vigilante committee for being vigilant. If it is accused of being a lynching committee, I think the accusation should be made properly by the persons who considered themselves in danger of lynching."

Marshall then expressed support for the curiously un-American premise that anyone on a blacklist was presumed to be guilty until they had proved themselves innocent. "Until proper charges have been brought by those accused in the bulletin, we can only assume that the accusations are justified, and we should thank the people who are interested enough to give their time to look for our interest."

As AFTRA debated the resolution, Hartnett and his allies enlisted reluctant support from a new source: Kim Hunter. Now hoping to end her own blacklisting, the actress agreed to oppose the AFTRA progressives publicly.

Earlier, an elated Hartnett wrote to Johnson in Syracuse: "Confidentially I had a good telephone conversation this morning with Kim Hunter who just returned to New York from the Bucks County Playhouse. I stressed to Kim Hunter that she *had* to take a public stand against Communism. She assured me that she would do so and if she comes through tomorrow night at the AFTRA meeting as she promised she would do, you will hear the comrades shrieking all the way from New York to Syracuse."

Sure enough, Hunter sent a telegram to her fellow AFTRA members urging them to drop their resolution condemning Aware. She wrote:

> Let those cited in Publication 12 seek redress. Don't go out on a limb. For your union to condemn Aware Inc. shouldn't it

> also bring suit against Aware for libel and defamation of character? Is AFTRA prepared to follow this through to its logical conclusion? And what earthly good do we hope to accomplish for the union or its members by passing this resolution?
>
> I'm neither a member of Aware Inc. nor a friend, nor am I in sympathy with any of its methods, but I urge you all to think very carefully indeed before voting for this resolution.

The message was less than ardent in its defense of Aware, but it was the most that Hartnett and his colleagues could expect.

And the telegram succeeded in wiping Hunter off blacklists. From that point on, Hunter reported later, she found she "worked quite frequently."

At a meeting on June 30, 1955, the resolution was put to a secret vote and passed 197 to 149. Shocked by this opposition, Aware supporters in AFTRA insisted on a mail referendum so the entire union membership could vote on the resolution. This result shocked even more: 982 to 514 in favor of the resolution.

During the summer of 1955, AFTRA's internal struggle boiled over into the mass-circulation press. Among those rallying behind Aware were columnists Leon Racht of the *New York Journal-American*, Bill Coleman of the *Tablet*, and George Sokolsky of the Hearst press.

Talk host Steve Allen devoted an installment of his NBC-TV show to the AFTRA move against Aware. He invited Schmidt and Hartnett to defend Aware against columnist John Crosby and actress Faye Emerson.

Schmidt wrote to his allies in Syracuse that he and Aware were far from distressed by all the publicity. He said:

> We benefit by the controversy and will benefit more; while our first ambition is to be right rather than popular, we have been brought to wide attention in and outside the field of entertainment communications.
>
> Our purposes have been proclaimed and are being discussed. We have found many new friends and some more of our opponents have identified themselves. And most heartening of

CHAPTER FOURTEEN: The John Henry Faulk story

all: the violence proves that Aware is hurting the Communist conspiracy. And that is our purpose.

No "condemnation" or criticism will deflect us from the objectives set forth in our Statement of Principles....So far as we are concerned the fight has just begun.

Schmidt took the opportunity to deny that Aware had interfered in the union's affairs, that it fed any information to show-business employers, or that it played a role in their operations. "It does not supply data to any employer, gratis or otherwise," he said.

However, seeking to keep the pressure on AFTRA, Hartnett urged federal legislators to look into the union. Other board members joined Hartnett and Aware in calling for a congressional probe.

The HCUA investigators responded by scheduling hearings in August and October 1955 to explore allegations of communist infiltration of the New York entertainment industry. Fourteen of twenty-seven witnesses at those hearings refused to answer questions on constitutional grounds. They were George Tyne, John Randolph, Stanley Prager, Martin Wolfson, Phil Leeds, Sara Cunningham, Elliott Sullivan, Madeline Lee, Peter Lawrence, Joshua Shelley, George Keane, Albert M. Ottenheimer, Alan Manson, and Zero Mostel. Subsequently, all their careers suffered, and most faced legal sanctions.

Singer Pete Seeger, who refused to answer questions but also refused to use the Fifth Amendment to do so, was cited for contempt and sentenced to a year in jail.

Aware, which had gathered names from the AFTRA vote, would note that all but one of fifteen members who refused to answer HCUA's questions had also voted for the resolution, along with "at least 50 persons with significant and unrepudiated Communist-front records."

Under this newest heat from Congress, AFTRA's anti-communist boldness evaporated. In August 1955, the membership voted 3,967 to 914 to allow local boards to punish members who refused to answer the HCUA's questions. Henceforth, uncooperative AFTRA witnesses could be fined, suspended or expelled.

Faulk said later that during this strained period he "began to take an active interest in AFTRA's affairs." It would be Faulk's vocal opposition to blacklisting and his successful run for the AFTRA board that soon prompted the anti-communists to place a big target on his back.

After *Publication 16*, although still employed by CBS, Faulk lost other radio work and became all but unemployable on television.

Unlike most who found themselves blacklisted, Faulk refused to quietly suffer and hope for the best. Blacklisting had damaged his career, and he wanted compensation and his name cleared. He never was a communist or a communist supporter, Faulk said later, so he was in a strong position to test in the courts the bigger issue: the "nefarious and racketeering practices (of blacklisting) which masquerade as patriotism."

'A LEGAL DECLARATION OF WAR'

Faulk planned to join a lawsuit with Charles Collingwood and Orson Bean, the two other performers singled out in Aware's *Publication 16*. But Collingwood and Bean decided not to seek legal relief, and Faulk was left to press on alone.

Friends and associates had urged Faulk not to sue for libel. They argued it could only hurt his career by compounding the controversy surrounding his name. Advertising executives from four agencies representing his sponsors also warned him that it was foolish to go to court.

However, in the spring of 1956, he arrived at the midtown Manhattan offices of Louis Nizer, the legendary trial lawyer dubbed by the media "Napoleon of the courtroom." Faulk found a swarthy man of medium height and build, immaculately tailored, dark hair brilliantined, with piercing dark eyes. Years later, Nizer's best-selling anthology of his exploits, "My Life in Court," prompted this accolade from Robert R. Kirsch in the *Los Angeles Times Book Review*: "Louis Nizer could have achieved excellence not only in the field of law (which he has) or in the field of authorship (which he has), but could have done so as a philosopher, a psychologist, a detective, literary critic and a research scholar, to name but a few pursuits."

CHAPTER FOURTEEN: THE JOHN HENRY FAULK STORY

After a short talk, Nizer agreed to represent Faulk, although the attorney warned that the process would be long and emotionally difficult.

"I don't want you to be misled that this would be an easy case. It won't be," Nizer said. "But you will win in the end."

On June 26, 1956, Nizer filed suit in New York State Supreme Court on behalf of Faulk, naming Aware Inc., Vincent Hartnett, and Laurence A. Johnson as defendants in an action alleging libel and conspiracy, and seeking $500,000 in damages.

From the start, Nizer envisioned the case not as a narrow dispute between Faulk and the defendants, not even a symbolic battle between the "Middlers" and anti-communists in the AFTRA union. Nizer sought a show trial exposing the dark side of blacklisting with the goal of shutting down the clearance role of the anti-communists in show business.

Nizer wrote later about the lawsuit:

> It was a legal declaration of war on the nefarious practices which pervaded the entertainment industry....The key language was that the defendants conspired maliciously to defame and injure Faulk, to destroy his livelihood, to remove him as an officer of AFTRA by certain "racketeering practices."
>
> The gantlet had been thrown down for a battle to the finish. The issue involved nothing less than the extermination of the entire machinery for reviewing an artist's record of loyalty. Whether it was called blacklisting or patriotic precaution, the validity of the procedure would be legally tested.

Faulk's accusers, now the accused in a major lawsuit, at first were not concerned.

"In all honesty, I thought it was a publicity stunt," Hartnett said years later. "I said, 'Well, how could anybody sue? What would be the basis for the lawsuit?'"

In retrospect, he could see that the lawsuit was not entirely unexpected. In the late summer of 1955, Hartnett said, he attended a panel discussion on "so-called blacklisting" in suburban Connecticut, where he and the novelist Rex Stout squared off on the subject. Their conversation touched on the struggle between Aware and AFTRA. After the program, a group adjourned to a restaurant, where Hartnett said he was approached by "a famous cartoonist whom I'll not name."

"He told me I'd better enjoy life while I could because I was going to be out of business within a few months because of a lawsuit," Hartnett said. "Now, this was even before the bulletin came out."

Hartnett and his colleagues at Aware had reason to feel confident they could overcome Faulk's lawsuit. In the hostile judicial atmosphere of the late 1940s and through the early 1950s, courts routinely rejected legal actions by show business plaintiffs, including the Hollywood Ten. These rejections took various forms, such as outright dismissals, reversals on appeal, occasional token settlements, and at least one hung jury. A plan by the American Civil Liberties Union for libel suits fell through. As the 1950s progressed, no one had succeeded in defeating the anti-communists in court.

Nevertheless, Hartnett decided news of Faulk's lawsuit was important enough to relay it without delay to Laurence Johnson, who was traveling overseas with his wife. At the time, Johnson was adjusting to the reality of no longer owning a supermarket. He was particularly disappointed the new owner showed no interest in the beloved historical exhibit in the South Salina Street store. "The first thing Victory did was come in and tear out the Old Country Store," Coyne said. When Johnson found out, she said, it "broke his heart." Victory Supermarkets, however, did allow Johnson to keep some of his collection in permanent storage at the store.

In the late June, Hartnett sent a terse message to Johnson at the Hotel Excelsior in Rome, Italy: "We got sued by John Henry Faulk. He wants half a million bucks."

After Faulk's lawsuit was filed, Johnson quietly ended his calls and letters targeting blacklisted entertainers. The Veterans Action Committee of Syracuse Super Markets also disbanded. In October 1956, *Spotlight* praised departing VAC president Francis Neuser, Johnson's fruit and vegetable buyer, as Patriot of the Month. The editors used the occasion for a tribute to the VAC members:

> There was no glory attached to the patriotic work they performed. Indeed they never sought any, for they fully realized

how distasteful it was to have to expose the records of certain individuals who appeared on TV or radio sponsored by products they sold over the counter each day.

Neuser's untiring efforts on behalf of everything American and his honesty, coupled with his sincerity of purpose, enabled his organization to slow down the efforts of the communist party in taking over radio and TV and other communications media.

The smears received by Neuser and the Veterans Action Committee from left-wing publications and from the communist party itself is a tribute to their success in their fight to save America.

Interviewed in the 1980s, Hartnett said the VAC's end certainly came in response to Faulk's lawsuit. "After 1956, with the lawsuit filed, the Veterans Action Committee was dead," he said. "I imagine it was the chilling effect of the lawsuit. The lawsuit did what it was intended to do."

Hartnett also drifted away from anti-communist activities. Hartnett would earn $17,658 in 1956, most of it from his "security consulting" work, a decrease from 1955. He and his family moved to Crestwood, a middle-class New York suburb, and he started to work on a show-business directory, mostly focusing on biographies of English theatrical people. The publication would have had nothing to do with communists, pro-communists, or communist-fronters. But the project never materialized.

"I was discredited, of course, by the lawsuit," Hartnett said.

As for Johnson, at least publicly, he kept his thoughts on the lawsuit to himself.

'THIS IS REAL SERIOUS'

Johnson's neighbor Burnett Haylor recalled how the topic of the lawsuit came up one day when he was having lunch with *The Post-Standard*'s Tink Keller. Like Hartnett, Haylor was inclined to dismiss the lawsuit as a publicity gimmick. Keller, who remembered all too clearly Senator McCarthy's lawsuit against the newspaper three years earlier, took a more cautious view.

John Henry Faulk, standing, meets with attorney Louis Nizer outside of court in 1962. (The Center for American History, The University of Texas at Austin photo)

"Barney, this is real serious. You don't know what the hell's going to happen to Larry," Keller said.

When Nizer filed an amended complaint on September 14, it became even clearer that Johnson was in for a rough time. The 42-page document listed count after count in a blistering attack on the defendants.

Nizer's summary was a compelling run-on sentence that portrayed Johnson and his allies as defamers, blacklisters, racketeers, and profiteers:

Since on or about February 1956, the defendants conspired and maliciously and willfully participated in a plan and course of action designed to defame and injure the plaintiff in his good name and reputation, in his professions of radio and television artist and lecturer; to destroy his income and his livelihood; to remove the plaintiff as an officer of AFTRA; and to eliminate and vitiate the declared opposition of the plaintiff, as such an officer of AFTRA, to certain nefarious and racketeering practices of the defendants, involving the use of intimidation and terror in order to procure the blacklisting of radio and television artists by the networks, sponsors, producers and advertising agencies and to censor and control all employment of such artists, and, upon information and belief, the extortion of monies in consideration for the "clearance" and even the mere "screening," of radio and television artists charged by the defendants, however baselessly, with subversive or former subversive associations.

FAULK'S TROUBLES MULTIPLY

At first, CBS stood by Faulk, despite the drop-off in sponsors and additional pressure from ad agencies resulting from the lawsuit and concurrent bad publicity. In December 1956, the network offered Faulk a five-year contract. He signed with relief. Faulk still had the support of CBS newsman Murrow, who donated $7,500 to help with his legal bills.

In April 1957, the New York State Appellate Division rejected a request from Godfrey Schmidt to dismiss Faulk's lawsuit, and the case was assigned to state Supreme Court Justice Saul Streit. From there, the legal process would drag on month after month.

A warning sign of career troubles ahead for Faulk came in June 1957 when the hardline anti-communist faction in AFTRA, led by Ed Sullivan, reasserted itself and wrestled back majority control of the union's board of directors, meaning Faulk could not count on the support of the union to keep his job at WCBS.

In July, an exhausted but still-hopeful Faulk left New York City with his family for a vacation on the Caribbean island of Jamaica.

On August 6, the day after they returned, Faulk learned that CBS had fired him. The network offered multiple reasons for letting him go. One was that Arthur Godfrey had pre-empted Faulk's half-hour time slot; another was overall stagnation in programming that needed reshuffling; the third was that Faulk's ratings had slipped.

No one at CBS would come right out and tell Faulk the network was giving in to efforts by anti-communists to push him off the air. In the mid-1950s, CBS, like many others, refused to publicly acknowledge that a blacklist even existed, let alone that it hired or fired based on one.

Whatever the reason, Faulk was out of work. In the days immediately following his departure from CBS, Faulk turned to the other networks looking for work. During his rise at CBS, he had passed on several tempting offers from the competition. After CBS let him go, these same outlets had no interest in offering him anything.

His hopes rose when WCCO-AM in Minneapolis initially reacted favorably to his overtures; however, that job opportunity fell through.

Late in 1957, Faulk found himself in line for a job in New York with the Mutual Broadcasting Company radio station WOR. When Hartnett heard about this, despite being out of the clearance business, he called Pat Winkler, a WOR executive. After Hartnett passed along details of the allegations against Faulk and the ensuing controversy, WOR ended its interest in hiring Faulk.

At one point he was about to accept a job offer from an old friend, Wendell Campbell, for a DJ slot with KFRC-FM in San Francisco when a letter arrived from Campbell. "Johnny, at this point I have to pass," Campbell wrote. "I want you to understand that it wasn't because of our reaction to your work, it's just that some other things have come up which preclude our asking you to join us."

The letter didn't specify these "other things." But Faulk learned the truth anyway when he received a letter Campbell had meant for Robert Leder, vice president of WOR Radio in New York. Campbell's secretary had mistakenly addressed the envelope to Faulk.

CHAPTER FOURTEEN: THE JOHN HENRY FAULK STORY

Campbell wrote that he was "concerned with Johnny's legal problems with Aware Inc. but have been given to understand that these are all cleared up. If this is so, then we will be definitely interested in him." Of course, Faulk's legal problems had not been "cleared up" at all—which is why Campbell lost interest in Faulk.

In 1959, KNOW-AM in Austin invited Faulk to go on the air in his old hometown. However, on March 3, eleven days before he and his family were to move, Faulk got the word: KNOW's programming plans made it impossible for him to be one of its radio personalities, and he would "just have to forget the whole thing."

As opportunity after opportunity disappeared for Faulk, he borrowed money from friends to get by. Faulk stayed in New York and went to work as a mutual fund salesman, which, by his own account, was a disaster.

Then he moved back to Austin. Faulk opened an advertising agency that barely paid the bills. While there, the Austin Anti-Communist League publicized his presence while closely monitoring the legal case unfolding in New York.

CHAPTER FIFTEEN:
The Antiquarian

Laurence Johnson suffered a devastating loss on May 11, 1957, when his wife died at age sixty-four after a painful fight with cancer. Hermione had shared his interest in antiquing—more so than in shopkeeping, and certainly more so than in fighting communism. And while daughter Lois readily admitted her parents didn't always have an "ideal marriage," her father deeply missed his wife's companionship. "They were both strong-willed people," Lois said. "And they both inherited genes of intellectual interest." Daughter Marilyn said that her father, mourning for Hermione, lamented: "My bobbin has run out."

Following the sale of his supermarkets, his wife's death, and the pending libel suit interrupting his anti-communist activism, Johnson returned to one of his first loves: Americana.

Johnson began to downsize his collection of antiques and memorabilia. By 1958, Johnson had sold a complete country store replica to Grover Robbins Jr., the owner of the "Tweetsie Railroad" tourist attraction in Blowing Rock, North Carolina. Johnson also sold a considerable portion of his political memorabilia and country store artifacts to the Western entrepreneur A.J. Bayless, who built the Bayless Cracker Barrel Country Store in Phoenix, Arizona.

Johnson threw himself into his historical research. He reconnected with an old friend, Jasena Foley. Together they would delve into local history and visit folklore conventions. They grew particularly close after Foley's husband died in 1961. Foley found it amusing when Johnson would express concern that people might gossip about all the time he spent with her.

"Now, I don't want to do anything that's going to reflect on your character in any way," he said.

And Foley replied, "Larry, I've never been talked about in my life and I'm just dying to get the experience!"

And Johnson would just laugh, she said.

"He liked devils like me," she said. "He never knew what I was going to say. And when we were going someplace, if he wanted pie for breakfast, it was all right with me. He was a good traveler. He'd take an extra pair of glasses, an extra set of teeth, and he said he was prepared for anything."

In 1958, Johnson expanded his folklore scholarship with an article in *Spinning Wheel*, a national antiques magazine. His topic was Bath brick, an abrasive for cleaning cutlery. As part of the background research, Johnson gathered material on a trip to England, where he learned how Bath brick was invented and manufactured from tidal silt deposits in Bridgwater, Somerset.

He also contributed an article to *The Chronicle*, published by the Early American Industries Association, on the history of the Hasher, a meat and vegetable cutter invented in 1865 by New England entrepreneur Laroy S. Starrett.

In the spring of 1959, Johnson was featured in an affectionate article in *Food Marketing in New England*. He was described as "a pioneer supermarket operator, nationally known food merchant and, as a sideline, an antiquarian and collector specializing in the equipment and merchandising of general stores and food stores of bygone days."

"He dropped in on us recently and told us many new and old things with his keen sense of what's interesting," the writer added.

Johnson talked about the ingenuity and canniness of the early shopkeepers—who were far from being primitive rural characters. "Don't write about the old-time storekeeper as just a comic figure," Johnson advised the journalist. "He was a smart man and his shrewd understanding of human nature and his skillful, offhand way of capitalizing on his knowledge are a fascinating chapter in the big story of the development of American food retailing."

When Johnson and the writer were getting ready to part, Johnson opened the trunk of his car and removed a cone-shaped, blue-papered package tied with string.

CHAPTER FIFTEEN: The Antiquarian

"Take this—the oldest food package known—a sugarloaf," he said.

Johnson was a big fan of sugarloaves, a mass of refined sugar, often produced in the past by pouring molten sugar into a mold to create the desired shape. "He called me one day," Foley recalled, "and said, 'Jasena, can you come over today? I've got sugarloaves all set up.' You know, you crack off your own amount. You have a sugar knife. You whittle it off."

Johnson also displayed his skills as an antiquarian in a charming short piece he wrote for the Winter 1960 issue of the *New York Folklore Quarterly*. Entitled, "A Texas Game in South Butler," the article told the story of 42, a domino game with bids and plays similar with the old card game Pedro.

Before chronicling his efforts to trace the Texas roots of 42, Johnson established the long-ago scene from his boyhood at the Wilson Brothers General Store in South Butler:

> When the hands of the old clock, advertising "Mulford's Cream Mustard," pointed to nine, one of the two Wilson brothers would bring out the large checkerboard and a box of dominoes. We knew then that the game would soon be under way. The privileged four who were to play took their seats....
>
> By the time the lights in front of the store were dimmed or out, pipes were lit and smoke curled above the huddled players. Silence was broken only by the clicking of the dominoes and the low deliberate voices of the bidders. Woe to any onlooker who had the temerity to break the spell while the hand was being bid and played!

Johnson wrote that, when he began wandering beyond Butler, he was surprised to learn that virtually no one had heard of 42. Wrestling with the mystery, he eventually came upon a games encyclopedia with an entry on 42, describing it as the closest thing to the "national game of Texas." Johnson said this jogged his memories of visits to South Butler by Texas relatives of the Wilsons and another local family, the Coxes. He wrote to the Dallas Historical Society, and sent letters to newspapers in Dallas, Fort Worth, and San Antonio, reaping a considerable harvest of responses sketching the possible origins of the game. Having thoroughly explored the "mystery," Johnson wound up his report on a wistful note: 42 was dying out in Central New York, what with the closing and subsequent demolition of the Wilson Brothers store and the advanced age of the surviving few players. Johnson wrote:

> When I pass the site, my thoughts go back to my boyhood. I can remember the dimly-lighted store late in the evening after most of the people in the village were fast asleep. On such an evening long ago a late straggler came into the store and looked down on the players hovered over the old checkerboard. For many years the episode has been told and retold. One of the Wilson brothers was minding the store that night. When the customer came in, Wilson was at the critical point of making his bid. He looked up rather reluctantly and said, "You don't want anything, do you?"

'OVER THE COUNTER AND ON THE SHELF'

Johnson's scholarship was sufficiently rigorous, and his energy and determination were still of such magnitude, that he would go on to complete by the late 1950s a book that he titled "Over the Counter and On the Shelf: Country Storekeeping in America, 1620-1920."

All he needed was a publisher. Before long, a publishing house expressed interest. It was the Charles E. Tuttle Company of Rutland, Vermont—suitably located in the heart of Yankee New England. Johnson signed with Tuttle. Then came a shocker. Johnson learned the book would be farmed out to editorial and manufacturing concerns in Japan. This was a bitter pill for Johnson, whose Americanism was a core value in his life.

"He was disappointed in having it sent abroad," Jasena Foley recalled. "This company sent it to Japan, and he didn't know it was going to be done that way. And the book says 'Rutland, Vermont' (on the title page) as if it had been published in Rutland, and it hadn't, it wasn't, it was done in Japan. And he didn't like that at all. Everything had to be American."

CHAPTER FIFTEEN: The Antiquarian

Laurence Johnson looks over a copy of his newly published book, "Over the Counter and On the Shelf," in March 1961. (Syracuse *Post-Standard* photo)

The book that appeared in 1961 was a thin, oversized volume bound in tan covers, profusely illustrated. The book was arranged mostly chronologically over seven chapters and 161 pages. The lively and fact-filled text showcased Johnson's eye for detail and direct, authoritative style.

While a passionate tribute to his predecessors in shopkeeping, the book had the added value, perhaps unintended, of offering insight into the makeup of Laurence Johnson and his aspirations as a businessman, as an antiquarian, and eventually as an anti-communist activist.

Johnson described the archetypal storekeeper of the 1800s as a common man of the world, the kind of person Johnson admired and tried to emulate. He wrote:

From earliest days the country store was head over heels in

THE GROCER WHO SOLD McCARTHYISM

political discussion. Around the cracker barrel, presidential campaigns were won or lost, and the grass roots of the nation, a phrase coined in later years, called the turn.

The storekeeper himself was a man of consequence, his opinions respected, if not always agreed with. Though he often lacked formal education, he was almost always exceptionally well informed. As postmaster he kept up with the times through the periodicals and newspapers that passed through the office. Yearly buying trips to Philadelphia, New York, Boston, or New Orleans introduced him to a wider world. Slack time in winter could be improved by reading and meditating on the books he carried in stock. Not at all unusual was the book selection of a merchant in a small Missouri town in 1829, who advertised volumes by Josephus, Byron, Shakespeare, Cervantes, Scott, Fielding, Herodotus, Hume, Smollett, Milton, Defoe, Homer, and Bunyan. No wonder, in an age of flowery harangue, the storekeeper was capable of Fourth of July speeches full of classical reference, and to holiday toasts second to none. In his political beliefs, he seldom hesitated to stand and be counted.

Curiously, Johnson, the zealous anti-communist, had some kind words for the "communism" of the Oneida Experiment in Central New York. Johnson praised the commune's lasting contributions to the American marketplace: Oneida silverplate and Newhouse animal traps. He wrote: "One of its cardinal tenets was that selfishness was the chief sin of human kind and that communism was the best method of overcoming it." However, he said, "Like other experimenters in communism in this country, the Community found it could not live up to itself."

An intriguing anecdote in Johnson's book is a description of what may be the country's first "anti-merchandising" effort. It involved the early years of processing coffee that involved various methods of glazing and polishing the bean. Competition was fierce among manufacturers. As Johnson told the story, Arbuckle & Co. once distributed an illustrated handbill suggesting its coffee-roasting rival, Dilworth Bros., ground up trash and sold it to the public as coffee. A picture on the handbill included a small crowd with a man remarking, "No wonder I have been sick," and a woman crying, "I see what killed my children." For eerie resonance, set that cry against the "anti-merchandising" display sign that Johnson reportedly concocted for his stores during the Korean War: "Buy this product and help kill American boys!"

The book had several features that set it slightly askew. The dust jacket carried a garish mishmash of calligraphy above a crude woodcut depicting a country store scene peopled by what looks like alien creatures. The foreword consists of two testimonials, including one by Rose Kiefer, secretary of the National Association of Retail Grocers of the United States. The narrative was interrupted by a single, 52-page chapter that grouped stories about product development. The final chapter covered the development of the modern supermarket in just four pages.

Johnson himself said of the book that he was "chagrined about a number of errors that crept into it." However, such glitches might not be noteworthy or even noticeable to the general reader.

TRAVELING ABROAD

Between March 20 and May 6, 1960, several months before the book came out, Johnson took an ambitious overseas trip, logging more than 5,000 miles in Africa and other countries. Johnson visited game reserves and cities in South Africa, where in Durban he rode up a skyscraper in an elevator marked "European," and down in one for Black visitors.

Johnson hired Amos Kahuha, a 44-year-old Kikuyu, to chauffeur him on the 2,280-mile motor trip through East Africa and into the Belgian Congo, then just weeks away from independence. Johnson later told *The Post-Standard* that, after witnessing some primitive conditions in the Congo's interior, it seemed unthinkable to him that natives were prepared for home rule. The newspaper reported that his was "probably one of the last such excursions into the Belgian Congo for a long while to come for it is not now safe to be a white tourist there. If you point a camera at a native these days he points back with a Sten gun." In another interview, Johnson noted that sugarloaves were made in parts of northern Africa.

Many years later, Hartnett recalled conversations in which Johnson discussed his travels and expressed bewilderment at some unethical practices that thrived in underdeveloped societies.

"I remember the puzzlement he expressed at the mores, for example of some ethnic groups abroad, in their attitudes toward crime. He found this actually to be staggering, the kind of casual attitude," Hartnett said. "He was a man who just thought that people should obey the law, and when he found in some foreign parts the casual acceptance of malfeasance, he was stunned—corruption, black markets, bribes, things like that. He was not naive, but just found this a puzzlement."

Johnson, then seventy-two, continued his travels. He and Jasena Foley drove in June 1961 to Staten Island to view the Richmond Town restoration program, visiting a re-creation billed as a typical American village of the 18th and 19th centuries in metropolitan New York. The city parks department and the Staten Island Historical Society sponsored the project.

Foley said she and Johnson had a ball, enjoying each other's company as much as the Americana. "He knew I didn't want to get married, and I knew he didn't want to get married, so we had a fine time."

The visit to Staten Island would be their last time together engaged in historical sightseeing.

CHAPTER SIXTEEN:
Pretrial Maneuvers

THE two sides in the Faulk lawsuit wrangled over the rules of engagement throughout much of 1956 and 1957. It quickly became clear that this wasn't like the HCUA and other congressional committees where immunity rules protected lawmakers from being sued for slander. Because a private publication had made allegations against Faulk, there was no such protection for the defendants. They also discovered the hard way that a court of law didn't allow the kinds of free-wheeling, unsupported accusations made before Congress.

As the court considered procedural matters, Louis Nizer relentlessly outmaneuvered his counterpart, Aware attorney Godfrey Schmidt. One by one, the court dismissed defense pleadings.

As the months went by, various judges heard pretrial arguments, and they ruled that familiar defenses used in libel cases—truthful reporting, fair comment, free speech, lack of cause—did not apply here as the basis for dismissal of the charges, nor could they be defense arguments during the trial. Schmidt also pleaded some novel defenses, including "provocation," "the right to reply" and even a retrospective defense alluding to the Bolshevik Revolution and the terrors of communism.

By the time Schmidt had exhausted his repertoire, Justice Saul Streit had died, and the case had passed to the first in a long line of successors. Before the pretrial hearings had concluded, a dozen more jurists would come and go: Walter A. Lynch, Jacob Markowitz, Sidney Fine, Aaron Steuer, George Tilzer, Samuel Hofstadter, Edgar J. Nathan, Owen McGivern, Samuel Gold, Matthew M. Levy, Nathan B. Gurock (who also died during the proceedings), and Irving Saypol.

Finally, yet another judge, Abraham N. Geller, would preside at the trial.

The pretrial examinations of Faulk, Hartnett, Johnson, and Aware's Paul Milton extended over three years, beginning in 1958. Hartnett's interrogation by Nizer's attorneys filled more than 2,500 pages of transcript. His first session took place in Nizer's midtown Manhattan offices on June 5, 1958.

To Nizer's surprise, it appeared Hartnett was trying to dissociate himself from the campaign against Faulk. Both Hartnett and his attorney Schmidt seemed more than willing to forget the whole thing, in effect, to admit that the Faulk attack had been a mistake. The session amounted to a forthright admission of error.

At one point, Nizer asked: "Would you be willing even now to issue a public statement...which would go to television companies and to agencies that could give him employment, that 'If this is the basis for your not giving him employment, I want you to know that...we are sorry, and he is clear as far as we are concerned'?...You would be willing to lend your name to it?"

Hartnett replied: "Yes, I would," explaining that someone sold him "a barrel of false information."

Nizer continued, "If Faulk today had an offer to appear on television for a paid, commercial proposition, so far as you are concerned, if your voice could be heard, or your writing...you would give your blessing to it and would want him to be employed?"

Hartnett: "Yes, I would."

Schmidt added: "That goes for me, too."

Figuratively, Schmidt and Hartnett were standing with hats in hand before an incredulous Nizer, their eyes on the door, looking for a way to get out of the room. Nizer wrote later: "It was apparent that the defenses had for all practical purposes been abandoned."

By and by, Nizer, acknowledging the "spirit of good faith with which we have exchanged this colloquy," proposed a settlement. He and Schmidt went to lunch where Nizer asked if the defendants would write a strong statement retracting their charges against Faulk, and pay the plaintiff a modest sum—say, $10,000—to cover his losses.

CHAPTER SIXTEEN: Pretrial Maneuvers

Schmidt told Nizer he thought he could arrange something along those lines. But he cautioned Nizer that Aware Inc. had no money, Hartnett was not wealthy, and Johnson wouldn't volunteer to pay a penny of any settlement.

Faulk was inclined to press on with the lawsuit. He was still trying to persuade Nizer to continue with the case when word arrived that a settlement had become moot: Former McCarthy aide Roy Cohn had replaced Schmidt as attorney for the defendants.

With the hard-charging Cohn in the picture, the defendants' strategy altered dramatically. There was no more talk of accommodation or out-of-court deals. Cohn insisted the case would go to trial—eventually. First, there was a delay when Cohn left town on an extended trip to the Far East. When the pretrial examination resumed in August 1958, Hartnett was a changed witness. He repudiated the damning admissions he had made in June, saying that after checking, he was more certain about the accuracy of *Publication 16*.

"Mr. Nizer had me wondering myself," Hartnett said. "I was pretty well brainwashed. I began wondering what was what. I checked further, and I found out that the Faulk mentioned in Club 65 was John Faulk of CBS."

Cohn associate attorney Thomas Bolan stretched out the process by raising one objection after another. He interrupted the proceedings hundreds of times, asking questions that had to be referred to a judge, who was sometimes not available. Weeks and months passed. When it was Laurence Johnson's turn to be questioned, the case was already four years old.

Johnson was examined in September 1960, and in April and August 1961. Nizer associate Paul Martinson handled Johnson's questioning, and he hosted the Syracusan at his law offices for his first session.

Johnson was "very polite and soft-spoken during the examination before trial," Martinson later said. "He appeared like a deacon of the church. He seemed elderly, not infirm. He was chagrined."

For all intents and purposes, defense attorney Bolan was the main "witness" at Johnson's three examination sessions. Bolan did most of the talking, while Johnson mostly limited his answers to "I don't know" or "I don't remember."

Martinson's questions delved deeply into Johnson's anti-communism threats, including statements about Kim Hunter in 1955 and Goodyear Tire and Rubber Co. in 1954; the Swanson and Colgate-Palmolive-Peet affairs in 1953; the Block Drug Company, Schlitz, and Proctor & Gamble campaigns in 1952; and the protest against The Weavers in 1951.

If Bolan were to keep this from becoming the show trial that Nizer was looking for, he would have to demonstrate the irrelevance of these previous cases. While Bolan ultimately failed in this quest, his frequent interjections did manage to tie up in knots the pretrial examination proceedings.

At one point, Nizer co-counsel Martinson tried to draw out Johnson on a pressure tactic that the Syracuse grocer used against the Hunt Foods company to get Adolf Dehn off Kate Smith's show. The lawyer asked about Johnson's claim at the time of declining Hunt sales in his stores.

Johnson started to reply: "Yes, that is due to the fact—"

Bolan interrupted. "Let's not go into that."

Martinson then asked Johnson if the discussion of this matter had "refreshed your recollection" that Hunt subsequently canceled its sponsorship of Kate Smith.

"Yes," Johnson replied.

That was more than Faulk's attorney often got from Johnson.

In another exchange, Martinson grew testy after Bolan, standing up, interrupted to explain a question posed to Johnson:

> Martinson: I don't think it needs any explanation, except from me.
>
> Bolan: When he (Johnson) says he doesn't understand the question, I think it needs an explanation.
>
> Martinson: Then ask me for an explanation, Mr. Johnson, please. Please sit down, Mr. Bolan.
>
> Bolan: No, I won't, I want to read the document myself.
>
> Martinson: You have no right to consult the witness during an examination.
>
> Bolan: I have a right to read the document.

CHAPTER SIXTEEN: Pretrial Maneuvers

Martinson: Confine yourself to reading it and refrain from talking.

Bolan: Then you will permit me to stand if I like?

Martinson: And not talk to the witness.

Bolan: Thank you for allowing me to stand.

Martinson: You have been doing a great deal more than that, as you know.

Bolan: I take exception to that.

Martinson: To the truth?

Bolan: Pardon me...

As Martinson and Bolan jousted, Johnson sat silently, his body language reflecting irritation with the process.

On the rare occasion when Johnson didn't answer a question with a claim of amnesia, he often lapsed into sly country-bumpkin jargon. "You will have to excuse me for not being very astute in catching all these little phrases," he told Martinson at one point.

Responding to a question about whether he intimidated salesmen with threats of product boycotts in his stores, Johnson offered one of his longest responses, but he largely danced around the issue:

"You mentioned something there, Mr. Martinson, will you read the question there? I thought the way you were phrasing that, that the salesman would be afraid his product wouldn't be sold in our store anymore ....That wouldn't have been said anyway, because we never did anything of that nature....There wouldn't have been any conversation with relation to the sale of the product.

"What I did was something that I did for lots of others. If they asked me to call their houses, I did. Because, as I said, we worked very closely with the salesmen. We helped him all we could."

Johnson was similarly evasive on other topics, such as the reason he was familiar with the New York Public Library, where he once pored over back issues of the *Daily Worker* for damning references to show-business figures.

"I checked down at the library lots of times, on matters that I was writing on— trade publications, making notes on my book, which thank the Lord the last few months has come out," Johnson said.

Martinson asked Johnson if the book was about communism.

"No, no," Johnson replied, explaining that it was a history of shopkeeping in America. Johnson said it was due to his interest in folklore that he recognized Henry Wallace's name in an Aware bulletin. "I am a collector of political Americana, and...Wallace was a Progressive candidate for president at the time, a cowboy from out West was candidate for vice president."

When Martinson asked if Johnson had learned anything about Faulk that suggested the radio host wasn't a dangerous pro-communist, Johnson chose semantic obfuscation: "That is kind of a hard question. You have definitions, I don't know if I am capable of answering on definitions."

Later, Johnson admitted that he had removed some correspondence from his office.

What documents? Martinson asked, apparently hoping to reveal a cover-up of blacklisting efforts.

"Correspondence on antiques and that nature—my hobbies," Johnson answered placidly. "Well, a better word is what the English call it: 'bygones.'"

A while later, he returned to the pretense of being the unsophisticated small-town grocer facing the big-city lawyer: "I can't follow you....You are asking me an opinion, and I am probably wrong giving that to you. This is all new to me."

When Nizer's team had finished with Johnson, they knew little more than when they had begun. Nevertheless, the cumulative effect of the evidence gathered, and Nizer's pretrial arguments, had helped to turn a narrow libel case into the showdown Faulk wanted over the general practice of blacklisting in entertainment.

A DATE IN COURT SET

By early 1962, Bolan and Nizer had completed their pretrial work. A trial date was set for April 16 when the attorneys would begin interviewing prospective jurors.

CHAPTER SIXTEEN: Pretrial Maneuvers

Around this time in Syracuse, Johnson threw one of his popular house parties. Close friend Jasena Foley remembered how the phone rang, and it was Johnson's lawyer, calling from New York. Something about the trial.

"Larry and I were in the kitchen alone," she said. "And Larry said, 'Well, that's not good, is it?' And the conversation went on."

Johnson spoke in a flat tone in the call with the attorney. After he hung up, he turned to Foley and said, "It's a shame it had to come just now. But I'll fight it all the way."

After that, Johnson returned to the party, saying nothing to anyone else about the phone call.

On January 30, 1962, fire ripped through Johnson's old flagship store on Salina Street. The fire gutted the building, causing an estimated $700,000 in damage. It also destroyed Johnson's grocery memorabilia collection, which was stored in a loft space where he had been assembling yet another old country store replica, complete with a vintage post office. Among the artifacts lost were 42-star flags, old wooden egg crates, antique shelving, advertising posters, a 1902 daybook, and an 1888 calendar.

Johnson was devastated. He told a newspaper that the "merchandising bygones" were only insured for a fraction of their value, and some were practically irreplaceable.

"It really took the steam out of him, the fire in the Salina Street store," said his daughter Eleanor Buchanan. "You could see the change in him." Johnson showed no interest in rebuilding the collection.

In the spring of 1962, Johnson was a guest of honor of the Early American Industries Association in Sturbridge, Massachusetts, where his book was a big hit. He was presented with a beautifully bound compilation of his articles that had appeared in *The Chronicle of Early American Industries*.

Without directly referring to the court case, Johnson hinted at his troubles during an interview published in the *Worcester Sunday Telegram* on April 29, by which time the libel trial had begun.

"There's never a dull moment," Johnson told the reporter.

CHAPTER SEVENTEEN:
Faulk Case Goes to Trial

THE trial in *John Henry Faulk v. Aware, Inc., Laurence Johnson and Vincent Hartnett* got underway on April 16, 1962, inside the New York Supreme Courthouse on Foley Square in Manhattan.

Roy Cohn was notably absent from the defense table. The renowned aide to Senator McCarthy during the height of the Red Scare had handed over to associate Thomas Bolan the task of representing Johnson and the other defendants at the trial. This would invite speculation that Cohn, who always seemed to relish a good fight, did not view the case as a winner for his clients.

From the start, Bolan aimed to present the defendants as law-abiding, patriotic Americans, not conspirators. He sought to persuade the jury that his clients' intentions were honorable, that they were diligent in their research and respectful of truth and propriety, that the only malice they bore was toward the menace of communist infiltration and influence. He would argue that John Henry Faulk had lost his job not because of the essentially accurate information published in the Aware bulletin but because of his shortcomings as a broadcaster.

Louis Nizer set out to show that Hartnett, Johnson, and Aware were part of a vicious conspiracy to deprive Faulk of his means of livelihood and good name. Nizer would hammer home that the defendants were racketeers, reckless in their charges, careless in their anti-communist methods, malicious in their intent. Finally, Nizer meant to place the case in the larger context of the McCarthy Era, painting the defendants as agents of a toxic process that systematically victimized innocent men and women in the name of ideological purity.

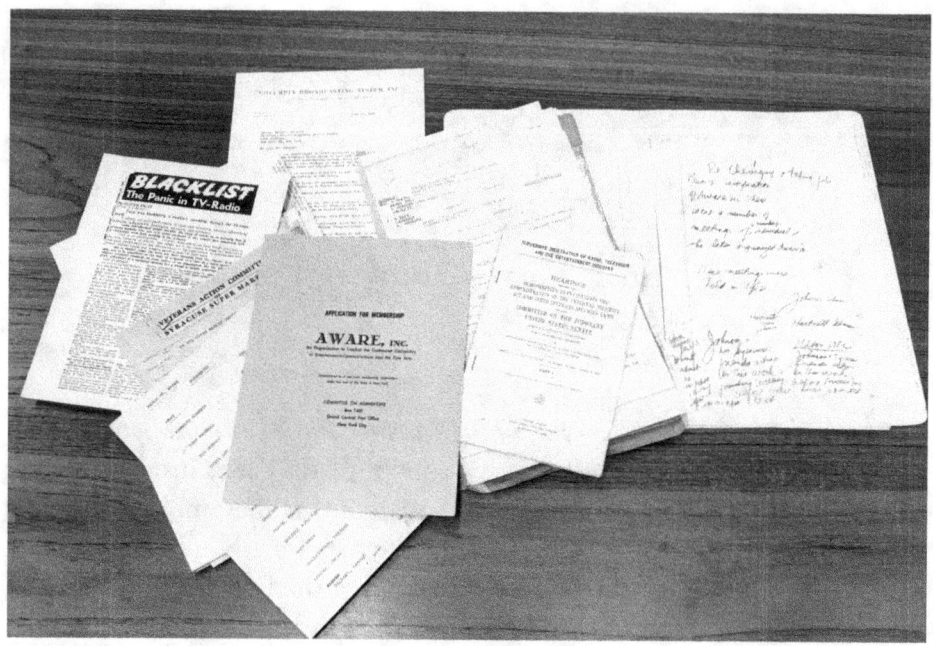

A collage of documents related to *John Henry Faulk v. AWARE, Inc., etc.* is displayed during a "For The Record" exhibit in 1984 at the Barker Texas History Center at the University of Texas at Austin. (The University of Texas at Austin photo)

After the first day of jury selection, Nizer asked Justice Geller for an attorneys' conference in the robing room. Nizer wanted to raise the stakes.

"At the time the suit was instituted, the plaintiff was still employed at CBS," Nizer reminded the judge. "Subsequently we learned, to our dismay, that not only was he to lose that employment, but he was to become unemployable....Under those circumstances, the damages which we had not anticipated would be as pervasive and extensive as they have turned out to be, are now evident to us from actual experience over a period of about five years."

In other words, since the damages to Faulk had worsened since the suit was filed, Nizer wanted permission to ask the jury for more than the $500,000 originally requested.

After hearing from both sides, Justice Geller approved increasing the claim for damages to $1 million, an amount when adjusted for inflation would equal about $10 million in 2024.

CHAPTER SEVENTEEN: Faulk Case Goes to Trial

At the heart of Nizer's case was the list of specific accusations leveled against Faulk by the Aware bulletins. Justice Geller ruled as the trial began that the defense could not justify the mistakes in the bulletins by arguing the writers had relied on the Attorney General's List or HCUA indices. "Those citations," Justice Geller said, "are not binding and do not constitute a finding—a proper finding. It must be a judicial finding ...."

As Nizer wrote later with evident satisfaction: "The defendants had the burden of proving that Faulk actually attended the functions he was accused of in the *Bulletin*, that they were Communist Fronts, and that he knew or should have known that they were."

Thus, even before the trial was underway, Nizer had cleared the way for a full examination of the blacklisting process. The defendants could still claim that they had relied on published reports, that they themselves had not fired Faulk, that they had not withdrawn sponsorship from his programs, and that they didn't directly call for Faulk's firing. But how would these arguments look to the jury, considering that the stated objective of the anti-communists was to keep blacklisted individuals like Faulk off the airwaves?

DISPOSING OF *PUBLICATION 16*

After his opening remarks, Nizer addressed the itemized charges in *Publication 16*, one by one. With Faulk on the stand, Nizer began his exposition.

"First," the lawyer said, quoting from the Aware bulletin, "according to the *Daily Worker*...Jack Faulk was to appear at Club 65...a favorite site of pro-communist affairs."

Nizer turned to Faulk. "Did you ever appear at Club 65 on that date or any other date?" he asked.

Faulk replied: "I did not."

"Did you know at the time you received this bulletin what Club 65 was?"

"No, sir. I don't recall ever having heard of Club 65 until the defendants put out this bulletin."

Nizer hammered further on that issue, all but suggesting that the "Jack Faulk" named in the Aware bulletin was some other person, raising the issue that Hartnett hadn't taken any steps to verify it.

"This item says 'Jack Faulk.' Have you ever been known as an entertainer or in private life as 'Jack Faulk'?" Nizer asked.

"No, sir...as John Henry Faulk or Johnny Faulk."

Later, Faulk allowed that at least twice his name had been listed as "John Faulk," including when he had supplied material for "Show-Time for Wallace," a New York City revue in 1948 for Henry Wallace, the Progressive Party candidate for president. The *Daily Worker* referred to him in the citation as "John Faulk." In any case, Faulk said, he had never considered the Progressive Party to be a communist front.

Likewise, Faulk admitted he was the "John Faulk" cited in the *Daily Worker* as attending the first-anniversary celebration of the United Nations at the Astor Hotel in New York City in 1946. However, Nizer noted the affair was co-sponsored by several reputable groups, such as the American Association of University Women, the American Bar Association, the American Jewish Committee, and the National YMCA. And yet Aware chose to focus on how Faulk shared the stage with "identified Communist Earl Robinson and two non-Communists." (Robinson was composer of the popular anthems "Ballad for Americans," "Joe Hill," and "The House I Live In.")

In his testimony, Faulk observed: "Out of all the names and sponsoring organizations, the only one Mr. Hartnett saw fit to mention was a man named Earl Robinson, who I never met before and who I did not invite."

Nizer asked, "Do you now know...anything about him?"

"I know he was a song composer," Faulk replied. "I know nothing about his communist relationships, if indeed there are any."

In this manner of questioning, Nizer continued to show that Aware had relied on published citations without taking basic steps to verify Faulk had actually carried out the cited activity—and had used information it did have in such a way as to misleadingly connect Faulk to communism.

Nizer asked Faulk, "Did you appear as an entertainer for Stage for Action?"

"No, sir. I did not."

CHAPTER SEVENTEEN: Faulk Case Goes to Trial

Did Faulk know Stage for Action had been designated a communist front?

No, he did not.

Nizer: Did you, in fact, send greetings to People's Songs on its second anniversary?

Faulk replied, "No," adding that he didn't do so for its first one, either.

"Did you know where the Jefferson School of Social Science was located until the bulletin was shown to you?"

"No, sir. I did not."

Nizer asked if Faulk sponsored the Congress for Peace held in Mexico City.

"I didn't even know they held one down there until that thing came out listing me," Faulk said.

"Did you attend...the Congress?"

"I did not."

Bolan objected over and over to Nizer's line of questioning, but the judge overruled the defense attorney.

In an interview years later, Hartnett argued that Justice Geller had created insurmountable obstacles by requiring the defense to prove Faulk attended or sponsored meetings as alleged in the bulletin. Hartnett also lamented that the judge had refused to let the defense offer findings from the Justice Department or the HCUA as evidence that Aware had acted in good faith.

"He placed the burden of proof on the defendants," Hartnett said. "No individuals could carry it; it was impossible."

Viewed another way, Hartnett and his co-defendants were getting a taste of their own medicine.

THE WITNESSES

After Faulk testified, Nizer began calling witnesses to describe their first-hand experience with the pressure tactics used by the defendants.

Thomas D. Murray and Samuel Dalsimer from the Gray Advertising Agency recounted their tangles with the defendants over Faulk, and earlier over the Amm-i-dent toothpaste account.

Another advertising executive, Fred Mitchell, told of his brushes with the defendants while handling Colgate's account.

Francis C. Barton Jr., formerly of the Lennen & Newell ad agency, told of his dealings with Laurence Johnson and his allies over Schlitz beer.

Reginald Allen, former director of operations at the Lincoln Center, testified about Johnson's unsuccessful attempt to keep Jack Gilford and the Metropolitan Opera Company's production of "Die Fledermaus" out of Syracuse.

Producer/director Hiram Brown described the pressure put on one of his stars, Joseph Cotten.

Actress Kim Hunter told of her years-long ordeal on the blacklist.

The actor Everett Sloane, who suffered years of unemployability because his name was confused with someone on a blacklist, took the stand to tell his story. Asked how he had reacted when Paul Milton had suggested he get himself cleared through Hartnett, Sloane stuttered vehemently while the gallery held its breath: "I said go f-f-f...fly a kite!"

Kenneth Roberts, a radio and TV announcer who suffered after being listed in *Red Channels*, expressed his resentment over the ominous letter he received from Hartnett that stated, "You will find it of the greatest importance to your career to get in touch with me without delay."

Mark Goodson, the impresario behind Goodson-Todman Productions, detailed how the show-business blacklist complicated the mechanics for his TV shows of the mid-1950s, including "The Name's the Same," "The Price is Right," "Stop the Music," and "What's My Line?"

Producer David Susskind described how Young & Rubicam hired Hartnett to screen talent for "Appointment with Adventure" on behalf of Camel cigarettes; how during a single year 5,000 names were submitted for clearance, at rates that varied from two to twenty dollars per name; and how Hartnett flagged one out of every three names.

Television personality Garry Moore described the dark shadow that blacklisting cast over the livelihoods of people in show business. "I was terribly frightened by what was happening to people, being blacklisted, suddenly becoming unemployable, for what reason they knew not, not even being confronted or told why they were made unemployable. It was

CHAPTER SEVENTEEN: Faulk Case Goes to Trial

a little like fighting with six men in a closet with the light out, and you can't tell who is hitting you." Moore said.

Moore was among several famous figures, including Susskind and Charles Collingwood, who testified that Faulk was on the verge of becoming a highly paid TV star before the Aware bulletin was published.

Nizer asked Gerald Dickler if he was still Faulk's business manager. He replied: "There isn't any business to manage."

Ad executive Lester Wolff testified that Faulk was so desperate for a job that he once offered to work for "scale" at just eighty dollars a program, but even then, clients turned Faulk down because he was too controversial.

The witnesses severely undercut defense attorney Bolan's contention that there was no such thing as a blacklist. They painted a convincing portrait of Hartnett as a full-time clearance consultant, and they linked him to Johnson and Aware in case after case.

This bold testimony stood in stark contrast to the early 1950s, when few producers or advertising executives dared to speak up against Johnson and the anti-communists. It was now 1962, and critics of blacklisting no longer feared paying a high price by going on the record.

In fact, when it was time for the defense to present its own witnesses, it learned it couldn't even count on everyone who in the past had been friendly with the anti-communists.

Jack Wren, who had handled clearance and screening work for Batten, Barton, Durstine & Osborn, once consulted regularly with Hartnett and Johnson. At the trial, Bolan confidently called Wren to support his clients' denial that they were agents of any blacklist.

"Mr. Wren, what were your duties at BBD&O in late 1955?" Boylan asked.

"Well, my duty, among other things," Wren said bitterly, "was to protect our clients against false charges made that we loaded our shows with communists, by Vincent Hartnett, who made these charges against us, who wrote poison pen letters behind our backs to our clients, wrote to our officers accusing us of loading our shows with communists."

Bolan foolishly pressed on.

"Did you ever send any communications to Mr. Hartnett at any time?"

"It is entirely possible," Wren said. "I had to treat him as a merchant treats a racketeer who sells protection."

Bolan's efforts also backfired when he attempted to show that Faulk wasn't dismissed from CBS because of the Aware bulletin, but rather due to low ratings.

Bolan called psychologist Sydney Roslow to the stand to explain Pulse, a TV and radio ratings system. Roslow noted that Faulk's radio listenership declined in the first six months of 1957 from a 4 rating to 3.1—a drop he measured as a loss of 36,000 households.

The data, on the surface, seemed to support WCBS's stance that it fired Faulk due to low ratings. But in cross-examination by Nizer, Roslow conceded that other Pulse data showed no statistically valid evidence of a decline.

And while Faulk's ratings declined by 9 percent between mid-1955 and mid-1957, overall ratings for the station fell by 20 percent in the same period. In other words, as Nizer summed up for the jury, "Faulk had done much better than the station."

DUELING DOCTORS

As the trial proceeded in the packed New York City courtroom, Hartnett and representatives of Aware took the stand in their own defense. However, Bolan stated that Johnson would not testify due to declining health. Nizer suspected this was a ploy by the defense to limit the liability of Johnson, the only defendant considered to have substantial financial resources.

While it was true Johnson had not masterminded *Publication 16*, Nizer demonstrated during the trial that the Syracuse grocer was every bit as involved as his co-defendants in the anti-communist cause in general—and in targeting Faulk in particular. If they committed libel, Nizer's argument went, so did Johnson.

So, at the trial, when a skeptical Nizer repeated his demand that Johnson take the stand, Bolan stuck to his story that Johnson was in ill health and should not testify—on doctor's orders. Nizer then asked that Johnson be examined by two physicians, one for the defendants, the other for the plaintiff. Justice Geller agreed.

CHAPTER SEVENTEEN: Faulk Case Goes to Trial

Bolan arranged for Dr. Wardner D. Ayer of Syracuse to examine Johnson. Ayer had sterling credentials: senior attending physician at Upstate Medical Center in Syracuse, consulting neurologist at the Syracuse State Psychopathic Hospital, and emeritus professor of internal medicine and neurology at Syracuse University. During his forty-five years in practice, he had been a pioneer in the study of brain hemorrhages and poliomyelitis.

After examining Johnson for two hours, Dr. Ayer traveled to New York City to testify to his findings. He described Johnson's most debilitating ailment: a cardiospasm, or constriction in the lower end of the esophagus. This condition caused burping, vomiting, and difficulty in swallowing, he explained. The doctor went on to describe Johnson's "flabby neck," and he said X-rays showed "an enormous dilation" directly above the constriction, where food tended to become trapped. Ayer reported other graphic evidence of declining health: "Rapid heart action, evident fatigue and nervousness, a top normal blood pressure, severe varicose veins, enlargement of the prostate with frequency of urination."

Bolan asked Ayer whether taking the witness stand would endanger Johnson's health.

"In my opinion, yes," the doctor replied, "on the basis of nervous strain, and aggravation of the cardiospasm with the fact that he would be having pain, would be possibly regurgitating and vomiting under the stress of harsh—I don't say you are harsh—but of severe cross-examination."

When Nizer questioned him, Dr. Ayer acknowledged that he was not a specialist in digestive disorders. He also confirmed that Johnson's constricted esophagus condition had been plaguing him for at least a decade and, during that time, the energetic merchant had run a supermarket chain with considerable success, traveled widely, pursued his avocation of studying and collecting Americana, and pressed his anti-communist cause. Dr. Ayer also confirmed that Johnson had gone on an extensive tour of Africa only two years previously and that the former grocer had published a book in 1961. In addition, Johnson had withstood several long sessions of examination before trial.

Nizer asked if Johnson arrived at the doctor's office independently, undressed by himself, and appeared well-groomed.

Yes, the doctor replied, although he thought Johnson "was a little uncertain and hesitant in his gait." He added that he saw no signs of edema (swelling of the tissues), that his heart appeared to be in good shape, and that there was no significant weight loss.

Did Johnson vomit during his physical examination?

"He was in pain," Dr. Ayer replied.

Nizer shot back that "pain is subjective. He didn't vomit?"

"No, he did not," Ayer said.

Nizer ended his cross-examination by asking, "Doctor, would you mind if I asked you how old you are?"

Replied Ayer: "I don't like to tell you. I am 73."

Then, as if to defend his diagnosis of Johnson, Ayer added: "And I have not got a sagging neck!"

Nizer left it to the jury to consider that if the doctor could testify, why couldn't the defendant, a man about the same age?

The day before Dr. Ayer testified, Johnson drove from Syracuse to New York City for a physical examination at Nizer's request by Dr. Jerome A. Marks, a gastroenterology specialist on the faculty at New York University.

Following Dr. Ayer to the stand, Dr. Marks reported that Johnson had conducted himself "calmly and quietly" during his examination. "He seemed to recall quite well the details of his illness, going back fifteen years, and he was on the whole an exemplary patient," Marks said.

Was Johnson fit to testify? Nizer asked.

"In my experience," Dr. Marks replied, "patients with this condition are able to carry on their usual duties and occupations....I should say with reasonable certainty that this man would be able to come into court and testify for any reasonable length of time."

Nizer left it at that. He still couldn't compel Johnson to testify. But he was confident he had made his argument to the jury that Johnson was healthy enough to appear in court, and that his absence betrayed the weakness of his case.

Faulk was equally confident that Dr. Marks had persuaded the jury. "They regarded Dr. Ayer as a fine gentleman but...they considered Dr. Marks the better qualified authority on Johnson's particular disorder,"

CHAPTER SEVENTEEN: Faulk Case Goes to Trial

Faulk wrote later. "It seemed clear that they accepted his judgment that Johnson was well enough to appear as a witness if he wanted to."

Also sitting in the courtroom was *New York Post* columnist Murray Kempton. In his next column, he nicknamed Johnson "Sick call Larry," and wrote derisively of the missing defendant:

> It is rather odd that a man like Laurence Johnson would not lust to face the enemies of his country; there is something pathetic in this image of him wandering from doctor to doctor, hoping for an exemption. He is the senior officer of an unspeakable crew. One might at least expect of him that he would stand up and answer "Here" at its last formation.
>
> But Vincent Hartnett sits and takes it, and all Johnson could do was to look for a doctor to certify that, in face of his enemies, there was danger that he might throw up.

'A LITTLE HEART TROUBLE'

A few weeks before Johnson had arrived in New York City to be examined by Dr. Marks, Jasena Foley had spent time with him, and she thought Johnson looked in pretty good health. He didn't say much about the trial, except to mumble that "things are sort of rough."

As the trial was underway in late May, Johnson visited his daughter Eleanor Buchanan and her family in Cranston, Rhode Island.

While there, he wrote to Foley in Syracuse: "Thanks for your nice card. Marilyn forwarded it to me. Have so much to tell you and to write someday." He noted that he had recently done some research in the Boston Public Library, and he enclosed a copy of an anecdote relating to Onondaga County history, which he asked her to pass on to fellow history buffs Richard and Caroline Wright, "with my best wishes."

He signed off "Cordially, Larry," with this postscript: "P.S. Awfully much better. Was laid up in the house here in the Buchanans over a visit."

Foley also received a short note from Johnson dated June 1962. "Thanks for your wonderful letter. It is nice to have friends like you....I am not feeling too great, have had a little heart trouble for the first time in my life."

Eleanor noticed her father had lost weight when he came for his visit. "He borrowed an ice pick to make a new hole in his belt," she said. However, she didn't think his health was exceptionally fragile. "Dumb me," she said. "I had just had major surgery. I was still in bed. He was able to help me—and he was ill, too. But he was able to travel."

Upon leaving Rhode Island, Johnson drove his 1961 Cadillac to New York City and eventually checked into the Town & Country Motor Lodge at 2244 Tillotson Avenue in the Bronx.

SUMMING UP

During the summations, defense attorney Bolan attempted to turn the tables to try to make the jury focus less on his clients' actions and more on whether it was Faulk telling the truth.

"I am going to start first with what I think is a very important issue and fact in this case," he said. "Namely, that is, that the plaintiff, Mr. Faulk, has deliberately lied to you on numerous occasions in this case on matters of great importance. There are so many lies that it's hard to list them all. I will give you about nine or ten for a start and mention many more throughout my summation."

One lie, Bolan said, was Faulk's claim that his sponsors dropped his show because of the Aware bulletin. In fact, Bolan said, the year after the bulletin appeared was the most successful of Faulk's career, when he enjoyed his maximum number of sponsors and earned his peak income.

Bolan continued that Faulk lied when he said WCBS fired him because of Aware. The defense attorney noted that CBS executives had testified it was because of Faulk's falling ratings, and there was no reason for the CBS men to lie.

"It is Mr. Faulk who is not telling the truth," Bolan said.

He also brushed aside the issue of blacklisting. He argued that employers have the right to consider an employee's loyalty record—for example,

CHAPTER SEVENTEEN: Faulk Case Goes to Trial

whether he had pleaded the Fifth Amendment, the constitutional right that barred a witness from being forced to testify against himself.

Bolan explained: "If a man asked, 'Did you steal $10,000 from your former employer?' and he says, 'I refuse to answer on the ground that an answer may tend to incriminate me'...wouldn't a prospective employer be foolhardy if he didn't doubt the man's honesty?"

As for Laurence Johnson, Bolan told the jury that the grocer had nothing to do with producing the Aware bulletin. It was improper to attempt to connect Johnson to any "conspiracy" against Faulk, the defense attorney said.

"I would like to contrast Mr. Faulk's many lies with Mr. Hartnett's testimony under five days, approximately, of cross-examination," Bolan said. "I submit, ladies and gentlemen, that I doubt if you will ever come across a man as truthful and honest as Mr. Hartnett is....I would gamble this entire case on your appraisal of Mr. Hartnett's frankness."

Bolan added that Faulk "seeks to put the blame on the defendants for what he calls blacklisting. But he is dead wrong. It is the American public that does not want identified Communist Party members on its radio programs or television programs. It does not want people who invoke the Fifth Amendment concerning communism on its program. It does not want people with records of communist-front affiliations, that have never been repudiated, appearing on their programs.

"And since the public does not want it, the sponsors don't want it, the advertising agencies don't want these people on their programs."

Bolan's summation took all day. The next morning, it was Nizer's turn. Faulk's attorney began by tackling the credibility issue Bolan had raised.

"They called my client a liar!" Nizer declared. "Any man would have had to hold on to himself. I admire Mr. Faulk for just keeping silent under that attack, because I had to grip my seat. At the last moment we are libeled again.

"And who is it that is held forth as a truthful man? Mr. Bolan says, 'I gamble my case on the integrity, on the truth of Mr. Hartnett.' I accept that unhesitatingly. Why...the bulletin that he wrote has already been held to be a complete lie....So how can he be a truthful man?"

Bolan leaped to his feet, objecting.

"This exhibit was not held to be a complete lie," he said of *Publication 16*. "In fact, no part of it was held to be a lie. All that was said—"

Justice Geller interrupted.

"It was held to be a libel by the court," he corrected.

Bolan persisted: "It was not held to be a lie in any part, Your Honor."

Geller dismissed the objection. "No, overruled, overruled."

Nizer continued: "I repeat that when a defense of truth is stricken out of a case and a defense of partial truth is stricken out of a case, that the document is not only libelous but a complete lie. I stand by that, and I wouldn't have been as strong about it, if they hadn't called Mr. Faulk a liar."

Nizer reminded the jury that Faulk was neither a Communist Party member nor a communist sympathizer.

"There is no issue here of communism," he said. "The question is whether we will permit our government to protect us under proper judicial and other procedures, or whether we are going to permit private vigilantes like this gentleman seated here," turning to Hartnett, "with the thin mouth and blue suit, who sneaks into the Blue Ribbon Restaurant, when there is a meeting of some union people, with a hidden microphone in his lapel. That is the question, are you going to permit private vigilantism for profit?"

Nizer said Hartnett and Aware sought to "destroy" Faulk because furthering the blacklist meant they would make more money. The attorney pointed out that Hartnett charged $300 for a report on playwright Arthur Miller, and collected twenty dollars for one on humorist James Thurber, "one of the great figures that we ought to be proud of in America. And then, believe it or not, on that list: 'Santa Claus, five dollars.' Despite the red suit, he got passed by Mr. Hartnett."

The damaging *Publication 16* bulletin, Nizer said, had been mailed to some 2,000 people, anyone who could have a role in damaging Faulk's career, people in newspapers, advertising, the movies, TV, radio, the unions, even the police department.

"Is it any wonder that Mr. Faulk is as dead as a doornail?" Nizer asked. "They covered every possible spot to injure him....It's like knocking a man down and pumping twelve more bullets into him."

CHAPTER SEVENTEEN: Faulk Case Goes to Trial

Nizer moved on to the third defendant, Laurence Johnson. Nine witnesses had linked Johnson to the blacklisting process under scrutiny in this case, Nizer asserted. The other side had produced no witnesses to deny the charges—not even Johnson himself.

"Whether he is sick or not, let's make this clear, ladies and gentlemen," Nizer said. "A man cannot answer charges by not appearing....The only question is whether there is an inference to be drawn from his not appearing....This was a plain pretense. This man who drives a car and can do everything else could have testified here, but, like all bullies, they are also cowards."

Nizer reminded the jury that Johnson "had this esophagus condition ten years ago, and five and six years ago he was crushing Mr. Faulk. The only trouble with him inside is guts, not the esophagus, and he should have appeared here and defended himself, and he didn't have the guts to do it."

At this point, Nizer asked for a brief recess. With the climax of his summation still to come, Nizer's strategy was to give the jury a break, and use the interval to collect his thoughts for the finale.

Suddenly, as Nizer got ready to sit at the counsel table, a young woman rushed into the courtroom and, with a trembling hand, gave a note to Bolan. The attorney opened the paper, and instantly he seemed to turn pale.

Looking up to see Nizer standing there, without a word, Bolan handed over the note.

It read: "Laurence Johnson has just been found dead in a Bronx motel."

CHAPTER EIGHTEEN:
The Verdict

Laurence Johnson had left word with his family that he would be staying for a few days at the Town & Country Motor Lodge at Exit 5 of the New England Thruway in the Bronx. When he checked in on Sunday afternoon, June 24, 1962, he told the motel clerk, "I'll be going to the dining room," but it seems he never went. He had ice cream brought to his room.

He apparently died that night, clad in pajamas and sitting up in bed, his unseeing eyes facing the flickering television screen, several medicine bottles nearby. The next morning, a maid opened the door to clean up Johnson's room, noticed what appeared to be a guest watching television, and left. On Tuesday, a different maid did the same thing.

By Wednesday, his family began to worry something was wrong because he wasn't answering the phone in his room. Finally, a family member called the motel to ask if someone could see if Johnson was okay.

At about 9 a.m., a clerk entered Johnson's room and found him dead. The police soon arrived, and they ordered the body transported to Jacobi Hospital morgue. Authorities told reporters there was no sign of foul play.

An autopsy report revealed that Johnson had taken his doctor-prescribed barbiturates that Sunday night and, while asleep, had suffered a vomiting attack—not unexpected for someone with his restricted esophagus. Since the barbiturates prevented him from waking, the regurgitated food entered his lungs, causing death by asphyxiation.

CAN A JURY AWARD A JUDGMENT AGAINST A DEAD MAN?

After learning of Johnson's death, the attorneys at the libel trial huddled with Justice Geller, who decided not to inform the jury of this news until the court had decided how to resolve the legal problems arising from it. Bolan argued that a jury cannot deliver a verdict against a dead man. Nizer disagreed.

As *The New York Times* noted in a report on the issue, it was clear that the estate of a man becomes liable if he dies after a judgment is made against him. Less clear was whether this was still the case if the man died before the jury reached its verdict.

While he considered the matter, Justice Geller asked Nizer to complete his summation despite uncertainty about whether Johnson's death might nullify the proceedings and force both sides to start over. "Knowing that, after all these years of preparation and 10 weeks of trial, we had at the very last moment received what was almost certain to be a mortal blow, it was necessary nevertheless to continue the argument with the same intensity as before," Nizer wrote later.

Returning to his closing remarks, Nizer recited the evidence of Faulk's unemployability and loss of potential earnings, and he urged the jury to award his client punitive damages.

"The real issue in this case, ladies and gentlemen," Nizer said, "is that there are people who try to take the law into their own hands. They try to, because they believe fanatically, and in this case, there was no fanaticism; it was malice. They didn't think Faulk, even fanatically, was a communist.

"I will not go on with the rest of the terrible story of this man's ordeal, but now I place his life in your hands, very literally, because this man's reputation is either going to be restored by a verdict that will ring to the world, or he will be besmirched all over again. I leave to your hands the doing of full justice, and if you do that, ladies and gentlemen, you can sleep well because God will be awake."

Justice Geller ordered the jury sequestered for the night while he and the lawyers wrestled with the implications of Johnson's death.

Bolan pressed for a mistrial or, at the very least, to have the claim against Johnson dismissed. However, Justice Geller sided with Nizer,

CHAPTER EIGHTEEN: The Verdict

and the judge granted his request to designate another lawyer to represent Johnson's estate temporarily. Justice Geller then ordered the estate to take Johnson's place in the Faulk case.

However, Justice Geller ruled out any punitive damages against the Johnson estate. Nizer succinctly paraphrased the judge's logic: "Punitive damages cannot deter dead men from repeating the offense."

On Thursday, June 28, Justice Geller finally told the Faulk jury of Johnson's death. He warned jurors not to draw any overt conclusions from this sudden development—nor should they make any particular connection between his death and his failure to testify at the trial.

At 5:35 p.m., the jury retired to begin deliberations. They had heard thirty-five witnesses over forty-seven days. The record now filled some 8,000 pages.

At 10:20 p.m., the jurors sent the judge a note. Justice Geller mounted the bench with a slip of paper in his hand, then read the message aloud in the courtroom.

On the issue of punitive damages, the jury asked if it could award "more than amounts" that Faulk requested. Justice Geller advised the jury that the size of the award was its business. The jurors left to resume deliberations.

The jury's note electrified the courtroom, where spectators crowded around Faulk and Nizer, congratulating them for what now appeared to be a victory in the plaintiff's favor.

Sure enough, at 11:40 p.m., the jury returned with its verdict, delivered by the foreman:

"We, the jury, have arrived at our decision in favor of Mr. Faulk. We have awarded the plaintiff, Mr. Faulk, compensatory damages in the sum of one million dollars against Aware Inc., Mr. Vincent Hartnett, and the estate of the late Mr. Laurence Johnson. We have also awarded the plaintiff, Mr. Faulk, punitive damages in the sum of $1,250,000 against Aware Inc. and $1,250,000 against Mr. Hartnett."

The jury's verdict totaled $3.5 million, far exceeding Faulk's and Nizer's expectations. It set a record at the time for a libel award.

Justice Geller asked if the decision was unanimous, and the foreman replied "no." The vote was eleven to one. One juror agreed with deciding in favor of Faulk, but not the size of the award.

Bolan immediately moved that the verdict be set aside as excessive. Justice Geller took the matter under advisement and dismissed the jury.

When the proceedings ended, Nizer and Faulk embraced. Nizer wrote later that Faulk was "almost carried out of the courtroom by his friends, who had shared his suffering through the years, and were now entitled to share his triumph."

In the courthouse corridor, Nizer encountered Hartnett. Almost whispering, Hartnett said emotionally, "We will appeal. Now, Mr. Nizer, it is all in God's hands."

Nizer replied, "What makes you think it hasn't been there all the time?"

A *New York Times* editorial viewed the verdict as the watershed event it would turn out to be: "The libel verdict should have a healthy effect in curbing the excesses of the superpatriots who sometimes show no more concern for the rights of individuals than the communists they denounce."

'ONE THAT LOVED NOT WISELY, BUT TOO WELL'

In Syracuse, where Johnson's death was front-page news, a *Post-Standard* editorial writer two days later put the trial in context with the extraordinary career of one of the city's most prominent citizens.

The editorial began with a famous quotation:

I have done the state some service, and they know't.
No more of that. I pray you, in your letters,
When you shall these unlucky deeds relate,
Speak of me as I am; nothing extenuate,
Nor set down aught in malice. Then, must you speak
Of one that loved not wisely, but too well.

The editorial followed:

> Those lines from Shakespeare's "Othello" might well be the epitaph for Laurence A. Johnson, retired Syracuse grocer, ardent patriot and devoted antiquarian, who was found dead

CHAPTER EIGHTEEN: The Verdict

Wednesday in a New York City motel as a million-dollar libel suit against him was nearing its close.

For if Larry Johnson had any fault, it perhaps was that he loved his country "not wisely but too well."

It was his love of America and his hatred of anything that he regarded as un-American that got him into deep legal trouble in the closing months of his life. Whether the lawsuit against him was justified we do not know, but we do know that whatever he did in his fight against what he regarded as Communist influence, his motivations were of the highest. If he erred in his facts or in his judgment about any individual, it is most regrettable.

But Larry Johnson was much more than a super-patriot.

His love of country was translated into a glorification of the past and into an effort to preserve in tangible form some of the fine old traditions of early American and colonial days. An avid collector, his home was a museum of treasured Americana, and he was known across the land for his "old country stores," which were authentic reproductions of the cracker-barrel era of merchandising.

One of the pioneer super-market operators, Mr. Johnson paved the way for much of today's chain-store retail operations....

A good friend, a delightful companion, Larry Johnson was entitled to live out his life in greater peace than he had had these past few weeks.

Years later, Vincent Hartnett recalled sitting in the courtroom when news of Johnson's death arrived. "It was a complete surprise to me," he said. "As far as I can judge it was a complete surprise to Bolan, because I was right by his side when the word came in about it. Everyone was absolutely staggered. It couldn't have been more dramatic."

His first thought? "That the trial had killed a very good man," said Hartnett, his voice cracking. "A wrongful death."

A grave marker on a hillside plot at the Butler-Savannah Cemetery in Wayne County, New York, marks the final resting place of Laurence and Hermione Johnson. (Fred M. Fiske photo)

Johnson's neighbor Burnett Haylor also blamed Johnson's death on the Faulk case. "That's what killed him," he said. "I probably saw him within a month of his death. He didn't sound very good."

Not everyone in Syracuse mustered much sympathy for Johnson's struggles in his final days. Lillian Reiner, a liberal adversary, said no one should forget all the innocent people who suffered from his anti-communist activism. "I suppose you have to give him credit for all he did—collecting Americana, developing grocery stores. I wish he'd stuck to it, doggone it!" Reiner said. "But all that surrounds my mind is the death and devastation that he caused to so many creative lives. You know I can't forgive this."

As for Faulk, he wrote later that, upon learning of his old adversary's death, he thought: "What a frail thing life is!"

CHAPTER EIGHTEEN: The Verdict

Johnson's funeral was held Saturday, June 30, 1962, in the chapel of Syracuse's Fairchild and Meech Funeral Home, where the services drew "a large attendance," the newspaper reported. Banks of flowers donated by Victory Supermarkets, the buyer of Johnson's stores, decorated the chapel. On the casket was a small, old-fashioned bouquet—"one suspects, a tribute from the grandchildren," the reporter wrote.

Johnson was buried in his native soil—Wayne County's Butler-Savannah Cemetery—in a hillside plot next to the remains of Hermione.

FINAL BUSINESS

Nizer and Faulk had insisted on tying Laurence Johnson securely to the other defendants on the assumption that the retired entrepreneur had the financial resources to pay a substantial judgment if the plaintiff won. After all, Johnson had enjoyed a highly successful career, building a multimillion-dollar retail grocery business that, for a time, intimidated the food industry, their advertising agencies, and the broadcasting establishment. As Faulk wrote later: "Laurence Johnson was worth millions, we had been told by one and all of the big companies which had caved in before his threats."

Even though Johnson's death had led Justice Geller to rule out punitive damages against the former grocer's estate, Nizer remained optimistic. He wrote in another best-selling memoir, "The Jury Returns," published in 1966: "Our hopes had been high that at least this defendant was financially responsible for the one million dollars in compensatory damages now assessed against it."

Everyone soon learned otherwise. The attorneys for Johnson's estate, Laurence F. Sovik and Harlow B. Ansell, reported that Johnson had left nothing like a multimillion-dollar fortune. The amount was reportedly closer to $500,000, a considerable sum in the early 1960s, but far short of paying the full judgment.

Eventually, Nizer and Faulk accepted a settlement of $175,000 from the Johnson estate. Faulk noted that the money allowed him to repay "at least part of my debts," including $100,000 in legal fees, and loans from Murrow, Susskind, and others.

Although the money did not restore him to financial solvency, Faulk said his disappointment was tempered by the rewards of vindication and restoration of his good name. "I could not help feeling good about the irony of it," he added. "Every network and advertising agency in town had trembled at Mr. Johnson's tread on Madison Avenue, yet any of them could have bought him out with a week's advertising budget. It didn't take much to make them run."

The other defendants—Vincent Hartnett and representatives of Aware Inc.—pursued an appeal with a new attorney, Charles E. Henry. Hartnett and his colleagues were intent on achieving vindication and were not about to make any deal—not that Nizer and Faulk expected much in the way of monetary damages from either defendant.

The Appellate Division of the New York Supreme Court, while unanimously upholding the jury's verdict, reduced the award. Since Hartnett had primarily conducted the campaign against Faulk, the court assessed $50,000 in compensatory damages against him. Aware was ordered to pay $10,000. The court also revised punitive damages downward to about $500,000, divided equally between the two defendants.

Aware and Hartnett continued their quest for exoneration, this time in the New York Court of Appeals. When this panel reaffirmed the lower court decision, defendants' attorney Henry petitioned for a hearing before the U.S. Supreme Court, which refused to hear the case—although justices Hugo L. Black and William O. Douglas dissented. The court also denied a second petition.

Nizer commented that the defendants, by pressing appeals, had done Faulk a favor by giving him a "stamp of vindication" while also making it clear that numerous courts condemned the practice of blacklisting in radio and television.

In death, Laurence Johnson had been spared the agony of witnessing these final repudiations of a cause he held so dear, as well as the lasting enmity of many whose lives and careers he damaged or destroyed.

From his studies of Americana, the old patriot understood, as well as anyone, that history's judgment can be harsher than any monetary penalty. After the Faulk trial, Johnson's reputation would forever be linked

CHAPTER EIGHTEEN: THE VERDICT

to a bitter epithet, one that his detractors found fitting for a groceryman they decided had left this world with blood on his hands.

His detractors' disparaging nickname for Johnson appeared in December 1964 in *Parade* magazine in its response to a query from a reader:

> Q: Who was the "Butcher of Syracuse?"
>
> A: He was the late Laurence Johnson, owner of supermarkets in Syracuse, who was charged with viciously and unfairly conspiring with Vince Hartnett, a TV script supervisor, to deprive actors, writers and directors of their livelihoods by listing them as Communists or Communist sympathizers.

The magazine noted that an account of Johnson and Hartnett's misguided crusade could be found in John Henry Faulk's new book, "Fear on Trial," just published by Simon & Schuster. Laurence Johnson loved to write about history, but in their landmark battle over blacklisting, it was Faulk who had the last word.

Epilogue

Despite winning in court, John Henry Faulk never regained the career momentum that came to an abrupt halt with the campaign of the anti-communists. CBS chose not to give him his old job back or to present him with any meaty television work. For a while, he hosted a mid-afternoon radio show on WINS in New York City and appeared as an occasional guest on television, including as a panelist on the game show "To Tell the Truth." He made personal appearances, including a speech before the Syracuse Section Council of Jewish Women in 1963, where Faulk was not shy about noting the city's role in the show-business blacklisting of the 1950s. "Syracuse was synonymous with pressure," he said, "even as far away as Hollywood."

Immediately after the jury verdict, Faulk mostly worked on writing "Fear on Trial," which earned overwhelmingly positive reviews upon its publication in November 1964. Soon, there was a deal for Dick Van Dyke to star as Faulk in a movie based on the book. However, the project would stall for years until the post-Watergate era made a 1950s blacklisting story palatable for a nation that seemed ready to reassess and repair the wrongs of the past.

But instead of the big screen, "Fear on Trial" was produced as a made-for-television movie that aired, believe it or not, on CBS. In this production, William Devane starred as Faulk and George C. Scott played attorney Louis Nizer. Character actor John Harkins played Vince Hartnett. As for Laurence Johnson, although mentioned several times, the movie kept his character off-screen, not unlike the real-life Johnson's no-show at the libel trial.

The actors George C. Scott, left, as attorney Louis Nizer, and William Devane as John Henry Faulk display a copy of *Red Channels* in this publicity photo for "Fear on Trial," a made-for-television movie that aired on CBS in 1975. (CBS-TV photo)

While Faulk's book had reached thousands of readers, the TV movie drew a sympathetic audience of millions, resulting in a surge in new opportunities for its central character. Faulk was soon on television in a recurring role from 1975 to 1980 on the Southern-themed variety show "Hee Haw." In his segments, he sat in a rocking chair, telling stories and cracking corn-pone jokes.

In 1986, Texas Monthly Press published another of his books, "The Uncensored John Henry Faulk," a collection of folk tales, columns, sermons, and essays. Included in the book was the script of a one-man show he wrote and performed, "Pear Orchard, Texas" inventing characters and telling stories about them. Faulk also appeared at colleges and universities, where he spoke about the U.S. Constitution.

During an interview in 1987, Faulk said he was making a "pretty good living" while speaking to colleges and business groups. When asked about the Syracuse grocer, Faulk said: "I never disliked Johnson. I felt sorry for him. He was a pitiful old man. He made a mockery of the Constitution, ironically enough, the very thing he wanted to defend most heatedly."

Faulk died April 9, 1990, at age seventy-four after being diagnosed with cancer.

Nizer, who would continue a long career as an attorney and author of several books, was ninety-five when he died in 1994.

One of Johnson's closest allies in the cause of anti-communism, John Dungey, editor of *Spotlight*, died unexpectedly in 1965 at age 53, reportedly due to a heart condition. Fellow Legionnaire Carl Tarver noted that Dungey had expressed sadness over the libel verdict. However, the loss in court had not stopped Dungey's anti-communist writings. "John was very active right up until his death," Tarver said. "I don't think it (the verdict) would have had an effect on John. John would keep on."

Francis Neuser, Johnson's vegetable buyer and head of the Veterans Action Committee of Syracuse Super Markets, did not respond to a request in the 1980s for an interview for this book. "When the trouble came with the trial, I think Fran became a nervous wreck," supermarket co-worker Mary Coyne said. "He was so upset over it." Neuser died in 1995 at age seventy-eight. (Coyne died five years later at age eighty-six.)

After serving time for perjury, Harvey Matusow kept reinventing himself with many relocations and a potpourri of jobs. He lived in England, Massachusetts, Arizona, and Utah. He tried the music business, joined a commune and a Mormon community, and played a clown on TV.

When interviewed while visiting Syracuse in December 1984, Matusow said he was surviving on $118 a month in veterans disability payments. "I've taken a vow of poverty," he said. Matusow later moved to New Hampshire to run a public-access television studio, and in 2002 he died at age seventy-five from injuries in a car crash.

THE GROCER WHO SOLD McCARTHYISM

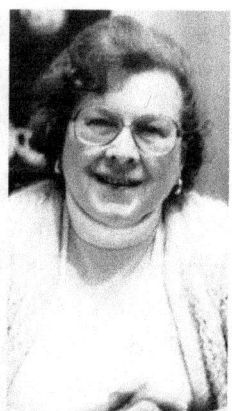

FROM LEFT: Vincent Hartnett, Mary Coyne, and Harvey Matusow are photographed by the author in the early 1980s. John Henry Faulk, right, appears in a publicity photo for a 1990 public television special, "The Man Who Beat the Blacklist," hosted by Bill Moyers. (Fred M. Fiske and KEDT photos)

Vincent Hartnett would spend two decades after the libel verdict in a quixotic quest for vindication. In 1976, he filed a $4 million lawsuit alleging the "Fear on Trial" movie libeled him. The suit targeted Faulk, Nizer, CBS, scriptwriter David W. Rintels, and producer David Susskind, who appeared as himself in the film.

Among Hartnett's objections was that the movie blamed him for financial losses suffered by people he claimed were communists. If they had losses, he said, it was their own fault for joining the Communist Party.

His suit dragged on until 1986 when New York State Supreme Court Justice Joseph H. Owen finally dismissed it. Owen in his ruling said, "It does not require much acumen to see by now that this action, legally baseless, is nothing more than an attempt to change what plaintiff perceives to be the verdict of history regarding his conduct."

Interviewed in 1982 at his home in Tuckahoe, New York, Hartnett acknowledged he was still required to make installments for the $500,000 judgment in the 1962 libel verdict. (It amounted to about $2,000 annually, or 10 percent of Hartnett's salary.) When Faulk was asked about the payments, he said, "It's not something we're depending on for survival."

Hartnett, who spent much of his later years teaching high school English in Pelham, New York, died in 2009 at age ninety-three.

FINAL THOUGHTS

Reflecting on history through the lens of modern America, the targeting of show-business people by anti-communists is perplexing. Today, dismissing actors solely because of their political beliefs is usually not unlawful, but it rarely occurs. After all, if an entertainer's work resonates with audiences and sells products, they keep working. So, what caused all the fuss during the McCarthy Era?

Consider this paradox: The American story is filled with examples of groups seeking to limit the freedoms they themselves fought to secure. We, as Americans, pledge allegiance to founding ideals that champion individual liberty, enshrined in documents like the Declaration of Independence and the Bill of Rights. Yet, we often fall short of these ideals, infringing on the rights of others, limiting their actions, and even scrutinizing their behavior and beliefs. Social scientists have long documented this disconnect, highlighting a persistent tension in the American experience.

A sign of improved mental health is when recovering patients notice their daily life transform from "the same old grind" to "one challenge after another." Similarly, a vibrant republic depends on avoiding the suffocating stagnation of tyranny and embracing a series of challenges. This essence of democracy lies in our ability to learn from our experiences, heal from setbacks, and rise to meet the next challenge.

The political tensions of the McCarthy Era took their toll, stifling dissent and ruining careers of many Americans. However, legal rulings like the Supreme Court's rejection of loyalty oaths for federal workers and shifting societal attitudes toward due process eventually brought an end to the Red Scare. Public attention then turned toward civil rights, Black empowerment, women's rights, and gay rights, each sparking passionate debate and ongoing struggles for equality.

From the fiery debates over slavery to the cultural clashes of the Vietnam War, contentious issues keep changing, yet the center generally holds. Institutions like a free press and an independent judiciary act as safety valves, restoring equilibrium over time. Progress, though never achieved in complete consensus and often amidst hostility, allows us, as citizens of a free and diverse society, to inch closer to a more perfect union. The journey is never easy and the destination ever-receding.

Laurence Johnson and his allies believed communist influence in entertainment was pervasive, subtly shaping scripts, productions, and performances. They argued that only by removing suspected communists could this influence be contained. However, discerning who truly held communist beliefs proved immensely difficult. There was no foolproof test for loyalty, and accusations often relied on circumstantial evidence or flimsy associations.

The anti-communist crusade in show business also faltered because it was ultimately futile. Despite their efforts, anti-communists couldn't extinguish the star power of figures like Charlie Chaplin, Marlon Brando, Arthur Miller, and Burt Lancaster, whose talents and bold ideas captivated audiences. Regrettably, countless others weren't so lucky. Blacklisting led to the loss of careers and stifled creative voices. Ultimately, the public was the loser, deprived of a wider range of talent and thought-provoking entertainment.

Johnson's strategy that the industry would cave to his demands did work for a while. One wonders what might have transpired had the industry refused from the start to give in to his threats. Imagine the cultural richness that might have been preserved, the careers that could have been salvaged, if artistic merit had been the sole yardstick for success, rather than the political affiliations of the creators.

It wasn't until John Henry Faulk challenged the status quo that Johnson's bluff was called. Although personally costly, Faulk's protracted legal battle played a pivotal role in ending the iron grip of anti-communism on the entertainment industry.

Art that challenges societal norms thrives in a free and tolerant society. An argument could be made to let the communists present their perspectives; if they compellingly engage with contentious issues, so be it. However, if their approach becomes dogmatic and preachy, it's unlikely to gain traction.

"(I)n a free society," wrote Ted Morgan in his 2003 book "Reds: McCarthyism in Twentieth-Century America," all styles "must be tested against peer review, market forces, and public indifference." Surely,

Johnson learned this on his way to becoming a merchandising legend. Whether you are selling toothpaste or performing on TV, if you pass Morgan's three-way test, the public will buy what you are selling. If the acting is good, who cares if the actor is a communist?

An irony of the McCarthy Era is that, as most historians studying that period have come to believe, it was not the communists but the anti-communists who posed the greatest threat to freedom. Johnson and his allies, in their zealous crusade against communist influence, undermined the very principles they claimed to defend.

In his powerful summation during the Faulk trial, Nizer observed that when people point a finger at someone, they also have several fingers pointing back at themselves.

Laurence Johnson and his cohorts trembled in the shadow of communism, their fears so palpable that they embraced methods imperiling the very democratic ideals they claimed to embrace. Nizer memorably made this point to the jury by quoting Robert Frost, who in the poem "A Hundred Collars," wrote: "There's nothing I'm afraid of like scared people."

A Note on Sources

Soon after moving to Syracuse, New York, in 1979 to work at *The Post-Standard*, I came across "Syracuse Guidebook '79," a lively, 320-page compendium of facts, tips, and stories about Central New York. On Page 79 was an entry about Laurence Johnson, the local grocer who became an ardent anti-communist activist in the 1950s. His mission was to help ban from the airways any show-business stars who had links to organizations listed as subversive by the U.S. attorney general, or who were cited as communists or sympathizers in congressional records and elsewhere. The short article by Carl Mellor was paired with a sketch of a stern-faced, bespectacled Johnson in a high collar, coat, and tie. It described his rise to commercial prominence as a supermarket innovator; his passion for Americana, particularly the artifacts of old country stores; and his decision to join the anti-communists and use his merchandising skills to keep blacklisted performers off the air.

In his article, Mellor noted Johnson's strategy of displaying a warning notice next to a product in his supermarkets if its manufacturer sponsored a radio or television show featuring a performer Johnson found objectionable. Mellor's story left a vivid image in my mind of Johnson putting up signs above Swanson frozen peas or Libby's canned carrots, and bending the will of food makers, advertising agencies and broadcasters. I was determined to learn more about a man savaged by his critics as the "Butcher of Syracuse" (Mellor and others thought the damning nickname originated with Faulk's attorney Louis Nizer; however, the earliest published usage I could find came from the pen of Gore Vidal in a November 1964 article reviewing Faulk's "Fear on Trial" for the *Book Week* newspaper supplement.)

Because Johnson and his wife died years before I began my research in the early 1980s, I turned to surviving members of Johnson's family, his friends, and his associates. In the early part of the project, I interviewed Johnson's three daughters, Lois Wangerman, Marilyn Giancola, and Eleanor Buchanan, who also made available family papers, including letters and photographs. Another rich source of information was Johnson's scrapbook collection; in five oversized ledger books Johnson preserved trade journal articles, newspaper clippings, store promotions and other material chronicling the evolution of his merchandising strategies and antiquarian activities between 1942 and 1954. Also helpful was Laurence Johnson's book, "Over the Counter and On the Shelf: Country Storekeeping In America, 1620-1920" (Rutland, Vermont: Tuttle, 1961).

Another source for Johnson's family history was an unpublished memoir by Edmund Roe Johnson, Laurence Johnson's uncle. Howard Williams, the unofficial historian of South Butler, New York, also sketched some vignettes of young Laurence Johnson as a farmer.

Johnson himself wrote a genealogical history of the family of Morris Craw, his great-grandfather. The unpublished manuscript is in the Genealogy and Local History section of the Onondaga County Public Library in Syracuse.

I also interviewed Jasena Foley, Johnson's close friend who spoke of his passion for local history and Americana; Mary Coyne, business manager of Johnson's supermarkets from 1940 until Johnson sold the chain in 1956; Robert Giarrusso, a senior vice president of Merchants Bank in Syracuse, who once was a clerk in Johnson's South Salina Street store; Thomas Higgins, retired president of Merchants Bank and a regular at the Schrafft's "roundtable" in the 1940s and 1950s; Burnett E. Haylor, retired president of Haylor, Hahn, Freyer & Coon Insurance Company and a member of Johnson's Kiwanis Club chapter; William A. Dyer and Henry "Tink" Keller, former advertising directors at *The Post-Standard*; Joe Ganley, a reporter and columnist at the *Herald-Journal* in Syracuse who occasionally was assigned to accompany Johnson on antique-hunting jaunts; and Jim McHale and Carl Tarver, members of Syracuse-area American Legion posts who were anti-communist activists working with

A Note on Sources

John Dungey. Tarver, historian for Post No. 41, made available a collection of back issues of *Spotlight*, the post's anti-communist newsletter published from 1951 to 1965.

Francis Neuser, Johnson's vegetable buyer and head of the Veterans Action Committee of Syracuse Super Markets, declined to be interviewed. His wife said that he had burned all his records, and that her husband felt recalling the turbulence of the era would be too painful. "Larry Johnson is a dead issue," she said.

Marguerite Fisher, professor emeritus at Syracuse University in the 1980s, described the mood on campus during the years of the Red Scare, and she told of her own adversarial relations with the anti-communist crusaders.

Retired Syracuse University Chancellor William Tolley provided additional background material on the Red Scare years.

Lillian Reiner spoke about Syracuse in Johnson's time from her perspective as an engaged liberal activist.

Anti-communist activist Vincent Hartnett offered his recollections. So did Harvey Matusow, who worked closely with Hartnett and Johnson. Johnson figures prominently in Matusow's confessional book, "False Witness" (New York, Cameron & Kahn, 1955).

Paul Martinson, an attorney in Louis Nizer's law firm who worked on the Faulk case, provided details of his pretrial examination of Johnson and made available transcripts and other documents related to the case. Thomas Bolan, the attorney in Roy Cohn's law firm who represented Johnson, Hartnett and Aware Inc. in the Faulk libel case, did not respond to a request for an interview.

John Henry Faulk spoke to me briefly in 1987, three years before his death. He told me he never met Johnson face to face, but Faulk had no shortage of opinions about the Syracuse grocer. "I never disliked Johnson," he said. "I objected to what he did, very strenuously."

In addition to archives of *The Post-Standard* and the *Herald-Journal*, the following books proved useful to me as key secondary sources:

"Fear on Trial," by John Henry Faulk (New York: Simon and Schuster, 1964).

"The Jury Returns," by Louis Nizer (New York: Doubleday, 1966).

"Journal of the Plague Years," by Stefan Kanfer (New York: Atheneum, 1973).

"Report on Blacklisting, Vol. II; Radio-Television," by John Cogley (New York: Fund for the Republic, 1956).

"The Political Blacklist in the Broadcast Industry," by Karen Sue Foley (New York: Arno Press, 1979).

I also found helpful a summary of Johnson's anti-communism in David Caute's "The Great Fear; The Anti-Communist Purge Under Truman and Eisenhower" (New York: Simon and Schuster, 1978). Caute's book contains a comprehensive bibliography of the anti-communist era.

Other published works I read in my research included:

"Tube of Plenty: The Evolution of American Television," by Erik Barnouw (New York: Oxford University Press, 1975).

"The American Inquisition," by Cedric Belfrage (New York: Bobbs-Merrill, 1973).

"Thirty Years of Treason," Eric Bentley, ed. (New York: Viking, 1972).

"Reds in Your Living Room," by Martin Berkeley, The American Mercury, Vol. 77 (August 1953).

"Communism in Central New York," by Luther "Gus" Bliven, *The Post-Standard*, (February 23-March 9, 1954).

"Red Masquerade," by Angela Calomiris (Philadelphia and New York: Lippincott, 1950).

"On the Air: Trial by Sponsor," by Saul Carson, *New Republic*, Vol. 123, No. 1, (September 11, 1950).

"The Nightmare Decade: The Life and Times of Joe McCarthy," by Fred Cook (New York: Random House, 1971).

"Due to Circumstances Beyond Our Control...." by Fred Friendly (New York: Vintage, 1968).

"The Committee," by Walter Goodman (New York: Farrar, Straus and Giroux, 1968).

"The Paranoid Style in American Politics and Other Essays," by Richard Hofstadter (London: Jonathan Cape, 1966).

"A History of the Cold War," by John Lukacs, (Garden City, N.Y.: Doubleday 1962).

"Trouble on Madison Avenue, N.Y.," by Merle Miller, *The Nation*, Vol. 174, No. 26 (June 28, 1952).

"Naming Names," by Victor S. Navasky (New York: Penguin, 1981).

"Blacklist," by Oliver Pilat, *New York Post* (January 26-31, 1953).

"A Quarter-Century of UnAmericana," Charlotte Pomerantz, ed. (New York: Marzani & Munsell, 1963).

"America's Mass Media Merchants," by William H. Read (Baltimore and London: Johns Hopkins University Press, 1976).

Red Channels: The Report of Communist Influence in Radio and Television, New York: Counterattack (1950).

"Freedom and the Foundation: The Fund for the Republic in the Era of McCarthyism," by Thomas C. Reeves, New York: Knopf (1969).

"Henry A. Wallace: Quixotic Crusade 1948," by Karl M. Schmidt (Syracuse, N.Y.: Syracuse University Press, 1960).

"Syracuse: From Salt to Satellite," by Henry W. Schramm and William F. Roseboom (Woodland Hills, Calif.: Windsor, 1979).

"Communism, Conformity and Civil Liberties," by Samuel A. Stouffer (New York: Doubleday, 1967).

After a long hiatus, and now in retirement, I resumed work in 2023 on this book, knowing that no one else had published a comprehensive biography of this influential Syracusan and that the broader issues raised by Johnson's story remained as relevant as ever.

In the years since I began research, new disclosures helped to clarify the surprising extent of intrigues, efforts, and activities of Soviet and American communists during the 1940s and 1950s. Starting in the mid-1990s, declassified transcripts of the so-called Venona project began revealing the contents of thousands of messages from Soviet spy agencies (NKVD, KGB, GRU), that were captured and decrypted by U.S. intelligence officers—and kept secret—starting in the 1940s. Archival records from the KGB and elsewhere were released after the demise of the Soviet Union in 1991. Several major texts reflect these new sources of information, including:

> "Red Scare or Red Menace? American Communism and Anticommunism in the Cold War Era," by John E. Haynes (1996).
>
> "Not Without Honor: The History of American Anticommunism," by Richard Gid Powers (1998).
>
> "Reds: McCarthyism in Twentieth-Century America," by Ted Morgan (2003).
>
> "The Age of McCarthyism: A Brief History with Documents," by Ellen S. Schrecker and Phillip Deery (2017).

— *Fred M. Fiske*

A Note on Sources

Laurence Johnson poses in 1946 for the Syracuse *Post-Standard*.

Index

A

Abraham Lincoln Brigade, 176, 208
Abbott and Costello, 159
Acheson, Dean, 128
Actors Equity, 183
Adams, Joseph H., 65
Adams, Val, 230
Adler, Larry, 100, 103
Advertising Club of Syracuse, 39, 112
Albers, William Henry, 49
"The Aldrich Family," 107
Allen, Reginald, 119, 122, 124, 292
Allen, Steve, 232
Ameche, Don, 159
American Association of University Women, 290
American Bar Association, 290
American Broadcasting Company (ABC), 93, 107, 177, 206, 253
American Business Consultants Inc. (ABC Inc.), 85–6, 90, 99–102, 107, 156, 206
American Civil Liberties Union (ACLU), 62, 264
American College Dictionary definition of McCarthyism, 200
American Committee for Cultural Freedom, 231
American Communications Association, 61
American Federation of Labor (AFL), 61, 163
American Federation of Radio and Television Artists (AFTRA), 189, 216, 218, 225–28, 230, 234–35, 248–49, 255–56, 258–64, 267, 309–10
American Federation of Radio Artists (AFRA), 92, 189, 255
American Guild of Variety Artists, 121
American Jewish Committee, 290
American Labor Party (ALP), 87, 93, 95, 117, 174, 183
American Legion
  salute, 3
  magazine, 81, 151, 164, 177, 187
  Duncan Paris Post, 185
  Illinois Anti-Subversive Commission, 107
  Peekskill Post, 95
  Post No. 41, Syracuse, 111, 113–14, 117, 124, 129, 134–35, 147, 155, 167, 174, 202, 204
  Spotlight newsletter, 113–14, 117–18, 121, 123, 125, 135–38, 156–65, 167–68, 179, 182–84, 201–4, 206–7, 210, 215–16, 219–20
American Peace Crusade, 138
American Peace Mobilization, 105
American Tobacco Company, 95, 139, 157

Boldfaced numbers indicate pages with a photo.

American Writers Congress, 78
American Youth for Democracy, 148
Amm-i-dent toothpaste, 141–44, 235, 291
Anthony, Joseph, 183
anti-anti-communists, 7, 86, 184, 245
anti-communism
  activists, 102, 109, 111, 131, 151–52, 201, 210, 216, 275, 322
  campaigns, 3, 27, 125, 128, 133, 168, 172, 176, 190–91, 216, 222–23
  Anti-Communist League, Austin, Texas, 269
Anti-Defamation League, 221
Appell, Donald T., 150
Appleby, Paul, 178
Arlen, Richard, 159
Army-McCarthy hearings, 195–200, 206
Ashland, Camilla, 176
Associated Foods Incorporated, 24
The Associated Press, 171, 191, 247
Astor Theatre, Syracuse, 135, 179–80
Attorney General's List of Subversive Organizations, 5, 85, 95, 107, 173, 289, 321
Atwater, Ralph, 53–54
Autry, Gene, 159
Aware Inc., 116, 188–90, 201–2, 221–22, 226–28, 232–34, 241, 244–45, 247, 258–64, 287, 290–91, 293–94, 305, 310
  AFTRA resolution condemning, 258
  AFTRA supporters, 260
  bulletins, 228, 230, 232, 234, 237, 284, 287, 289–90, 293–94, 298–99
Ayres, Ida, 12-16, 20
Ayres, Margaret Louise, 13, 16
Ayres, Nathaniel, 9
Ayres, Stephen Beckwith, 11–12

B
Ballard, Charles, **114**
Barrett, Leslie, 255
Barton Jr., Francis C., 155–56, 292
Batten, Barton, Durstine & Osborn, 54, 216, 293
Bayless Cracker Barrel Country, 271
Bean, Orson, 225–28, 230, **231**–32, 262
Belfrage, Cedric, 106, 324
Bell, Matthew, 139, 141
Bentley, Arvilla, 151, 191
Bentley, Elizabeth, 77
Bergen, Edgar, 112
Berkeley, Martin, 157–58, 324
Berle, Milton, 110
Bernstein, Leonard, 103
Bernstein, Walter, 142, 183–84, 206

Berra, Yogi, 152–53
Bessie, Alvah, 79
Blackburn, Harry J., 237
blacklisting
   Cogley report on, 116, 118, 176, 241–49, 255, 324
   critics of, 162–64, 185–86, 218–19, 228, 244, 255–60, 293
Blessing, Wayne, 53–4
Bliven, Luther "Gus," 117, 202, 324
Block, Leonard A., 141–45
Block Drug Company, 141–42, 144–45, 282
Bloomgarden, Kermit, 108
Bolan, Thomas, 8, 281–84, 287, 291, 293–95, 298–301, 304, 306–7, 323
Bond, Ward, 159
Borden Co., 112, 157, 167, 177, 216, 218
Brando, Marlon, 159, 318
Bridges, Lloyd, 156, 180
Broome County American Legion, 114
Brown, Hiram, 139, 141, 292
Brownell, Herbert, 211–12
Buchanan, Eleanor, 1, 4, 15–16, 18, 21, 24, 59, 68, 109–15, 122, 222, 242, 285, 297–98, 322
Buchanan, Jack, 98, 111
Buckley Jr., William F., 202
Bucks County Playhouse in Pennsylvania, 259
Budenz, Louis, 125, 202
Burrows, Abe, 103, 139, 253

C

Capra, Frank, 80
Careccia, Maria, 98
Carson, Jack, 110, 159
Carson, Saul, 164–65, 324
Catholic War Veterans, 107, 134, 145, 164, 166, 202
Cazenovia Seminary, 13, 16–17
Chambers, Whitaker, 77, 210
Chaplin, Charlie, 107, 179, 318
Charney, George Black, 151, 212
Chef Boyardee, 56
Chiang Kai-shek, 75, 85, 125
Chodorov, Edward, 158
Churchill, Winston, 75
Citizens Foundation, 88
Civil Rights Congress, 95, 105
Clamage, Edwin, 107–8
Clap, Captain Roger, 9
Cobb, Lee J., 103, 159
Cogley, John, 116, 118–19, 154, 167, 176, 241–47, 324
Cogley Report, 241–49, 324
Cohn, Roy, 8, 70, 134, 147, 150, 172–**74**, 190–191, 194–97, 200, 202, 210, 213, 281, 287, 323
Colgate-Palmolive-Peet Company, 142, 180–81, 232, 292
Collingwood, Charles, 225, 227–28, 230, 238, 262, 293
Columbia Broadcasting System (CBS), 92, 100,

106, 108–10, 112,
144–45, 154, 171,
193–95, 206, 226,
231–33, 236, 253–54,
267–68, 298, 313–14,
316
Columbia University, 91
Communist Party USA, 1–3,
5, 8, 61, 78, 80, 83,
87–88, 90, 103, 118,
121, 123, 125, 147–50,
158–59, 175, 189, 213,
265, 299–300, 316
Congress of Industrial
Organizations (CIO),
61–62
Consumer Reports, 62, 136–37
Consumers Union, 62, 136
Cooper, Gary, 79
Copland, Aaron, 103–104
Corcoran, Thomas J., 53
Cotten, Joseph, 138–41, 167, **231**, 292
Counterattack, 80, 85–86, 90,
92, 99, 102, 106,
111–13, 119, 151–53,
156, 188, 201, 244–45,
247, 325
Country Playhouse,
Fayetteville, New York,
137–38
Coyne, Mary, 27–28, 30–31,
33, 37–38, 51, 59, 64,
124, 134, 143, 205–6,
264, 315–**16**, 322
Crain, Thomas, 227
Craw, Morris, 10, 322
Crosby, Bing, 159
Crosby, John, 218–19, 260

Cultural Conference for
World Peace, 104–5
Cvetic, Matthew, 77, 177

D

Daily Compass, 117, 165
Daily Worker, 86, 88, 99,
104–5, 112, 128, 130,
145, 150, 182, 195,
227–28, 238, 244, 283,
289–90
Dalsimer, Samuel, 142, 235, 291
Daly, John, 253
Davis, Ossie, 217–18
Debs, Eugene V., 251–52
Deery, Phillip, 326
Dehn, Adolf, 158, 282
Dekker, Albert, 108, 179–80
Devane, William, 313–**14**
Dewey, Governor Thomas,
89–90, 95
Dickler, Gerald, 293
"Die Fledermaus," 110,
119–25, 135, 152, 159,
182, 292
Dies, Martin, 62, 64
Dilling, Elizabeth, 63, 102
Dimock, Edward J., 151, 212
Dobie, Frank, 254
Dorsey, Lew, 140
Doty, Edward, 18
Dougherty, Paul S., 169
Douglas, William O., 2, 94, 310
Draper, Muriel, 159, 164
Draper, Paul, 100
Dumont television network, 91

Dungey, John K., 113–**14**,
   117–19, 121–25, 129,
   131, 135–38, 142, 153,
   156–58, 161–65,
   167–69, 174, 179–84,
   204–5, 210, 212,
   218–19, 221, 232–34,
   315, 323
Dyer, William A. "Bill," 55,
   322

E
Eakins, Ruth and George, 37
Early American Industries
   Association, 254, 272,
   285
Eastern Frosted Foods
   Association, 48
Eckel, Rhea, 220–21
Edmiston, Martha, 150
Eisenhower, Dwight D., 130,
   148, 174, 193, 195, 215,
   324
Eldridge, Florence, 85
Emergency Civil Liberties
   Committee, 206, 231
Emerson, Faye, 227, 260
"The Emperor Jones," 217

F
Fagan, Myron C., 102
Fairbanks, A. Ray, 53
Farrell, Jack, 152–53
Fast, Howard, 159, 183
Faulk, Henry, 252
Faulk, John Henry, 116, 223,
   225, **226**–38, 249,
   257–**66**, 267–69,
   279–81, 287–91,
   293–94, 296–301,
   304–6, 308–11, 313–**16**,
   318, 321, 323
   early life and career,
      251–55
   "Fear on Trial," book, 311,
      313–14, 321, 323
   "Fear on Trial," movie,
      316
   firing, 289, 293
   "Johnny's Front Porch,"
      253
   libel lawsuit, 8, 262–67,
      287, 303–06, 310, 319,
      323
   "Uncensored John Henry
      Faulk" book, 314
Federal Bureau of
   Investigation (FBI), 1,
   77, 85, 92, 128–29, 147,
   149–50, 175–76, 207,
   217, 219, 222, 232, 256
Federal Communications
   Commission (FCC), 81,
   134
Federal Theatre Project, 63
Feiner, Irving, 93–94
Ferguson, Tracy, 129–30
Ferrer, Jose, 104, 113, 135,
   159
Fine, Sidney, 280
Fisher, Frederick G.,
   196–198
Fisher, Katherine, 69
Fisher, Marguerite, 71–73,
   94, 124, 161, 197–98,
   323
Flack, Jack, 22, 74
Flood, Robert P., 204
Flynn, Elizabeth Gurley, 153

Foley, Jasena, 22, 271–72, 274, 278, 285, 297, 322
Foley, Karen Sue, 324
Food Field Reporter, 52–53, 186
Ford Foundation, 172, 241, 248–49
Ford Motor Company, 20, 100, 238
Foreman, Arnold (aka Vincent Hartnett), 166
Fox, John M., 169
Francis, Clarence, 92
Friendly, Fred, 92, 106, 193–194, 324
Fuchs, Klaus, 77
Fund for the Republic, 172, 207, 220, 241, 245, 248, 324–325
Fur Workers Industrial Union, 61

G
"Gang Busters" radio show, 91–93, 227
Ganley, Joe, 322
Garfield, John, 104, 163
Gary, Harold, 258
Gelbart, Abe, 178
Geller, Abraham N., 280, 288–89, 291, 294, 300, 304–6, 309
Genant, William A., 20
General Electric Co. (GE), 269, 174–75
General Foods Corp., 92, 107, 168, 232
General Maximum Price Regulation (GMPR), 40, 66–67

Giancola, Marilyn, 18, 21, 23, 45, 51, 143, 271, 297, 322
Giarrusso, Robert, 29–32, 48, 145, 322
Gilbert, Lou, 159
Gilford, Jack, 104–5, 110, 119–**20**, 121-25, 135, 152–53, 159, 182, 247, 292
Gilman, Sam, 179
Godfrey, Arthur, 109–10, 119, 254, 268
"The Goldbergs," 159, 226
Goodman, Walter, 325
Goodson, Mark of Goodson-Todman, 138–39, 292
Gordon, Ruth, 159
Gorman, Leonard, 74
Gorman, Reverend Ralph, 166
Gough, Lloyd, 157–58
Grand Union supermarkets, 237
Grant, Lee, 142, 258
Gray Advertising Agency, 141–42, 235, 291
Green, Judson, 16
Griffiss Air Force Base, 72–73
Grocer's Digest, 51
Grocers' Topics, 35

H
Hagen, Uta, 116, 158
Hagerty, James C., 174
Harrington, Michael, 91, 245
Harris, William H., 182
Hartnett, Vincent W., 31, 59, 66, 80, 86, 91–93,

99–103, 108, 115–16,
119, 134, 141, 151, 166,
172, 175–77, 182,
188–89, 216, 218,
227–28, 230–31, 238,
241, 244–**47**, 256–61,
263–65, 268, 280–81,
290–94, 299–300, 305–
7, 310–11, **316**–17
Hatlo, Jimmy, 49
Hayes, Arthur Hull, 238
Hayes, Helen, 160
Haylor, Burnett, 21–22, 48,
70, 73–74, 265, 308, 322
Hazel Bishop Inc., 82
"Hee Haw" TV show, 314
Hellman, Lillian, 104
Henry, Charles E., 310
Herring, Charles F., 209
Higgins, Thomas, 22, 74, 322
Hiken, Nat, 104
Hill, Joe, 290
Hilton, Peter, 139–41
Hinerwadel's Grove, 4, 130
Hiss, Alger, 75, 97
Hoff, Syd, 182
Hoffman Beverage Co, 235
Hofstadter, Richard, 325
Hofstadter, Samuel, 279
Holliday, Judy, 104, 135,
158–59, 162, 181–82,
231
Hollywood Ten, 79, 86–87,
103, 139, 180, 264
Hoover, J. Edgar, 1, 128, 232
Hope, Bob, 173
Hotchner, Howard, 189
House Committee on
Un-American Activities
(HCUA, also informally
as House Un-American
Activities Committee)
62, 64, 82–83, 104,
112–13, 115, 117,
122–23, 150, 156–57,
178, 209, 213, 227,
229–30, 245–47, 261
Hubbard, Elbert, 36
Hunter, Kim, 137, 156,
182–83, **231**, 259, 282,
292
Hunt Foods, 158, 282
Huston, John, 80
Hutchins, Robert, 172, 241

I
Independent Citizens
Committee of the Arts,
Sciences and
Professions, 229
Ingram, Rex, 217–18
International Fishermen and
Allied Workers, 61
International Longshoremen
and Warehouse
Workers Union, 61
Irving, Charles, 167
Isaacs, Ted, 180
Ives, Burl, 104
Ivory Soap, 53–54

J
Jagger, Dean, 160
Jahoda, Marie, 246
Jansen, William, 133, 172
Jefferson School, 209, 229,
291
Jencks, Clinton E., 209–10,
212
Jennings, Edgar, 19

Jewish War Veterans, 164
Jimmie Higgins, 251–52, 255
John Quincy Adams
    Associates (JQAA), 85
Johnson, Anceanda Craw,
    11–12
Johnson, Cecil A., 182
Johnson, Edmund Roe, 13,
    322
Johnson, Francis Marion,
    12–14
Johnson, Hermione Cartner,
    18–**19**, 20-21, 122, 124, 245,
    271, 308–9
Johnson, Laurence Ayres
  boycotting products, 6,
    139, 145, 208, 211, 283
  death, 301, 303–08
  estate, 305, 309
  funeral, 309
  health, 294–97
  memorabilia destroyed in
    fire, 285
  nicknamed "Butcher of
    Syracuse," 311, 321
  old country stores, 13, 23,
    28, **45**, 47, 274-**75**, 307,
    321–22
  "Over the Counter" book,
    274-**75**, 276-77, 322
  sugarloaves, 273, 277
Johnson, Thomas, 10, 13, 19
Johnson Wax, 157
Johnson-Welch, Ida, 14
Jukoski, Laurence, 114

K
Kahn, Albert E., 209–10
Kallet, Arthur, 136
Kanfer, Stefan, 91, 101, 110,
    123–24, 324
"The Kate Smith Hour," 158
Kaufman, George S., 159
Keel, Howard, 179
Keenan, John G., 85, 102
Keene, William, 189
Keith, Richard, 189
Keller, Henry "Tink," 22, 56,
    59, 74, 265, 322
Kempton, Murray, 297
Kendrick, Alexander, 104
Kennedy, Arthur, 183
Kennedy, Raymond J.H., 221
Kent, Rockwell, 89–90
KFRC-FM, 268
Khrushchev, Nikita, 171, 215
Kilgallen, Dorothy, 253
King Kullen supermarket, 24
Kingsley, Jesse E., 130
Kirk, Dorothy, 41–42
Kirkpatrick, Theodore "Ted"
    C., 85, 99–100, 107,
    151, 165
Kirsch, Robert R., 262
Kiwanis Club, Syracuse, 73,
    112, 207, 222, 322
Klein, Harvey L., 257
Kohlberg, Alfred, 85, 201–02
Korean War, 81, 98, 111,
    134, 277
Kraber, Tony, 108
Kraft, John, 217
Kraft Foods, 112, 168, 205,
    217–18
"Kraft Television Theatre,"
    218
Kreuzer, Melanie A., 221
Kroger Co., 24
KTRC-AM, 208

Kudner advertising agency, 177, 227

L
Labor Youth League, 183, 208
Laird, Donald A., 43
Lake, Veronica, 159
La Manna, Father Joseph, 204
Lampell, Millard, 106, 184
Lancaster, Burt, 180–81, 318
Lasky, Victor, 70, 187, 202
Latimore, Robert M., 129
Lattimore, Owen, 125, 195
Lawrence, Peter, 261
Lawson, John Howard, 79, 83, 87, 159
Leder, Robert, 268
Lee, Canada, 95
Lee, Gypsy Rose, 104, 107
Lee, Madeline, 176, 182, 261
Leeds, Phil, 261
Lennen & Mitchell (also. See Lennen & Newell), 154–56, 211
Lennen & Newell (also. See Lennen & Mitchell), 211, 292
Lever Brothers, 142, 157–58
Levy, Matthew M., 279
Liebmann Breweries, 237
Liggett & Myers Tobacco Company, 109–10
Lincoln's Birthday Party of Radio Industry Committee, 105
Lippmann, Walter, 76
Lipton, Sir Thomas, 32
Lipton soup, 206

Loeb, Philip, 159, 163–64, 226, 228
Loew's State Theatre, Syracuse, 55, 119, 121, 123, 135, 179
Los Alamos, 77
Lucky Strike, 157, 159
Lukacs, John, 325
Lux Toilet Soap, 157
"Lux Video Theatre," 157
Lynch, Walter A., 279

M
Magee, Warren, 129
Maltz, Albert, 81
Mansfield, Senator Mike, 170
Manson, Alan, 157, 261
March, Frederic, 85
Markowitz, Jacob, 279
Marks, Jerome A., 296
Martinson, Paul, 234, 281–84, 323
Marvin, Rolland B., 130
Masaryk, Jan, 76
Matusow, Daniel "Danny" B., 148
Matusow, Harvey, 133, 141, 143, 145, 147–57, 170–72, 190–94, 208–13, 315–16, 323
  "False Witness" book, 191, 210–11, 323
Maxwell House, 21, 56
McBride, Mary Margaret, 85
McCarran Committee, 162
McCarthy, Senator Joseph R., 3–**4,** 7, 40, 97–98, 125–31, 134, 135–145, 147, 150–51, 162, 170–71, 173-**74,** 275, 178,

188, 190–203, 205,
207–9, 211, 213, 287,
317, 319
  death, 201
  libel suit vs. *The
    Post-Standard*, 125–131
McConnell, Joseph H., 169,
  180–181
McCullough, Hester, 100–01
McGivern, Owen, 279
McHale, Jim, 70, 204, 222,
  322
McNamara, Frank, 152, 247
McNett, Charles, 88–89
McTernan, John T., 209
McWilliams, Carey, 183
Mellor, Carl, 321
Metal Workers Union, 61
Metropolitan Opera
  Company, 119, 120–22,
  124
Midtown Theatre, Syracuse,
  179
Miller, Arthur, 80, 83, 104,
  108, 300, 318
Miller, Marvin, 175
Miller, Merle, 162, 325
Milton, Paul, 93, 115, 176,
  189, **247**, 280, 292
Minton, Sherman, 94
Minute Maid Corp, 169
Mitchell, Fred, 292
Moe, Janet F., 199
Montgomery, Robert,
  156–57
Moore, Garry, 227, 292–93
Morgan, Henry, 92
Morgan, Ted, 318–19, 326
Morley, Karen, 183
Morton, Harold, 123

Moss, Annie Lee, 194, 200
Mostel, Zero, 104, 261
Motion Picture Alliance, 175,
  182
Moyers, Bill, 316
Muir, Jean, 107, 163
Mundt, Senator Karl,
  196–98, 200, 248–49
Munsel, Patrice, **120**
Murphy, George, 179
Murphy, Wayne, 234
Murray, Thomas D., 235–36,
  291
Murrow, Edward R., 106,
  193–95, 238, 267, 309

N
National Broadcasting
  Company (NBC), 82,
  112, 152, 156, 158, 169,
  206, 218, 221, 260
National Education
  Association (NEA), 96
National Grocers'
  Association, 232
National Lawyers Guild,
  196–97
National Miners Union, 61
National Review, 225
National Teachers Union, 61
National Textile Workers
  Union, 61
Navasky, Victor S., 325
Neal, Patricia, 183
Neff, John W., 181
Neuser, Francis W., 134, 141,
  147, 203, 217–18, 234,
  265, 315, 323
Newhouse, S.I., 54, 128–131

Newhouse newspapers, 54–56
New York Central Trades and Labor Council, 61
New York Folklore Quarterly, 204, 254, 273
New York Folklore Society, 204
New York Herald-Tribune, 67, 90, 210, 218
New York Journal-American, 194, 245, 260
New York Post, 90, 185, 187, 221, 297, 325
New York Public Library, 99, 103, 227, 283
New York Sun, 69
The New York Times, 49, 90, 98, 128, 171, 191, 198, 230, 242, 304, 306
New York World-Telegram, 194, 245–46
New York Yankees, 152–53
Niagara Mohawk Power Corp, 169
Nizer, Louis, 8, 91, 122, 124, 262–63, **266**, 279–82, 284, 287–91, 293–96, 299–301, 304–6, 309–10, 314–16, 319, 321, 323–24
Nolan, Lloyd, 159
Novak, Bob, 189

O

Odets, Clifford, 158
Office of Price Administration (OPA), 66–69
Ohio County Women's Republican Club, 97
Ohio Un-American Activities Commission, 133
Oneida Experiment, 276
O'Neil, James, 87
Onondaga County Veterans Council, 180–81
Onondaga County War Memorial, 70, 117–18
Onondaga Historical Association, 24–25, 207
Ottenheimer, Albert M., 261
Oxnam, Bishop G. Bromley, 151, 209

P

Pabst Brewing Co., 233–35
Pall Mall, 157, 238
Palmer, Walter, 9
Parker, George, 89
Patton, David H., 96, 137
Peekskill riots, 95
Pegler, Westbrook, 86, 100, 202
People's Songs Inc., 104, 118, 229, 291
Peress, Irving, 173–74
Perlstein, Harris, 233
Philbrick, Herbert, 210, 222
Philip H. Lord Agency, 91–93, 103, 166, 189
Pidgeon, Walter, 179
Pierce, Madeline, 176
Pierce, William E., 48
Pilat, Oliver, 185–86, 325
"Pins and Needles" theater show, 148
Prager, Stanley, 261
Price, Mary, 76

Printer's Ink, 34–35, 52
Proctor & Gamble, 53, 167, 206, 282
Progressive Citizens of America (PCA), 87, 105, 228–29
Progressive Grocer, 37, 54
Progressive Party, 8, 76, 89, 290

Q
Quinn, Anthony, 159

R
Racht, Leon, 260
Radio Writers Guild, 163–64
Randolph, John, 157, 261
Ray, Aldo, 135
Reader's Digest, 38, 69
Reagan, Ronald, 71, 222
Ream, Joseph H., 108
Red Channels: The Report of Communist Influence in Radio and Television, 5, 99–109, 111–13, 116, 119, 122, 134–35, 139, 156, 165–66, 175–76, 185, 188, 244, 258, 292, 314, 325
Reeves, Thomas C., 133, 325
Reiner, Lillian, 87–88, 94, 117, 125, 308, 323
Reschke, Joe, 31, 59, 64
Revere, Anne, 81
Rheingold beer, 236–237
Riesel, Victor, 164
Lardner Jr., Ring, 83, 87
Rinso laundry soap, 157
Rintels, David W., 316
RKO Pathe, 51

Robbins Jr., Grover, 271
Robbins, Jerome, 182
Roberts, Kenneth, 292
Robeson, Paul, 95, 117, 229
Robinson, Earl, 229, 290
Rogge, O. John, 93
Roosevelt, Franklin D. (FDR), 2, 46, 60, 62–64, 72, 75, 125
Roseboom, William F., 325
Rosenberg, Julius and Ethel, 77, 173, 183, 218
Roslow, Sydney, 294
Royal Crown Cola, 145
Russell, Bertrand, 62

S
Saile, Warren, 22, 74
Sampson, Harold B., 48
Saturday Evening Post, 175, 182
Saypol, Irving, 279
Schappes, Morris U., 62, 204
Schenck, Thola Tabor, 124
Schine, G. David, 173–**74**, 195–96, 200
Schlitz Brewing Company, 154–55, 282, 292
"Schlitz Playhouse" TV show, 154–55, 156, 211
Schmidt, Godfrey P., 63, 86, 116, 189, 202, 216, 219, 221, 244–45, **247**, 258, 267, 279–80
Schmidt, Karl M., 325
Schnabel, Stephen, 157
Schrafft's luncheonette, 73–74, 322
Schramm, Henry W., 325
Schrecker, Ellen S., 326
Schuyler, George S., 71, 204

Scott, George C., 313–**14**
Scott, Hazel, 176
Scott, Martha, 176
Scourby, Alexander, 183
Screen Actors Guild, 107
Screen Writers Guild, 78–79
Scribner's Magazine, 136
Seabrook Farms, 139–41
Seeger, Pete, 94, 104, 118, 204, 261
The Self-Service Grocer, 51
Sellin, John, 129
Senate Internal Security Subcommittee (SISS), 98, 125, 150, 163, 173, 178, 188, 231
Senate Judiciary Committee, 98
Shaw, Artie, 104, 118–19, 159, 162
Shean, Jim, 189
Sherwood, Robert E., 80
Silvera, Frank, 154, 156, 159
Skelton, Red, 159
Slack, Alfred Dean, 77
Sloane, Allan E., 175
Sloane, Everett, 175–76, 292
Smith, Art, 137, 159
Smith, Ferdinand, 87
Smith, Kate, 158–59, 282
Smith Act, 62–63, 117, 151, 153, 210, 212–13
Somerville, Jeanne, 189
Sondergaard, Gale, 247
Spellman, New York Cardinal Francis, 189
Stahl-Meyer meats, 238
Stalin, Joseph, 2, 7–8, 61–62, 72, 75–76, 78, 102, 139, 144, 165, 171, 181, 195, 215
Stanley Pennock VFW Post 2893, Solvay, New York, 202
Stanton, Frank, 144
Stanton, Thomas, 9
Stapleton, Frank M., 128
Stevens, Robert T., 174, 193, 195–96
St. Louis Post-Dispatch, 90, 128
Stouffer, Samuel A., 206–7, 325
Streit, Saul, 267, 279
Stripling, Robert, 199
Subversive Activities Control Board (SACB), 98, 208–9
Sullivan, Ed, 100–101, 232, 234, 267,
Sullivan, Elliott, 156–57, 261
Sunday Worker, 2, 149 (also, *See Daily Worker*)
Super Market Institute, 47, 49, 67, 110, 145, 152, 205
Surine, Donald A., 129
Susskind, David, 216, 292, 309, 316
Swanson, W. Clarke, 139
Swanson food company, 139, 181–82, 282. 321
Syracuse Film Society, 137
Syracuse *Herald-Journal*, 45, 54–56, 65, 70, 124, 129, 322–23
Syracuse Lions Club, 48
Syracuse Peace Council, 73, 219

Syracuse *Post-Standard*, 19, 22,
    45–46, 54–56, 59,
    64–65, 74, 89, 96, 113,
    117, 124–31, 198–200,
    202, 211, 223, 275, 277,
    306, 321–23, 327
Syracuse Rotary Club, 73,
    112
Syracuse Section Council of
    Jewish Women, 313
Syracuse University, 48, 94,
    124, 129, 295, 323
  College of Law, 73
  Daily Orange, 162
  Maxwell School, 66, 71–73,
      94, 178
  Syracuse University Press,
      72, 325
Syracuse Women for Peace,
    73, 184

T
Taft-Hartley Act, 209
Tarver, Carl, 73, 113, 138,
    315, 322
Taylor, Robert, 179
Tenney, Jack B., 62
Thomas, Representative J.
    Parnell, 63, 112
Thurber, James, 300
Tilzer, George, 279
Tolley, William, 178, 323
Tompkins Square
    Communists, 148–49
Town & Country Motor
    Lodge, 298, 303
Trachtenberg, Alexander,
    151, 212
Truman, Harry S., 75, 87,
    89–90, 97, 170, 324

Tweetsie Railroad, 23, 271
Twentieth-Century America,
    318, 326
Tydings, Senator Millard,
    97–98, 127, 131
Tyne, George, 261

U
United Auto Workers, 61
United Nations, 175, 290
United War Fund Campaign,
    69

V
Vadeboncoeur, E.R. "Curly,"
    220
Valentine, Anthony J., 88
Van Dyke, Dick, 313
Van Horne, Harriet, 194, 253
Van Volkenburg, J.L.,
    109–10
Victory Supermarkets, 223,
    264, 309
Vidal, Gore, 321
Vincent, John Carter, 125–26
Voorhees, Robert L., 128
Veterans Action Committee
    of Syracuse Super
    Markets (VAC), 134,
    141–45, 147, 153, 155,
    177, 184, 203, 217, 234,
    244–45, 264–65, 315,
    323

W
Wagner, Edwin R., 175
Walker, Robert, 160
Wallace, Henry A., 8, 62,
    89–90, 125, 178,
    228–29, 284, 290, 325

Wallach, Eli, 183
Wangerman, Lois, 18, 20–22, 66, 271, 322
Ward, Carl, 236
Warner Bros., 64, 80
Warren, Earl, 89
Warsaw Pact, 215
Washington Post, 128
WBAI-FM, 269
WBAP-TV, 149
WCBS-AM, 225, 233, 236–37, 267, 294, 298
WCCO-AM, 268
The Weavers, 94, 118, 159, 183, 189, 282
Wegman, Jack, 37
Weinstock, Louis, 136
Weisman, Frederick, 158
Welch, Joseph, 196–98
Welch, Michael, 14–16
Welles, Orson, 104
Whipper, Leigh, 189
White Rock Beverages, 238
Whitmore, James, 179
Wierum, Howard, 159
Wilder, Russell M., 69
Williams, Howard, 18, 322
Wilson, Henry, 74
Wilson, Lois, 183
Wilson Brothers General Store, 16, 43, 273–74
Winchell, Walter, 100
WOLF-AM, 159
Wolff, Lester, 293
Woman's Home Companion, 41–42
Wood, John S., 122
WOR Radio, 268
WPIX-TV, 107
Wright, Richard and Caroline, 297
Wright-Patterson Air Force Base, 150
WSYR-AM, 81, 88

Y

Yates County Chronicle, 12
York, Amos, 10
Young & Rubicam, 92, 177, 216, 227, 292
Young Communist League, 246
Young Progressives of America (YPA), 93

Z

Zwicker, General Ralph W., 174, 193

About the Author

Fred M. Fiske was born in Cambridge, Massachusetts. He lived in Iowa and Washington, D.C., then abroad as the son of a U.S. diplomat. Fiske earned degrees in history from Harvard University and journalism from Columbia University. He retired in 2013 after a forty-year newspaper reporting and editing career that included writing editorials for *The Post-Standard* in Syracuse, New York. He was president of the National Conference of Editorial Writers in 2001, and a Pulitzer Prize juror in 2002 and 2003. He lives near Syracuse.

www.ingramcontent.com/pod-product-compliance
Lightning Source LLC
Chambersburg PA
CBHW072147070526
44585CB00015B/1024